THE POWER OF FREEDOM

Henry Allen Moe

LONG MAY OUR LAND BE BRIGHT . . .

THE POWER
OF
FREEDOM

IN HUMAN AFFAIRS

BY

HENRY ALLEN MOE

INTRODUCTION BY JOHN SLOAN DICKEY

THE AMERICAN PHILOSOPHICAL SOCIETY

PHILADELPHIA, 1977

FOREWORD

MY husband Henry Allen Moe died on October 2, 1975. In going through his papers, I found to my complete surprise that he had been planning to publish some of his writings. He had written an introduction and had chosen seven essays to illustrate his passionate belief in the "Power of Freedom." This plan must have been made quite some time ago, because the last essay he chose to include was written in 1951. He had written many others before that, and many since then, always related to the same subject—that without complete freedom of the mind and spirit little can be accomplished.

I have followed his plan, using his own introduction as a preface, and adding more essays, chosen from the many which were written to be spoken before audiences with a great variety of interests. Those who have known him will hear him speaking. They will understand that the frequent repetitions are like the text in a sermon or the theme in a symphony. Some essays in this collection were edited for publication by my husband himself. The others I have edited, as I am sure he would have wanted me to do.

The tributes in the appendix, the first by the Reverend Justin Hartman delivered October 8, 1975 in Sherman, Connecticut, followed by others given at a ceremony at the Museum of Modern Art on December 8, and some received later, will give an idea of the wide range of his mind, and of his character and abilities. They are truly biographical.

He would be pleased that his passionate belief in the Power of Freedom and his undaunted faith in our country should be

Foreword

made available to be read at this time when we are celebrating the founding of our nation and thinking about what made us a beacon light for the highest hopes of mankind. I am profoundly grateful that I have been able to do this for him.

New York   EDITH MONROE MOE
1977

Long May our land Be Bright...

Essays on the Power of Freedom
in Human Affairs

by

Henry Allen Moe

CONTENTS

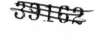

Contents

ACKNOWLEDGMENTS

THIS acknowledgments page lists the names of some of the many who have shared both the enthusiasm and duties of publishing this book.

Whitfield J. Bell Jr.   Rensselaer W. Lee
George W. Corner   Christian and Carolyn Moe
Charles Frankel   Henri Peyre
Charles and Nancy Farnsley   Marie A. Richards
W. Bentley Glass   James Kellum Smith Jr.
Constance W. Greene   Charles and Emily Smyth
Sally Earle Inda   Julieta C. Velasquez

INTRODUCTION

IT is wonderfully appropriate that these essays were assembled during the nation's Bicentennial. Taken together, the philosophy and career etched here come as close to being a celebration of the American idea as any solitary life is privileged to be. Freedom, American style, never produced a truer believer than Henry Allen Moe.

If by some divine arrangement one twentieth-century American were to be chosen to convey the thanks of our time to the Founding Fathers for the heritage they bequeathed to posterity, my nominee for the assignment would be the author of these essays. There may be others who personify American society at its quiet, private best, but I am confident that no one who meets Henry Moe through these essays, let alone anyone who was privileged to enjoy his friendship, will quarrel with the qualifications of this practicing American for such an awesome mission.

Indeed, it is doubtful that any other contemporary American would have been more at home in mind, spirit, and manner with that nonesuch trinity: Franklin, Jefferson, and Madison. This is not to assert a fatuous comparison of our author's talents in statecraft with the outer-edge creative powers of their genius. It is to say, however, that few, if any, among us have had a closer personal affinity with the best of our intellectual and cultural heritage. It might well be added that this immensely civilized successor to Benjamin Franklin and Thomas Jefferson in the presidency of the American Philosophical Society would have graced such a mission to the

Introduction

Founders with a spirit and style—in fine, a presence—that made him good company in any company.

Henry Moe's early life as the son of striving, appreciative Norwegian parents had a home-grown, Middle Western quality of simplicity and strength about it that fashioned his sturdy character and his life-long outlook of, as he put it, an "irrevocable American" whose faith in his country as "the best . . . ever" never wavered. On first acquaintance, some who had previously known him only by reputation as a sophisticated intellectual and foundation leader, occasionally found themselves surprised by the polite but unabashed Americanism of this Rhodes Scholar Anglophile. Needless to more than say, this "convinced American," as he also called himself, was no "professional patriot" who felt any need to wrap himself in the flag or, even for that matter, to flaunt it on his lapel. The seeming paradox disappears, as the reader of the essays will quickly discover, when one learns the "why" of his devotion. He was a truly *convinced* American who welcomed saying why.

In addition to being free of any hint of chauvinism, the dauntless quality of his national commitment took its positive strength from a mature, thoughtful assessment of the human experience, powerfully informed as it was by his professional learning as an Oxford-educated lawyer and by his constant recourse to history, particularly legal history. Although he never practiced law, he liked to think of himself intellectually as a "case-law lawyer." He had great confidence in the case-by-case processes of the common law but, as the essays bear eloquent witness, he was not afraid to reach out to general propositions while invoking the concreteness of history to validate his judgments. He took pride as well as assurance from, as he said, "thinking like a lawyer," but the polestar of his intellectual venturing was always history.

His understanding of history gave him unshakable conviction that "belief in the sacredness of the individual . . . is the

Introduction

foundation of all the good there is. Human individuality, protected as individuality, is the basis of every value in life." Strong words, yes, but also a considered judgment from which he never strayed in either his veneration of his country or in his leadership of the John Simon Guggenheim Memorial Foundation.

Freedom under law was the essential condition for human happiness and individual fulfillment. He was far, however, from being soft, let alone naïve, about the need for both self-imposed responsibility and the ultimate restraint of law to curb abuses of freedom. But important and indeed necessary as these disciplines were, in the large strategy of human affairs they were merely subordinate corollaries of the great purpose of law (the elementary origin of which he traced back to the kings of Mesopotamia): the protection and furtherance of individual rights.

If a man is to be known by the heroes he keeps, we do well to be mindful of the exalted position Henry Moe accorded in his pantheon of wise men to Frederic Maitland, the eminent English legal historian, and especially to the great American jurist, Oliver Wendell Holmes. Mr. Justice Holmes is singled out for approving mention perhaps twenty times in the essays, and when their author faces the testing question on freedom of thought and speech his response is pure Holmes: there must be "even freedom to be wrong." Mr. Justice Holmes himself might have preferred to say "especially" instead of "even," but on the basic proposition and in the larger domain of intellectual venturing Henry Moe was unmistakably and significantly a Holmes follower.

Beyond the factors of family and education which of a certainty powerfully fashioned his character and outlook, it is tempting to seek a causal relationship between his staunch Americanism, particularly his confident optimism about the nation, and the environment of his time.

Even accepting the factual limits involved in any effort to

Introduction

match a man to his times, one need not hunt under stones to support a judgment that in the "long view" he liked to take of things. Henry Allen Moe, if not exactly "a product of his times," was thoroughly at home in his time. Indeed, in the shaping years of today's America, from World War I through the Vietnam war, he was himself undoubtedly one of the influential shapers and shakers—albeit mostly vicariously and as a private person—of the American scene. By and large his time was far more than merely a comfortable fit. Intellectually, artistically, and in public affairs it provided a ferment that nurtured Henry Moe's convictions about freedom as the prime value of human affairs—both historically and individually. And perhaps even more critically, when the McCarthyism of the early Fifties and later the tumult of the late Sixties, put American freedoms to their proof and his faith was tested by a witches' brew of fears and selfrighteousness, including the taunts of some in the academic community, he had the satisfaction of being able "to take it" and yet quietly prevail—the clinching experience, I suspect, of his convinced Americanism.

For readers whose experience has been largely of a later time than the two middle quarters of this century, it may be useful to recall that Henry Moe's career as the directing head of the Guggenheim Foundation spanned most of this period of what, until its last decade, can fairly be characterized as a self-confident America. Indeed, the decade of the Twenties with its pursuit of "normalcy" (e.g., "two chickens in every pot") and of isolationist policies abroad, carried national confidence to levels that must now be regarded as so lacking in critical insight and sensitivity as to have been perilously self-satisfied.

During the Twenties, except for that first great leap on the way to today's women's liberation, the Nineteenth Amendment to the Constitution granting women's suffrage, official concern for the state of American freedom, particularly in

Introduction

matters of thought and social legislation, was largely confined to the dissents of Justices Holmes and Brandeis of the U.S. Supreme Court. Critically important as these seeds of change were to prove, the surface of society remained generally serene; only a few foresaw that such tremors as the Scopes "Monkey Trial" and the Sacco-Vanzetti case were far more portentous than merely casual stirrings of concern about the functioning of freedom.

The Thirties brought drastic weather-changes in American society. Dominated by the misery of the depression at home and the hardening grip of militarism and Hitlerism abroad, these years went far to dissipate any lingering self-satisfaction with the world of the Twenties. At the same time, Franklin D. Roosevelt's confident political leadership, with its unprecedented governmental stimulation and regulation, introduced the vitality of fresh controversies, as well as new concepts, into public affairs. The traditional boundaries of the freedom debate and of the reach of the democratic process in ministering to social welfare were drastically extended. World War II consolidated these changes in American society and, even more importantly for our purposes, the heroic national effort and the personal sacrifices required to defeat an enemy that personified as never before in modern times the antithesis of freedom, deepened the nation's concern with the quality of its own freedom beyond anything since the slavery issue was settled by the Civil War.

Retreat into the McCarthyism of the late Forties and early Fifties may well have been inevitable, but its acceptance and its virulence were surely heightened by the nation's recent experience with the monstrous evil of Hitler's totalitarianism. Be that as it may, as indicated above, not a few self-proclaimed defenders of freedom enlisted under the banner of the flailing Senator from Wisconsin, until finally he was brought down by the realization of his colleagues that an essential corollary in the defense of democratic freedom is fairness. Along with damage done, McCarthyism may have served a useful purpose in alerting some unwary, well-intentioned ones among us to the oft-repeated lesson of history that zealots are not always the truest guardians of freedom—a lesson, almost needless to say, historian-lawyer Henry Allen Moe knew well.

World War II, however, yielded a far more positive aftermath, namely, the national commitment launched in the late Forties under the aegis of President Truman's first Committee on Civil Rights, at long last to stop temporizing with American freedom's worst festering wound, officially sanctioned racial segregation. In subsequent years the struggle to gain equal freedom for all in America has spread from classical civil rights to education, jobs, housing, and other areas touching the quality of life. In a parallel cause, the Sixties and Seventies produced an irresistible momentum behind the ongoing effort to free women from situations of sanctioned economic and professional inequality. At the same time, the inherent power of freedom in the American judicial system was reasserted to strike down restrictions on individual freedom in such matters as family planning.

Finally, for those who find the most convincing proof of freedom's power in tangible triumph, the Sixties saw Americans voyaging to the moon, while the Seventies, not to be outdone, fittingly prepared for the nation's Bicentennial with a reassuring demonstration of freedom's capacity to work a self-cleansing of its own processes—Watergate, the Federal Bureau of Investigation, the Central Intelligence Agency, and all that.

Even such a brief sampling of recent American experiences with the idea of freedom makes clear that the furtherance and protection of this supreme value of our society is, as Henry Moe deeply believed, a work that is never done. Indeed, as recently as the late Sixties, even the American academic community had the bitter experience of relearning the ancient truth that its prime professional treasure, the maintenance of a free and open market place of thought and speech, could as quickly—in truth, perhaps more quickly—be lost from within by shortsighted zealots as from without by those of little faith or understanding.

Henry Moe was not disposed to dwell on such disappointments in either social conversation or in his speeches, but neither did he attempt to mask his awareness that some from whom he might have expected more had been swept downstream by passing freshets. His own confidence in the durability of freedom as the prime value of a civilized, happy society took substantial strength from his view of freedom's payoff during his time, including especially his great and merited satisfaction with the results it had yielded as the fundamental operating principle of his own daily work in the Guggenheim Foundation. He even pushed this professional confidence to an eloquent plea in behalf of more support for what he termed "academic outlaws" as essential to nurture the creative individualities of a pluralistic society.

But in the long view of human experience that he cultivated, his own experience was merely particular proof of the creative truths of history and of the processes men have learned to use for pursuing truth. As a lawyer he believed strongly in process and continuity. He could have avowed with his favorite preceptor, Mr. Justice Holmes, that he had "no belief in panaceas and almost none in sudden ruin." And with Maitland, he believed in the cumulative, coral-reef strength of "small successes."

Henry Allen Moe for all his confident conviction about the power of freedom was not much given to pontificating on public policy issues beyond the expertness of his learning or experience. Where he felt at home with the subject he did not shy from capacious generalization, but he was no dogmatist;

and lest his strongly stated positions be misjudged, he frequently warned his learned audiences "that one of the difficulties about saying anything is that it cannot be said all at once."

He was a realist, but in his long view realism and idealism were not beyond being bedfellows. It had been important to win both World Wars, but it was also important to realize that both were holding actions:

> . . . in this present world of power, more power will not do for the long haul. It may serve for the short term, fighting the holding actions which may be needed at the moment—and let us pray that it will serve—but for the long term the use of power is self-defeating for the life we would consider worthy of the vision of America. Somewhere, sometime must come men who will break through the encrustations of time and place and tradition and motive, of ignorance and greed and self-interest. . . .

*　　*　　*　　*　　*

Here, then, is the harvest of understanding, a treasury of minted wisdom, from a career spent judging and betting on someone else's opportunity to enlarge the truth and beauty of the human lot. Above all else, here is the testament of "a missionary for the belief that all we have, all that we can do here, all that we in America are—all this is the product of freedom."

JOHN SLOAN DICKEY

THE POWER OF FREEDOM

*"The secret of Happiness is Freedom,
and the secret of Freedom is Courage."*
—PERICLES

AUTHOR'S PREFACE

OPPORTUNITY AND FREEDOM

IN ONE MAN'S LIFE

MY wife's people on her father's side—Monroes from Scotland
—arrived in New England in the 1630's and on her mother's
side—Van Kowenhovens from the Netherlands—arrived in
New Amsterdam about the same time. Mine, both my mother
and my father, went to Minnesota from Norway in the 1880's
—250 years later. It is clear that—a quarter millennium apart
—they came for the same reasons: freedom and opportunity,
and of these the greater was freedom for themselves and
their children. And I shall add, old-fashioned though it be to
say so, they came for the pursuit of happiness, which they
found. So far as I can learn, none of them—neither collaterals
nor in the direct lines—ever went back to Europe except tem-
porarily for purposes of business, education, and the Grand
Tour.

When I was first married, I learned, to my astonishment,
that the flame that is America burned more brightly for me
than for my wife or her people. It had burned so long for
them that they noticed it but seldom and largely took it for
granted. We—my family—on the contrary, were aware of it
at all times. We talked about it as we studied around the
dining room table after dinner and learned all the fundamental documents of American history by heart, as we worked our

3

summer garden, as we fished and skated the Minnesota lakes and skied her hills.

We worked very hard and we never were sorry for ourselves; for we had no doubt that we were masters of our fates and captains of our souls. We were. And we had a whale of a good time while pursuing the strenuous life. We were practicing the doctrine before Theodore Roosevelt recommended it, and you may imagine my astonishment when—as an Oxford student traveling in the home of my ancestors, Norway —a cousin, a doctor, who had visited us in Minnesota told me that I had never had a childhood; for I had always worked too strenuously and had been too busy to play. He did not understand what Theodore Roosevelt had proclaimed, and less did he understand that it was profoundly American: "I wish to preach not the doctrine of ignoble ease, but the doctrine of the strenuous life." If ease meant happiness—which certainly it did not—we had had none.

We were newcomers and we had a funny little name— which not incidentally we deliberately declined to change. It was a family name of which we were proud, that of the Norwegian poet and folklorist Jørgen Moe. We were a convinced American family—that is in the same sense that some are convinced Quakers rather than birthright Quakers—and as convinced Americans, we believed that we should work hard, that that was the way to learn, to create, to contribute, to do our share, indeed to pursue happiness. We knew that in the U.S.A. even before the Clayton Act declared it in 1914, "The labor of a human being is not a commodity or article of Commerce." And being Republicans we knew that the ancestor of that statement was paradoxically Mark Hanna. However, in spite of hard work sometimes belts had to be tightened. We knew bank failures and we knew the Panic of 1907, but we remained bulls on the United States, in a sense no different from J. P. Morgan. Meanwhile all the children—and there were four who grew to maturity—continued our education in public school and by jobs after school and by armsful of books from the public libraries. We all got our college degrees and all had graduate study. We never had much money but we were rich—rich enough in things—our own home, with fine furniture, and farmlands to boot—but infinitely richer in hopes that we knew were certainties. And so they became.

A man cannot know the depth of a devotion until it is put to the test. One does not speak of being offered a permanent appointment in the University of Oxford and of refusing it; and I was not and I did not. But the facts are that, following my Rhodes Scholarship, during which I studied law and was admitted to the Bar of England at the Inner Temple, I held a lectureship in law in the University; and one evening during that year conversations were begun looking to the future. I walked the streets of Oxford late that night and before dawn I knew that I was irrevocably an American and had better be getting home. When my decision was known, my friends— both English and American—asked me what I could hope to have if I made a million dollars at the law in New York that I would not have in Oxford. The only answer was that I would be where I belonged; and then I knew that I belonged with a longing that made all other considerations nothing. England and the English I love, respect, and admire; but America and Americans are my own, myself. The difference is crucial.

But I did not practice law in New York, nor make a million dollars—either before or after taxes. Instead, I was given opportunity to meet Senator Simon Guggenheim, to assist in organizing the Foundation which Mrs. Guggenheim and he set up in memory of a son, and thereafter to become its principal executive officer. It was clear from the beginnings that Senator Guggenheim had a clear vision of America: he believed in freedom and he believed in opportunity—without distinction of race, color, creed, or economics—for the freest development of those who have the brains and talent and character and spirit, in the Senator's luminous saying, to "dignify, ennoble and delight mankind."

I tell these things, not to praise myself but to show my prejudices. The days of my youth were days of faith—faith in America, in its institutions and ourselves—and faith that was fulfilled. I know that I am a product of the faith of that period; and I will add that I feel sorry for those who are not. I know that, as Mr. Justice Cardozo has shown in *The Nature of the Judicial Process*, I cannot shed my innate convictions, my ways of looking at things; I cannot give up the faith in this constitutional republic in which I was reared. And I don't want to, and I shall not.

For that it is the best country the world ever has included, I know with clarity. That it is not perfect, I admit, but only as a mother admits some slight failings in her first-born.

The papers in this book are working papers, all written as invitations were offered, to state the Foundation's principles and plans to provide opportunities, in the American way, to develop talents and to guard the freedom which—and only which—makes that development possible to its fullest extent. The reader is asked to pardon a persistency which derives from the conviction that these are the most important things in the world.

Whether stated or not, whether admitted or not, whether understood or not, what the world—by and large and basically —wants is what we have, are, and can do here. To any one who will take the trouble to read the following papers, that statement will not convict me of being either a jingo or a pollyanna; but he will see clearly that I am a missionary. I am a missionary for the belief that all that we have here, all that we can do here, all that we in America are—all this is the product of freedom.

I have learned much from my wife and the long history of her people in America and she has come to see—and I no less

Author's Preface

—that meaning poignantly in the doubts and fumblings that now beset our country. "He has broached and divulged new and dangerous opinions against the authority of magistrates," declared Massachusetts as she banished Roger Williams. We now see clearly that a century later his "new and dangerous opinions" had captured Massachusetts.

Long may our land be bright, with freedom's holy light. If it be so, the future of the world—no less—is secure; if not, America will become just another indifferentiated part of the earth's surface.

HENRY ALLEN MOE

THE FUTURE OF

LIBERAL ARTS EDUCATION

UNIVERSITY OF MICHIGAN, ANN ARBOR,

OCTOBER 15, 1941

I HAPPEN to be a lawyer by profession with, I hope, a lawyer's sense of the continuity in human institutions. The law is always adopting new ideas from life at one end, and it always retains old ones from history at the other. Thus, we commonly speak of the body of our law, and when we do

> we use a metaphor so apt that it is hardly a metaphor. We picture to ourselves a being that lives and grows, that preserves its identity while every atom of which it is composed is subject to a ceaseless process of change, decay and renewal. At any given moment of time—for example in the present year—it may, indeed, seem to us that our legislators have, and, freely exercise, an almost boundless power of doing what they will with the laws under which we live; and yet we know that, do what they may, their work will become an organic part of an already existing system.

These words are not mine, written in this year of domestic stress and external war; but were written by that incomparable historian of English law, Frederic W. Maitland, in the year 1893. And he continues:

> Already, if we look back at the ages which are the most famous in the history of English legislation—the age of Bentham and the radical reform, the age which appropriated the gains that

had been won but not secured under the rule of Cromwell, the age of Henry VIII, the age of Edward I ("our English Justinian")—it must seem to us that, for all their activity, they changed, and could change, but little in the great body of law which they had inherited from their predecessors. Hardly a rule remains unaltered, and yet the body of law that now lives among us is the same body that Blackstone described in the eighteenth century, Coke in the seventeenth, Littleton in the fifteenth, Bracton in the thirteenth, Glanvill in the twelfth. This continuity, this identity, is very real to us if we know that for the last seven hundred years all the judgments of the courts at Westminster have been recorded, and that for the most part they can still be read. Were the world large enough to contain such a book, we might publish not merely a biography, but a journal or diary, of English law, telling what it has done, if not day by day, at least term by term, ever since the reign of Richard I; and eventful though its life may have been, it has had but a single life.

Now, a man is a lawyer because he thinks as a lawyer, not because he knows how many years in jail his client may get for forging a check or punching a traffic cop in the eye. And I shall do my best to write as a lawyer because the law affords a very accurate and long record of man's career; and what we need in these days—or what I need at any rate—are aids to long-range thinking.

When I say that a man is a lawyer because he thinks like a lawyer, I would illustrate that the words "convey in fee simple," for instance, flood a lawyer's mind with the memories of a thousand years of estates in land—pervading, embracing, filling his mind so that he cannot help thinking as fifty generations of his kind have thought. Similarly, however much we may legislate, this legislation will be but a phase of continuous growth for it will be dealt with, interpreted, by judges trained in the past which the law embodies. The lawyer's way of thinking will in time make the new legislation, however radical, into "an organic part of an already existing system" of law.

Liberal Arts Education

The process has its disadvantages, and to defend it nowadays is to be dubbed the worst of conservatives. But, nevertheless, I would say that *at its best* the process is unbeatable. The process was recently under heavy attack by the present Solicitor General of the United States while he was yet a professor of law; but the fact is that his career is the best defense of the process; for he now has opportunity to introduce new growth at one end of the process while not being able to neglect history at the other. He now is in the position of the man about whom Mr. Justice Holmes wrote, a man who—given his personal preferences, his articulate and inarticulate convictions, and his views of public policy—nevertheless must form his judgments not only out of experience but also under the burden of responsibility. It has always been thus in Anglo-American law. The conveyancer working for his clients the Barons at Runnymede drafted a reactionary document, Magna Carta; but the judges of England converted it into the charter of our liberties. When the law is administered by able and experienced men who know too much to sacrifice good sense to a syllogism or to history, the old rules always receive new content and often in time a new form. "The life of the law is not logic, but experience," wrote Mr. Justice Holmes at the age of forty, and then had a balance of a long lifetime, fifty years, to make that view effective. That has happened often enough in our own time for us to be sure that the process is still going on. And it does not matter that the engine and the brake are not often found in the same person. Nor does it matter much, except to the manners of the road, that some drivers prefer to accelerate up to the red light, then jam on the brakes, and honk their horn for the light to change; or that others prefer to slow down, catch the light as it turns to green, and make continuous progress. They arrive at the same place about the same time.

It was not long ago that all this would have sounded too full of sweetness and light, and it may be so yet, I concede.

Liberal Arts Education

The idea of progress toward an ultimate millennium was pretty prevalent, and revolutionary schemes to speed things up were in the air. But more recently it has become apparent that we shall not be badly off if we merely are able to hang on to what we have in a legal sense, which, do not forget, includes all the "freedoms" and a good deal more—experimenting, extending, and innovating here, patching there, providing for ever new wants, expressing ever new ideas, assimilating fresh elements of the most diverse kinds, and yet never ceasing to be under the system of law that has ruled us so long.

It is one of the few benefits of the wars that we are no longer ashamed to confess allegiance to the simple and enduring truths, of which this is one.

But what has this law got to do with the problems of the liberal arts college? The moral will come later, but meanwhile it will adorn the tale to quote the refrain of some ribald verses now going the rounds of the taverns and juke mills, the docks and the factories, and which I hope are going the rounds of the colleges and universities. The refrain is:

The line has changed again!

The great structure of British and American liberty has been built up century after century without any change of "line." There were and are the *essentials*, and there were and are the *experiments*; and I think it an accurate generalization to say that we have always held on to everything essentially good that we have ever had in the system. We have never changed the "line," we—in the sense of any proportion of persons that amounted to anything, numerically or otherwise —have never undertaken to begin over again and build up a new system with the idea that we could do it better.

But this does not mean that things will be well if we just let them ride along. It has taken the highest type of ability and leadership to adapt, in a continuous process of adaptation, the Anglo-Saxon jurisprudence to the needs of modern industrial society even so far as that ability and leadership have yet succeeded in adapting it—and the end of the need for brains and character and historical understanding is not yet in sight.

In this place it will be interesting to mention that the very first recorded words of Anglo-Saxon jurisprudence, in the laws of Ethelbert, king of the Kentish men, set down in the year 600 A.D., "God's fee and the Church's, twelve-fold" have undergone a continuous process of adaptation to the circumstances of the foundations of the Carnegies, Rockefellers, and Guggenheims, and the University of Michigan. How that was done is a long and fascinating, though minor, story in the history of the law. But it was done in response to a definite human need.

And so likewise must the greater job be done in response to a simpler and more urgent human need, that of eating regularly, of devising a legal concept adequate to cope with the facts of the cycles of industrial production and demand, and hence employment, and man's constant need for food, shelter, and clothes. Sir Henry Maine's generalization that "The progress of society is from status to contract" evidently needs extension. But from contract to what? It is an intellectual problem of the first order, and I know not the answer; but it must be solved, else misery may grasp at quick solutions which in other areas as well as in the economic might cause the loss of the gains of a thousand years.

Pressure for quick solutions is always upon the foundations and the universities, pressure to do the immediate thing, and the stress of war increases these pressures; but the fact is that the foundations and the universities, by and large, do their jobs well only insofar as they hold out against the pressures. At the moment the pressure for immediacy is from the proponents of hasty plans for saving civilization from wreck. But the hard fact is that improvisations will not do; for civilization will not ever be safe unless it is alive and healthy in root and

12

branch when the stresses come; and civilization will not be saved in times of future stress unless the men of the future maintain it. It is the principal business of the foundations and the universities to assist in making provision for that future maintenance.

How is this to be done? That is the essence of the question before this house. It has several aspects: natural science is on the high road; it has its method, and, more important, it attracts men of the highest pioneering ability. And it is important to keep them going; for, greater than the results of the study of the natural sciences, as a long-term proposition, probably is their example of what is called research. Because of it, as nobody disputes nowadays, not only has man's control over nature been vastly increased to his present good as well as to his harm, but also man's whole intellectual environment has been transformed.

But this research of theirs, what is it? It is certainly not what it is usually said to be, passionate intellectual inquiry, which, stripped, means piling fact on fact. To an outsider it seems that its largest ingredients are imagination and ingenious instrumentation—in short a combination of the virtues of the artist and the artisan—fused into creative efforts of the mind.

This seems to me largely to be forgotten in other disciplines, and while there are exceptions nobody, I suppose, would be heard to say that research in the liberal arts and the social sciences is in as good a state as research in the natural sciences. That is what I mean, and I can point it up sharply by the generalization that the trouble with the liberal arts in the universities is that their exponents are not creative in the same sense that chemistry's exponents, for example, are creative chemists.

The philosophers long have made a distinction between the world of value and the world of fact, a distinction now showing signs of crumbling. But be that as it may, I should suppose that even the most rigorously factual physicist, for example, necessarily lives very largely in the world of value. If this be true, it points to the easier task of the natural scientist; his data are less numerous, his factual material less diverse and complex. But I should also suppose that the humanists, had they been on the job these two thousand years, could have narrowed the world of value by enlarging the world of fact. But they cannot do it by burrowing into the past and hiding therein. By and large, I fear, that is what they are doing and have been doing for a long time. By way of evidence I quote the director of one of the country's great art museums in perhaps the greatest confession of failure I have ever seen. He was writing to a contemporary artist, and this is what he said:

> I have read a good deal on aesthetics and I confess that the older I get, the more bewildered I get. This does not sound well coming from a noncreative historian of art, but it has the merit of truth. The odd part of it is that I still arrogantly assume that I can tell a good painting when I see it, even though I do not know why. This holds, however, only for the art of the past and some contemporaries.

There is material for a sermon in every sentence but perhaps the most damning might be found in his reference to himself as "a noncreative historian." As you see, he had gained no notion in a long and well-paid life what being a historian involves.

Then I would cite the letter from a university friend, a professor of English, commenting on a list of Guggenheim Fellowship awards which contained a fair percentage of poets and such-like workers denominated "outlaws" by my friend's colleagues. Why did we give Fellowships to chaps like that, asked my friend by way of giving me opportunity to say an obvious say? I did, in this form:

> There was once a chap named William Shakespeare, who never spelled his name twice alike. But he wrote some plays and poems while living on what we would call fellowships. He got the fellowships although he was what the law called a

vagabond. Thousands of fellowships have been granted for studies of what he wrote on his fellowship. We are giving fellowships to literary vagabonds, "outlaws," to provide for our future business—to insure a supply of poets for your successor's colleagues of the year 2100 A.D. to study when they apply for Guggenheim Fellowships about that time.

That answer is, of course, only a jest; and such jests answer nothing. The real answer is that the Guggenheim Foundation grants fellowships to the academic outlaws—the poets and novelists, the painters, sculptors, and photographers, the composers and all kinds of other two-gun men—because they are trying (and we think with a fine measure of success) to do the important work which Emerson, in his unheeded Phi Beta Kappa oration delivered 105 years ago last month, gave as the charter, the blueprint indeed, for the American scholar. Here it is, neglected but yet magnificent, much honored but yet unheeded, very American but scrapped for an alien tradition:

> I ask not for the great, the remote, the romantic; what is doing in Italy or Arabia; what is Greek art, or Provençal minstrelsy; I embrace the common, I explore and sit at the feet of the familiar, the low. Give me insight into to-day, and you may have the antique and future worlds. What would we really know the meaning of? The meal in the firkin; the milk in the pan; the ballad in the street; the news of the boat; the glance of the eye; the form and the gait of the body; show me the ultimate reason of these matters; show me the sublime presence of the highest spiritual cause lurking, as always it does lurk, in these suburbs and extremities of nature; let me see every trifle bristling with the polarity that ranges it instantly on an eternal law; and the shop, the plough, and the ledger, referred to the like cause by which light undulates and poets sing; and the world lies no longer a dull miscellany and lumber-room, but has form and order; there is no trifle, there is no puzzle; but one design unites and animates the farthest pinnacle and the lowest trench.

This, no less, is what the outlaws are trying to realize. Listen to what one of them wrote me concerning the work he is trying to do. To understand it is not easy but neither was the concept of the quantum mechanics when it was in process of gestation *en ventre sa mère*:

> A motif is needed—one Yankee to thread all Yankees on. His dimensions are clear to me; he is the Land as one man can absorb it; all the Folkways touch him somewhere, color his mind. And he is the focus of my interest, the key to the fragments that I have, a multidimensioned legend of the old and the new. The particular gait of his lead waits on the attending experience; but what he carries, and where he is bound, I already know.
>
> . . . .
>
> The photographs will *look* rather than examine; the prose will be brief, the accent on manner rather than detail. Though he will serve as a device he is a fact of Folk experience. I need go no further than myself to know that he is real.
>
> . . . .
>
> At a time when our exterior is defined so that our interior may be defended, there is a need to reestimate what that interior is. After the warm bath of patriotism we are wrapped in the flag. The chill following our eventual unwrapping is always severe. It might be lessened, I believe, by occasional drafts of fresh air. And this the Folk will supply from their store of fresh air places: no single winter freezes them all, nor Spring finds them green. For the Land, white and green at a moment, holds them both. And when the Land, as a Folk, is seen, integration will also be there; for it is the Land, as the Land is more than the sum of its parts. This is not a thesis but a fact of experience not peculiar to me. This project is a first step toward its communication.

I hope you will see what he is driving at; but at least you will concede that he is trying. How hard he is trying and how aware he is of what he is trying to communicate!

And do not think that academic outlaws live only in the present. They have an accurate insight into the past, the good ones. They read always, they observe, they study on the things which concern them, they think, and they are not "meek young men," who in Emerson's words, "grow up in libraries believing it their duty to accept the views, which Cicero, which Locke, which Bacon, have given; forgetful that Cicero, Locke, and Bacon were only young men in libraries, when they wrote these books." "Real scholarship," Dean Charles Homer Haskins once said to me, "is a rough-and-tumble game." He meant exactly what Emerson meant. This fact of great knowledge in my academic outlaws is so contrary to the general impression that I would stress the point. I mean exactly that. I mean that, dealing with the same subject matter, they would hold their own in any academic company. And I would add that they can analyze contemporary production with a precision, with a deftness, with a sense of elegance, as the mathematicians use that word. with an insight into the past and with a feel for the future that I find nowhere else except among the natural scientists.

When I first read Frederic Maitland's remark that Sir Henry Spelman invented the feudal system it shed a bright light; for Spelman was a sixteenth-century scholar. Those who lived under the feudal system *lived* but they did not live under the feudal system. Not so far as they knew, they did not. So I cannot give a name to what we live under, but that they are great days of the spirit I have no doubt. It is not a Renaissance—presupposing a return to greatness—but it is greatness, I have no doubt; and perhaps a Spelman of the twenty-second century will give it a name.

Says Emerson:

> If there is any period one would desire to be born in—is it not the age of Revolution; when the old and the new stand side by side and admit of being compared; when the energies of all men are searched by fear and by hope; when the historic glories of the old, can be compensated by the right possibilities of the new era? This time, like all times, is a very good one, if we but know what to do with it.

The right possibilities of the new era—this renaissance which is not a renaissance—are not being fully shared by the liberal arts colleges. They stand aloof. They bury themselves in the past.

And why should I be concerned about the consequence of that? Simply because they are powerful: they are a power for the future because they control the minds and bodies and spirits of more of the ablest young men and women of the country than any other organizations. For that reason they might be able to kill these possibilities of which I have tried to speak. I do not think they can but I should much prefer that they were in it than aloof. The world needs the realization of those possibilities desperately, and this is the time and this is the place, and here are the people.

I have long tried to find out how it was that the experimental scientists achieved academic respectability. I gather that in the seventeenth-century England they stood just about where my Emersonian outlaws stand now. I think they just sneaked in, largely through metaphysics and mathematics, and I think so because the fact is that experimental science was taught at Oxford, and later at Cambridge, long before the curriculum shows it at all. You may read this fascinating story in the *Conway Letters* of Marjorie Nicolson, a very distinguished member of this university.

I should be quite content to have my Emersonians—let me call them—achieve their places in the colleges and universities through the back door. Indeed I think that would be the best way; for an announcement of policy converted into headlines by a news bureau is not my idea of the way to start anything good.

But very seriously, we are too much concerned with the academic machinery in this country and with changes of instructional policy: that "line," I might say, has changed too often. But the big job, and the only real job, in any college or university is choosing men. Getting together a great faculty is the only thing that makes a great institution. I hope I have called attention to some neglected sources of supply.

Liberal Arts Education

The difficulty about saying anything is that it cannot be said all at once. Hence I have had to neglect my friends, my enthusiasms, of the present faculties. I have been trying to make a point in which most of them have little part. But to them I now would say that I not only recognize but also insist that there are great traditionalists as well as great innovators: Bach is at least the equal of Wagner from any cosmic or near-cosmic view.

At the beginning of this paper I described the processes of Anglo-American law: adaptation to the needs of the present under a constant awareness of the line of history. I suggested that the process had gone forward, not because the virtues of the historian and the virtues of the radical were often combined in the same person, but because the virtues of both had free play. I stated that science, as we know it, had its beginnings when the skills of the artisans, the glassblowers, and cunning workers in metals, were added to the resources of the imaginative mind. I adopted the Emersonian concept of the job of the American scholar. I tried to show how the humanistic radicals might contribute to the doing of that job, and I would further suggest that they might contribute to that job in somewhat the same way as the radicals of the law have contributed to our legal processes. I pleaded for their incorporation into the colleges and universities to that end. And finally, I would meet the inevitable charge that the Emersonian concept and what I have been saying about it does not make practical scholarly sense by quoting a considered statement by Professor L. J. Henderson of Harvard, biochemist, starred in *American Men of Science*, who, coming to this matter with materials vastly different from mine, has arrived at the same place:

> Here is a body of evidence and of carefully formed inductions. It points to a clear conclusion, to a conclusion that has been almost completely obscured because the makers of the intellectual tradition, and still more its transmitters, like the politi-

cal scientists of whom Aristotle speaks, have rarely known human societies intimately at first hand. And when the facts have obtruded themselves, "intellectuals" have too often regarded them as expressions of ignorant prejudice or superstition, unworthy of their notice, and as an impertinent intrusion of nonsense into their more serious concerns. The conclusion, greatly over-simplified, is this: The acquired characters of men are of two kinds. One kind is chiefly intellectual, the other arises chiefly from conditioning, and from rituals and routines. This it is that has been neglected by intellectuals; yet this is the older, the more primitive, and in many respects by far the more important of the two.

. . . .

A suitable dose, neither too much nor too little, of such acquired characters, harmoniously interrelated, seems necessary to the stability of individuals and of societies, and as a foundation for orderly change. When social change is too rapid, a suitable dose is less often acquired. Without a very great deal of the resulting regular conduct, what we call liberty is impossible.

THE ONLY GREAT DECIDER

THE AMERICAN ACADEMY OF ARTS
AND SCIENCES, BOSTON, MASSACHUSETTS

APRIL 11, 1945

NOT very long ago your president and I were engaged in what might have seemed, to someone who does not know your president and me, a heated correspondence upon the subject of this paper. By way of giving him the *coup de grâce* I sent him a paper I once had read on the subject and suggested, not quite innocently, that perhaps I ought to publish it. Your president replied:

> I'm against publishing it anywhere. I'm against your committing yourself in cold print. Because the next thing you know, some injured applicant or endorser will say: But look here, in the Journal of Speculative Education, in that article you wrote, you said so-and-so, and if you meant what you said, you are doing me wrong in turning me down. No, no, publish a neat little article on bronze crucifixes dug up near Athlone as an index of Gaelic culture, but don't publish anything about how to pick people out.

But, though he thought the paper quite unpublishable, your president thought it had points as oral discourse. So here I am.

There are not many of you, I suppose, who have not been bothered by me, asking for a judgment of someone, or of his research proposal, and usually of both. An average of ten thousand such requests for judgments go from my office every

21

year. Believe it or not, the figure is accurate, and it is ten thousand. The dragnet for information and judgments on applicants is spread very widely and it brings in a lot of stuff. What it brings in is read, remembered, and filed; it often starts new lines of inquiry. What I get is usually accurate factually: but its value as judgment varies within very wide limits. Some people, I have concluded, have no judgment; so naturally they cannot give it. Some people have a judgment but for reasons of friendship with the applicant, dislike of me, and for lots of other reasons do not give it. The discrepancy between the apparent truth and the statement is known, in the broad lingo of those who are in this peculiar business, as the "coefficient of mendacity" in letters of recommendation. We make some claims to estimate the coefficient in respect to a large number of persons. But, some people both have a judgment and give it to us and they are the bright jewels, the apples of our eyes, the white-haired boys, or what you will.

You would ask me, properly, how I know that they have judgment. In the first place, there is experience: I have been reading these letters, these statements of judgment for more than twenty years. I have an office system which is good enough so that in five minutes I can see, together, every letter any referee has written me about persons through twenty years. I also have a good many records of the persons about whom the referee has written me in the past. Putting these data together, the predictive value of the referee's statement is fairly clear. It also is pretty clear whether or not his intellectual arteries are hardening or his spirit is drooping. And as important as anything, we can get inklings whether his failures are due to belief in intellectual daring that did not quite come off or to belief that the safe and sane is best. In this business the gilt-edged stuff pays, as about usual, two per cent, and two per cent is not to be despised; but your portfolio is not a good one unless you have a fair amount of speculative stuff in it—say forty per cent. It ought to be higher in specula-

tive stuff, but the plain fact of the matter is that good intellectual gambles are rare—just as good business gambles are rare.

But I have digressed somewhat from the main point: and
the main point, for anybody granting research funds, is related to the persons from whom you get judgments. The plain
fact of the matter is that any organization granting research
funds is utterly dependent upon the quality of advice it gets.
No administrative staff, no committee from within the organization, unless the research interests of the organization
be very special, can stand close enough to all frontiers to have
any judgment of the value of those working at the frontiers.

The difficulty of trying to say anything is that it cannot be
said all at once. You may have noted my referring to the
"apparent truth of referees' statements," their "predictive
value," "working at the frontiers." These, as they stand, are
question-begging phrases. Who am I to say, or who is anybody
else to say, what is truth about any person? Who can know in
advance what the predictive value of any statement is? Who
can say what horse, in the words on the program, is going to
win the race? Who can tell where the main front line is? Who
in the thick of the battle can tell Tarawa from Iwo Jima, or
even from Bougainville?

The only honest answers I can make to these questions is
that I do not know complete answers to them.

But however impossible it be to come by complete answers
to these questions, partial answers can be had, good indica-
tions can be had, and on the basis of them a shrewd, honest,
imaginative, and informed committee can come up with conclusions, a substantial percentage of which the future will
show to be valid. By valid I do not mean anything more than
that it would appear to me that a reasonable person would
think, on the future evidence, that the committee had not
made a mistake.

All this, I realize, is very abstract. But you will understand
that I cannot name names nor instance instances. I cannot,

for example, name Dr. So-and-So and say that he has no judgment, only a desire to get for his own doctors as much as he can. No more could I name Dr. Y who, while he recently has achieved international recognition for the work he did as a young man amid the scoffing of his colleagues, now has a closed mind as to the possibility of young men being in the same position he was in thirty years ago. Neither could I name Professor X, who while no great creative scholar himself, nevertheless seems to us to have a very high batting average when it comes to recognizing the real thing. I cannot even mention by name the horse that won the futurity with our backing, which had been granted despite much testimony that he was off on the wrong track. There have been such. I hasten to add that I cannot mention either the horse that won the race without our backing—withheld sometimes because scholars who ought to have been in the best position to judge judged that he did not have what it takes. This kind of instance is the most humbling of all. If a young scholar gets your backing and proceeds to success, the suspicion will not down that he might have done it anyway. The suspicion becomes very deep when someone who did not get your backing does it anyway. But the real point to remember is that no foundation or other educational or research organization stands alone and that the assistance that one of them grants would be useless if it stood alone. Naturally, I have had a considerable interest in our "misses" and so far as I have been able to run things down, I have found that these persons, at some stages, have received assistance from other foundations. This, of course, is the reason why there should not be interlocking directorates among foundations: the result of pooling judgments inevitably would be a combination in restraint of legitimate intellectual trade.

But the assistance given by other foundations to our "misses" affords small comfort to a man in my position who takes his job seriously. What I should like to be able to do after twenty years is to look at a field and know that practically everyone of significance, in say the twenty-five- to fifty-year age range, in it has had the Foundation's assistance and that there is not, on the other hand, a high percentage of duds in the field who have had our assistance. This is not often possible for the reason that most fields get support from several foundations, and so no one foundation has a fair shot at all the people in it. It is, however, the fact that there has been one field that has been clear for us, and, while it is not strictly germane to the subject of this paper, it will serve to illustrate what I have in mind. It is the field of musical composition. In that field it may be said with assurance that our Fellows in musical composition, of say between twenty-five and fifty years of age, are at the top of the heap and that they, with one or two additions, occupy the whole top; it may also be said with assurance that while we have made mistakes of appointment in this field they are very few in number.

How did this occur? In the first place, we had the field practically to ourselves. Secondly, we had Mr. Thomas Whitney Surette, whom many of you doubtless knew. He was sixty-three years old when he first began to act as our adviser and that certainly was one strike against him. He knew practically none of the younger composers personally, and that might be a second strike against him. But in fifteen years he did not strike out. On the plus side: he had time and he had unlimited interest in young composers and the future of music in the United States. He was not a composer of any consequence, he was not a rigorous historian of music; but he could read a score and hear it in his mind and he had that unpredictable ability called judgment. This judgment was not exercised vaguely: it was analyzed. He always asked a series of questions and those questions were: what training has this man had, as a matter of fact, training in school and self training; what has he done, as a matter of fact, in writing music? And then questions of judgment: what does his production show of his knowledge of what has gone before, what originality has he brought to the work of the past, how much has he got in him for the future, what is the intrinsic quality of his own work regardless of whether one likes it or not? These are all matters of judgment, and so far as I can judge, after twenty years, Mr. Surette came up with the right answers a very high percentage of the time; but here the point is that these are exactly the questions which also must be asked and answered, in relation to choosing grantees of research funds. All this Professor John Livingston Lowes in his incomparable *Road to Xanadu* has said better.

> The road to Xanadu, as we have traced it, is the road of human spirit, and the imagination voyaging through chaos and reducing it to clarity and order is the symbol of all the quests that lend glory to our dust.

All the quests, be it noted: science, liberal and social studies, the arts and engineering.

And Professor Lowes continues:

> The notion that the creative imagination, especially in its highest exercise, has little or nothing to do with the facts is one of the pseudodoxia epidemica which die hard. For the imagination never operates in a vacuum. Its stuff is always fact of some order, somehow experienced: its product is that fact transmuted. . . .

That transmutation is what makes all scholarship and all art worthy of their place. The intake is fact, the output should be fact transmuted. Only the person who can make that transmutation is worthy of special opportunities to carry on his own work.

Doubtless you all are familiar with Mr. Conant's statement of the division of the field of secular learning into three parts: accumulative knowledge, philosophy and poetry, in his words. In his speech of acceptance of the Priestley medal, after outlining the division, Mr. Conant said:

> Accumulative knowledge is distinguished from the other two divisions of the field of human learning by the fact that we can

readily recognize a progressive increase in our capacity to answer questions which have attracted the attention of inquiring minds for generations. For example, there can be no doubt that if the pioneers in chemistry or physics or mathematics were brought to life today they would exclaim with delight and wonder at the progress which has been made. . . . But one has only to imagine a meeting of Galileo, Newton, Faraday and Maxwell, with a group of modern physicists on the one hand, and a meeting of Machiavelli, Hobbes, Locke, Adam Smith and Mill with a group of modern social scientists on the other, to recognize the difference I have in mind. . . .

I wonder whether the difference is what Mr. Conant says. I do not myself think that Faraday would wonder more at radar, than Machiavelli would at lend-lease. I doubt that Newton would marvel more at the Einstein gravitational work than Thomas Hobbes would at the Declaration of Independence and the Constitution of the United States. I would even go so far as to say that I am pretty sure that Adam Smith would be mightily impressed by the Keynesian economics although he might not like it from the point of view of a value judgment.

Mr. Conant is of course right if he was thinking, as he undoubtedly was, about advances all along the line in the several fields. The social sciences have no such record of steady advances as the natural sciences have. Neither have the humanistic studies. The sciences have their method and, what is equally important, the sciences attract men of the highest pioneering ability. They also have large public support. They are generally attractive, not only because what they have done has resulted in a vast array of things like radio, hybrid corn, rustless wheat, sulpha drugs, and synthetic rubber, but also because, apart from technological advance, they represent something on which everybody can get together without serious differences of opinion resulting from differing value judgments.

In short, in the serious business of the advancement of learning, the sciences now have the easiest part, and selection from among scientists, for fellowships and as grantees of research funds, is easiest because there usually is respectable agreement among all who ought to be in position to judge. The difficult problems of decisions in the sciences are in relation to men opening up what they think are new veins, new sciences, not yet recognized. I do not, let me say earnestly, think less well of the advice we get about scientific matters, nor feel less obliged to scientific advisers, because their advice is not usually controversial. It is really fine, on a job where too much has to be decided, to have some things that can be decided fairly easily.

I wish other fields were like that; but in scholarly fields, outside the sciences, it is not easy to find agreement about much. This year, for example, we had thirty applications in the field of English language and literature. After all the evidence I could get was in, I submitted this group of applications to five separate referees—all scholars whose judgment we esteem and who have had long familiarity with what we are trying to do. All judged that about a half-dozen of this group of applications should be appointed to fellowships, but, only two names appeared on all the lists of recommendations.

The trouble was that these experts did not ask consistently and did not try to answer the series of questions Mr. Surette always asked and answered. So far as I could see they did not consistently remember that the test of the power to transmute the knowledge with which the applicant intended to deal is the test which should be applied to all who call themselves original scholars and original workers in the arts.

That power may be of higher or lower degree: its possession in some degree is the *sine qua non*. The problem of selecting recipients of research grants is to find those who have it: those who do not have should be denied research funds.

We had an application the other day which I can disguise sufficiently so that I may mention it. A man wanted to make a finding list of works in a certain area of English prose and he wanted a fellowship to help him to get on with it. It was admitted by the more honest or discriminating of his eminent backers that he lacked originality and imagination: it was even admitted that his "is the way of the beaver rather than the eagle" but the backers then went on to try to make the case in terms of need for the product.

Upon this point a critic commented cogently: "Of course, a finding list is a useful tool to get at needed material. But I find that, as in Butler's *Erewhon*, machines breed machines, so scholars no sooner get one bibliographical aid under way than that breeds other demands of the same kind. I think, if scholarship is to be a steadying influence in the years ahead of us, that we have to look for interpreters and not for compilers; and because X or Y or Z is a competent compiler, we tend to say he must have a grant in aid because this is in the interests of disinterested scholarship or research or some other mystic value. I would rejoice exceedingly if the Foundation would set its face against grants in aid of creating more bibliographies, finding lists, and other items of scholarly machinery, and insist that its primary duty to society is to search out and subsidize the merchants of light that Marjorie Nicolson pleaded for some months ago before the American Philosophical Society. 'There is no use deploring the unhuman quality of American scholarship on Tuesday, and voting sums for more mechanisms on Wednesday.' "

I agree with that. Sometimes, often in this business we have to take the position, as Emerson put it, that "a pop-gun is a pop-gun although the ancient and honorable of the earth affirm it to be the crack of doom." Conversely, we sometimes have to have the nerve to say that while it is *not* the crack of doom it nevertheless is very important, though the ancient and honorable of the earth affirm it to be a pop-gun. It is best not to say much about this kind of thing but the fact is that to do a job of creative selection, you have to take a gamble once in a while based on the belief that only Jim is in step.

29

The Only Great Decider

I take great comfort in Emerson's statement: it gives such fine scope for the application of big prejudices. It gives such fine incentive for taking a chance against the best and most eminent advice. I also take comfort from the example of Mr. Joseph Couthouy, for knowledge of whom I am indebted to Dr. Isaiah Bowman.

The Association of American Geologists and Naturalists met in Boston on April 26, 1842, and Professor Edward Hitchcock of Amherst College read a paper on "Glacio-Aqueous Action in North America." Mr. Couthouy, a merchant skipper who had sailed in Antarctic waters on his way around the Horn, heard the paper and commented upon it. The secretary of the meeting, reporting upon the matter, wrote:

> Mr. Couthouy observed that . . . in relation to the production of
> . . . glacial furrows he had no preconceived views of his own
> to support; but that when he first heard them attributed to the
> grating of icebergs along the bottom, he was convinced, by the
> recollection he had personally witnessed of the action of ice
> under such circumstances at the present day, that this never
> would have produced such results. . . . He felt persuaded that
> no person who had seen the actual movements of a stranded
> iceberg, would ever afterwards entertain for a moment, the
> idea that such a cause would produce the furrows under con-
> sideration. . . . It was with much diffidence that he dissented
> from the opinion entertained by some eminent geologists. . . .
> He offered these suggestions with no small hesitation, fully
> sensible how presumptuous it might seem in him to venture
> a difference in opinion with those eminent geologists who had
> addressed the Association on this topic. They were, however,
> such as rose naturally in his mind while reflecting on what had
> passed under his observation. . . .

In the spirit of Mr. Couthouy, we too have ventured, sometimes to dissent from the opinion of eminent scholars, on fresh evidence contra to their views; and usually we have been pleased that we took the chance.

The program refers to dark horses, including scientific ones. There are such in all fields but they are much fewer in science than in other fields. The reason for this situation is that scientists in this country, with the practical disappearance of the old-time naturalists, are only those who have had long training in centers with adequate, and usually expensive, instrumentation and other materials. By and large, scientists come from those centers.

But the Foundation also operates a plan of Latin American fellowships and there the scientific dark horse is not an unusual phenomenon. I remember well showing to Dr. Hans Zinsser some clippings from a provincial Chilean newspaper, the only place an applicant had found to publish his bacteriological observations. We gave the man a fellowship to work with Dr. Zinsser. Under that great scientist and human being, the young man blossomed and the crop of his scientific fruit is now very large and fine indeed. We had been told, by eminent Chilean scholars, and this apparently closed the matter in their minds, that there was no science in Antofagasta: they were wrong, as Dr. Zinsser saw. They were wrong because they would not look at the evidence as he did.

But, as Bishop Butler said in his Sermon on Balaam, "Things and actions are what they are, and the consequences of them will be what they will be: Why then should we desire to be deceived?"

This is my text, if I have any. In selecting persons for research fellowships you need to follow the evidence as far as it will take you and only so far, no matter who says it takes you further or who says it takes you less far. (How far is matter for dependable experts to decide?) But the next step, that of selection, is a creative act in which the subliminal, as in all creative acts, is the most important part—the subliminal self using the materials gathered by the work-a-day consciousness.

If there be persons here who think that the word "prejudice"—which I used a little while back, as a factor of decision in some non-clear cases—connotes something wrong I should not defend the use of the particular word in that connection;

but I *should* maintain that it does give the general idea of what goes on. Lawyers have examined, more closely than any other group, the bases of decision and I commend to all grantors of research funds a careful study of Mr. Justice Cardozo's "The Nature of the Judicial Process." Properly, the selection of persons is a judicial process and lawyers know that tight decisions, on cases outside the main streams of decision, are made on the basis of personal preferences, articulate and inarticulate convictions, formulated and unformulated views of general policy. In all honesty, tight cases at law are decided the way they are because the decider is what he is, and in all honesty that is the basis of tight decisions in making fellowship awards. The only great decider in law and at the fellowship bar is that court that really can think and which, making its inductions out of experience under the burden of responsibility, can for a moment be greater than it is—that is, rises to a creative act.

SCIENCE'S PROPER SHARE
OF THE NATIONAL POOL OF ABILITY

AMERICAN ASSOCIATION

FOR THE ADVANCEMENT OF SCIENCE,

BOSTON, MASSACHUSETTS, DECEMBER 28, 1946

AT the 1946 Annual Meeting of the AAAS, there was a Symposium on the Shortage of Scientific Personnel. I was asked to speak on the importance of the problem. I had recently been Chairman of a Committee which had reported to Dr. Vannevar Bush, Director of the wartime Office of Scientific Research and Development, on the discovery and development of scientific talent in American youth. That Committee consisted of Dr. Henry A. Barton, Director of the American Institute of Physics; Dr. C. Lalor Burdick, special assistant to the President, E. I. du Pont de Nemours & Co.; Dr. James B. Conant, President of Harvard University; Watson Davis, Director of Science Service; Dr. Robert E. Doherty, President of the Carnegie Institute of Technology; Dr. Paul E. Elicker, Executive Secretary of the National Association of Secondary School Principals; Mr. Farnham P. Griffiths, lawyer of San Francisco; Dr. Walter S. Hunter, Professor of Psychology in Brown University; Dr. T. R. McConnell, Dean of the College of Science, Literature and Arts in the University of Minnesota; Mr. Walter S. Rogers, Director of the Institute of Current World Affairs; Dr. Harlow Shapley, Director of the Harvard College Observatory; Dr. Hugh S. Taylor, Professor of Chemistry; Dr. Edwin Bidwell Wilson, Professor of Vital Statistics in the Harvard School of Public Health; and myself. We set up and recommended that the nation should search for and train for the national welfare

Science's Proper Share of Ability

*scientists and engineers of the highest ability without regard to
where they were born and reared and without regard to the size
of the family income. And, also unanimously, we warned, "The
statesmanship of science . . . requires that science be concerned
with more than science. Science can only be an effective element
in the national welfare as a member of a team, whether the condition be peace or war. . . . Science must not try to hog it all."*

*This paper is a statement of the considerations why science's
share of the pool of our country's high ability must be related to
the other needs of our society for high ability.*

I AM no authority on the history of science nor on the history
of support for science; but, along the line of my need to know
what our problem has been, I remember that in my early days
at the Guggenheim Foundation, beginning in 1924, I was
made aware of the fight which had been made and won for
financial support for science in the United States. The cause
then had centered about the worthwhileness of support of
science: would it pay out in social return? In the light of what
has happened since, the labored arguments to show that there
would be an adequate pay-off for science support have the
look of insisting upon the obvious; but it is worth remember-
ing that it was a real issue then.

In the procession of arguments for support of science, there
was Bulletin No. 1—significantly, I think, No. 1—of the National Research Council, entitled *The National Importance of
Scientific and Industrial Research*. It was written by Dr.
George Ellery Hale and other giants of those days and in it
we find Dr. Hale saying:

> Throughout the civilized world the national importance of
> science and research is appreciated as never before. . . . Scien-
> tific research was the first requisite [for winning the war] and
> both men and funds had to be provided without delay.
>
> No intelligent statesman, however, could meet such a situa-
> tion without appreciating its obvious limitations. Successful
> research demands trained investigators and these cannot be
> produced in a day.

34

Science's Proper Share of Ability

Later on in the paper he says:

We find industries which have awakened to the importance of research drawing from the universities and research foundations, by superior financial inducements, the men on whom we must depend for fundamental contributions to knowledge from which industrial progress springs. . . . It is plain that the skilled investigators needed in rapidly increasing numbers to man the laboratories of industrial research must be developed by the universities and schools of technology. But it is also clear that the draft of competent research men must not seriously deplete the ranks of those who are advancing knowledge. The universities should have ample means to support research, and the industries, especially those that profit from science, should aid them by establishing fellowships, professorships and adequately endowed laboratories.

We find Dr. J. J. Carty saying:

Let us arouse the people of our country to the wonderful possibilities to support it [research] which rests upon them, and I am sure that they will respond generously and effectively.

We find Dr. James Rowland Angell saying:

Among the many lessons which the war taught us, few have made a deeper impression upon the public mind than that of the part played by science and technology in the prosecution of any of the great undertakings of modern life. . . .

When the United States was drawn into the war one of the first problems which presented itself was the securing of the necessary number of scientific experts to organize and direct the tremendous technical enterprises which had promptly to be put on foot.

The price of a sound progressive national life is in these times widespread and intelligent scientific research. . . . This obligation to foster research means, first, the providing of a greatly enlarged personnel with much better fundamental training than is at present available. It means second the securing of the necessary facilities of laboratories, apparatus and all the physical conveniences that are involved in scientific work. It means third the procuring of sufficient freedom from other duties to permit research workers to give their full and undivided attention throughout such periods as may be necessary for the completion of their research undertakings.

It sounds like today—but not quite. History repeats itself but never exactly—or as Mr. Holmes put it we must not ask too much of history.

The fight for support of science was won, and then science entered into an era of apparent peace, prosperous and sure of itself. Yet today most of the elements in the scientific situation that we are thinking of were present in the 1919 situation —the need for science, the shortage of scientific personnel, the raids by industry on the producers of scientists, the necessity for public support.

Today our symposium is on one of these elements, the shortage of scientific personnel, and to me has been assigned a statement concerning the importance of the problem. I assume that Dr. Trytten, your next speaker, will go into the question of the present extent of these shortages. Concerning him, I should like to say in gratitude that when preparing material for the Bush Report, the advisory committee of which I was chairman went into the question as it then appeared, and relied to a very considerable extent upon Dr. Trytten's studies.

In view of Dr. Trytten's paper, it will suffice for me to say on this head that it was the considered conclusion of Dr. Bush's advisory committee upon scientific personnel that the shortages at the time we wrote the report were a matter for serious concern to all informed and thinking men, and now certainly the situation is no less serious.

Assuming that no one, in this day, needs to argue the necessity for a healthy and adequate science in this country, we need, however, to put into the record why the situation as respects scientific personnel now, in the United States, is a serious one.

It is partly because in our usual way, when we set out to do a job, we do it to the exclusion of everything else; the long-term considerations we put off. We set out to do the job of winning the war to the whole extent of our ability to contribute to victory, and that is the job we did. We stopped almost completely the training of men not only in fields of science and technology but in all fields. With the exception of students of medicine and engineering in Army and Navy programs and some 2,400 men on the reserved list who were taken from their studies for civilian war research, all physically fit students, graduate and undergraduate, and those ready for college over eighteen years old, were taken into the armed forces and were kept there. This went on for five years. What you take five years to undo in reference to training people for a vital function in the nation's interest, you cannot make up in any lesser amount of time, and unless you do twice as much training for five years following the five blank years as you were doing before the blank years you are going to lose up to five years of production of scientists. This is just elementary arithmetic, and, furthermore, serious as arithmetic shows the situation to be, there is no doubt that a higher calculus, if it can be made, will show it to be more serious still.

Those of us who wrote the report on the fourth question of President Roosevelt's letter to Dr. Bush, concerning the discovery and development of scientific talent, looked long and hard at a lot of figures concerned with the nation's future needs for personnel in science and technology. But in the end we confessed that we knew no way to calculate the nation's future needs for scientists and engineers. We all were convinced, however, that the needs would be greater in the future than they had been in the past.

In 1919 Dr. George Ellery Hale quoted with approval a statement by de Tocqueville in *Democracy in America*:

The French made surprising advances in the exact sciences at the very time when they were completing the destruction of the remains of their former feudal society; yet this sudden fecundity is not to be attributed to democracy, but to the unexampled revolution which attended its growth.

And Dr. Hale himself similarly concluded:

The intellectual stimulus accompanying great upheavals, however they originate, finds expression in unusual achievements in science.

However valid these theories may be, the situation, here and now, in short, is that we stopped for five years doing what it takes six years to do—that is, to take an eighteen-year-old and train him to the point where he is a producing scientist—and then at the end of the five years' stoppage we are faced with an increased and increasing demand for the product.

That is what this symposium is about, and following Dr. Trytten's paper on the supply and demand for scientific personnel I shall certainly listen with high interest to the papers on what government, the universities, and industry are doing about the problem.

My committee, if I may use a convenient shorthand, on the Bush Report concluded that the magnitude of the problem was such that the best prospect for solving it was through the Federal Government.

We proposed short-term ways of doing something about the problem and also a long-term way. The short-term ways all were related to what the Army and Navy ought to do following victory in Europe, none of which we judged would in any way weaken the war effort against Japan. But none of those things were done, and that water is all under the bridge, although I am going to say for the record that those short-term plans look, in retrospect, even better than they did at the time they were made. We pointed out that, in our judgments and in the judgment of all patriotic informed citizens—at least we could discover no contrary views—amelioration of the scientific deficits then piling up was necessary for military security, good public health, full employment, a higher standard of living after the war, and indeed was necessary from whatever angle anyone looked at the situation. But, as said, we drew a blank on any results from those recommendations.

They were short-term recommendations and are in the past. That bus was missed completely and it will never come back.

But we also made long-term recommendations for discovering and developing scientific talent in American youth through the foreseeable long future.

We studied the evidence concerned with the future needs—what in Mr. Holmes's words the problem tends to become—of the nation for scientists and engineers. Having regard to what appeared to be reasonable prospects for assistance in training them from colleges, universities, private sources, foundations, and local and state governments, we concluded, on the basis of an executive judgment of the total evidence we could get at, that providing scholarships for about 24,000 students of science and technology—6,000 entering a year—would be about right, with provision for about 300 graduate fellowships annually. There was not in our minds any sense of sacredness of these figures: the future might revise them down or up without objection from us. Nor were we so naïve as to think that these scholarship and fellowship provisions would increase the supply of scientists and engineers by the annual figures of recommended scholarships and fellowships. We knew that federal money in the area of science and technology would drive other money into other areas—that is, drive at least some of it into other areas. This, let me say at once, in my view, would be a good thing; but of that I shall say more later on.

Perhaps this talk is too elementary for this professional scientific audience; but about some things, I have concluded, it is impossible to be too elementary.

I have been asked *why*, since we had gotten as far as we had scientifically and technologically, and *why*, if the greatest war of all time was won on the basis of scientific advance—as it is arguable it was—why do we need to discover and train x thousand more scientists a year? The question may not sound sensible to this audience, but it makes sense, I assure you, to lots of people. Personally I have respect for the question and to the askers of it I respond as thoughtfully as I can. My answer goes like this.

It is a wholly safe assumption that in the United States, before the present overloading of all institutions of higher learning, practically all young people of brains and character who knew what they wanted and who could afford to pay for it could get and did get a scientific or technological or any other education. But now, on all the evidence we can find, that prewar total will not be enough to satisfy the nation's needs for scientists and engineers. Hence we must increase the prewar total.

You will have noted that there are two conditions to my statement about the total number of persons who got a scientific or technological education in prewar days: *first*, that they knew they wanted a scientific education and *second*, that they could afford to pay for it.

The first of these conditions is tantamount to saying that they must have been somewhere in touch with science and that means usually in a good secondary school. But it is painfully true that in some parts of the country good secondary schools are rare. Where this condition holds there will be much loss of high ability to training, simply because that high ability does not get interested in further training—in science or in any other field of the mind and spirit. But, while I recognize this, I am not a perfectionist and I would propose that before we as a nation tackle this situation we take first an easier road to producing a larger number of trained minds.

That easier road, and cheaper and quicker road, is to select those young persons who want to go on in their studies, who have shown that they have the brains and character for it, but who cannot afford it—select them on their merits and pay for their education on a modest scale of payment. There are reliable studies which show that the probability of college attendance for a high school graduate who is the child of a professional father is several times higher than for the child of a laborer. There are other studies which show that a large percentage of superior high school students do not get higher education simply because their parents cannot afford to pay for it.

The intelligence of a country's citizenry is obviously its greatest natural resource. Yet here we are wasting an appreciable part of ours by not giving it a chance to develop through higher education. We provide higher instruction at practically no charge to the student; but we pay very little attention to the important question of what he is going to use for subsistence money while getting the instruction. We provide board and lodging and institutional care for our feeble-minded; but lots of people have the idea that to provide food and lodging for our best young minds during the period of their education somehow is wrong or at least is not a proper function of government.

However, we who wrote the report on scientific personnel in the Bush Report saw it as an entirely proper function of government, and we proposed to select 6,000 of these fine young minds each year and stake them to an education, grub-stake them, with modest subsistence money, to a scientific or technological education that they otherwise probably would not get. It would cost about $20,000,000 a year; but if anybody has figured out how better to spend $20,000,000 annually for the long-term good of our country, it has not come to my notice. And if there is anything wrong with spending federal money for such a purpose I have not yet heard wherein the wrongness lies.

My committee on the Bush Report was charged with formulating a plan for the discovery and development of scientific talent in American youth, and we did what we were required to do: we confined our recommendations to scientific talent. But we also pointed out that:

> The statesmanship of science . . . requires that science be concerned with more than science. Science can only be an effective element in the national welfare as a member of a team, whether the condition be peace or war.
>
> As citizens, as good citizens, we therefore think that we must have in mind while examining the question before us—the discovery and development of scientific talent—the needs of the whole national welfare. We could not suggest to you a program which would syphon into science and technology a disproportionately large share of the Nation's highest abilities, without doing harm to the Nation, nor, indeed, without crippling science. The very fruits of science become available only through enterprise, industry and wisdom on the part of others as well as scientists. Science cannot live by and unto itself alone. . . .
>
> The uses to which high ability in youth can be put are various and, to a large extent, are determined by social pressures and rewards. When aided by selective devices for picking out scientifically talented youth, it is clear that large sums of money for scholarships and fellowships and monetary and other rewards in disproportionate amounts might draw into science too large a percentage of the Nation's high ability, with a result highly detrimental to the Nation and to science. Plans for the discovery and development of scientific talent must be related to the other needs of society for high ability: science, in the words of the man in the street, must not, and must not try to, hog it all. This is our deep conviction, and therefore the plans that we shall propose herein will endeavor to relate the needs of the Nation for science to the needs of the Nation for high-grade trained minds in other fields. There is never enough ability at high levels to satisfy all the needs of the Nation; we would not seek to draw into science any more of it than science's proportionate share.

And we further said:

> As emphasized, this report is concerned with discovering and developing scientific talent, but in its proper setting and

relationship to other needs for talent for the Nation's welfare. In the report we shall suggest, as befits our mandate, the appropriation of federal funds to be applied only to the purpose of discovering and developing scientific talent; but, as we have pointed out, we recognize that there is need for the discovery and development of talent in all lines and we point out that most of the plans and procedures recommended herein for science are equally applicable to the discovery and development of talent in other fields.

If this audience runs true to the form I have seen in other audiences, some of you will now be thinking: "Just why does he think he has to drag this social science controversy in? Doesn't he know that he is supposed to be talking about the importance of the problem of the shortage of *scientific* personnel?"

All such I shall take back to the beginning of this paper and say again: In order to know what a problem is, we must know what it was, and what it tends to become. If you are interested in shortages, you are interested in at least lessening the shortages. If you lessen a shortage by taking material from a field where the supply is limited, you necessarily affect others' needs for that material. If others' needs for that material significantly affect your own operations you would be unwise to lessen your own shortages by increasing theirs. In the context of this paper, it is clear to me that our problem of lessening our scientific shortages *tends to become* something besides that particular problem and that is why I consider a discussion of the needs for high ability in fields other than science to be germane to the topic assigned to me.

For our observations on this subject—those quoted above— we were at first let off scot-free. But when the President, in his message recommending science legislation, added five words, "and in the social sciences," we were told by some scientists that we, or somebody, had very much gummed the works. I have no way of knowing how you or a majority or a minority of you stand on this proposition, but if you will listen to me with your minds and not with your prejudices I shall state two truths—they are so to me—which ought to convince you, I think, that the President was right to include the social sciences in his proposed science legislation—at least insofar as the need for discovery and development of talent in American youth is concerned. "Truth to me," Mr. Holmes used to say, "is just what I can't help believing"; and I can't help believing this:

First: Science is not properly a game, played by its participants for their own benefit and satisfaction. Science, like anything else paid for out of the public's purse, is justifiable only insofar as it results, as a long-term proposition, in a fuller and more fruitful life to the people at large—by the improvement of standards and satisfactions of living, by the creation of new enterprises, bringing in new jobs, etc. But these results are not merely matters for science. They are also in very important ways matters of economic organization, of systems of taxation, of fair public administration, of resistance to pressure groups, and of many other social science factors. We, quite simply stated, shall not get the benefits of science in the best manner in our national life unless really scientific studies are developed in connection with many broad economic, social, and political items in our national organization. To get those studies we need to develop social thinkers—more of them and better ones than we now have. And not only do we as a nation need them, but the world also needs them; and science as socially useful science needs them. For without those studies, free science is going to be something your successors may read about but will not have.

Moreover, as we increase the tempo of scientific advance, the more shall we need to better the quality of thought over the whole spectrum of the human mind and spirit. For this reason do I devoutly hope, as I said earlier, that, if support for scientific training comes from government, and no gov-

Science's Proper Share of Ability

ernmental support goes to other training, funds now used for science training will be driven into other fields.

Second: There is a very elementary and self-evident reason for not restricting a program for the discovery and development of talent in American youth to the sciences. The reason is this: In youth, say at the end of high school, it is too early to say whether or not a boy or girl should be committed to a career in science and be given a scientific education. True it is that certain tests can be given to youth which show with some degree of accuracy whether or not they are oriented toward scientific pursuits; but it is also true that those same tests point to success in fields other than science. And science has no business, neither for the nation's good nor for its own good, to try to grab too large a share of the available brains.

Those of you who have followed what I have been saying may tell me that it leads to the logical conclusion that all high ability should be included in the talent search and its development; that potential literary critics, poets, composers, painters, theologians, and all those who can profit from higher training should be included. If that be said I should respond *yes*, I think so; for I agree with Dr. Raymond Fosdick, President of the Rockefeller Foundation, who said recently: "Certainly in our search for the means to control our own fate we must not overlook the possibility that the unity of mankind may be achieved by art or music, a poem or song, perhaps more effectively and lastingly than by engineering, medicine, or economics."

The point of view that poets and painters and composers, humanists and social scientists have as strong claims to support as scientists in any plan for the development of those who will lead mankind is the point of view of the John Simon Guggenheim Memorial Foundation; and for more than twenty years we have made our appropriations in that belief.

But, having said this in respect to the Foundation's funds,

45

Science's Proper Share of Ability

I shall go on to say that while I hope I am pure—in a mathematician's use of that word—I also hope I am not too pure and that I am not so politically simple, where the question is on the use of government funds, as to insist upon ultimates or end-of-the-road conclusions.

Time brings many innovations, as the founders of early universities, State and other, would see if they could see now the present breadth and inclusiveness of their institutions. They might not be content with what they would see; but, as for me, I should be content to wait for many logically foreseeable developments and not be distressed if they did not work out according to my or anybody else's logic.

I have come around again, you see, to Mr. Holmes's saying that:

> The felt necessities of the time, the prevalent moral and political theories, intuitions of public policy, avowed or unconscious, even the prejudices which judges share with their fellow-men, have had a good deal more to do than the syllogism in determining the rules by which men should be governed.

In this constitutional republic it cannot be otherwise and *it should not be otherwise*. Whatever scientists may think of the importance of the problem of the shortage of scientific personnel, they will get no amelioration of it by government unless and until amelioration is one of "the felt necessities of the time." And if we get it we shall get it only in accordance with "the prevalent moral and political theories" of this country at the time of legislative enactment, in accordance with "intuitions of public policy" and in accordance with the prejudices which members of Congress and the Executive share with their fellow-men.

Those prejudices—and neither Mr. Holmes nor I are using the word invidiously but in its primary sense—will not now permit poets to be educated by federal funds; but I hope and believe that in any science legislation the wisdom of the Congress—which I believe in—will demand the development of the

46

social and humane sciences concomitantly with the natural sciences. If not, you or your successors will, some day, wish the Congress had.

John Stuart Mill writing *On Liberty* wrote my conclusion:

The worth of a State, in the long run, is the worth of the individuals composing it; and a State which postpones the interests of *their* mental expansion and elevation, to a little more of administrative skill, or that semblance of it which practice gives, in the details of business; a State which dwarfs its men, in order that they may be more docile instruments in its hands even for beneficial purposes, will find that with small men no really great thing can be accomplished.

THE DOCTOR AS CITIZEN*

AMERICAN COLLEGE OF PHYSICIANS,

NEW YORK, MARCH 30, 1949

I START from the premise that what distinguishes the professional man is that he has a history, a history in his profession, and a concern, as the Quakers say, for the future. For you, some of that history and some of that hope is embodied in the pledge you all have made upon being admitted to the fellowship of this College. But this is a very small part indeed of the history and the hope which the medical profession has long maintained. As citizens we are all laymen; as professionals we are all citizens; and only as citizens, of whatever form of government, do we, as professionals, fulfill our deeper hopes, have our chance of success, exercise our motives, and live our lives. This is my theme: The Doctor as Citizen is conscious of history and he has a concern for the future.

The thought of the citizen in these days is dominated by the cliché that there is "so little time," or expressed in another way, "it is later than you think": we are going to Hell fast, the clichés all affirm, and we have got to do something about it *fast*. Perhaps so; but we, as professionals, cannot do anything about it fast—not a thing. Perhaps government can; but we cannot. Perhaps any government, in any present, can only skirmish on the battle lines of civilization, perhaps only fight

* Reprinted by permission from *Annals of Internal Medicine* 32, 2 (February, 1950).

holding actions—important holding actions to be sure, but nonetheless only holding actions. Perhaps the real battle is ours to fight; perhaps the slow gain called progress is ours to make. It is, I think.

A few examples from our long history that, in the relationship of man to man, things do not happen fast, seem worth mentioning:

When Julius Caesar parleyed with the German King Ariovistus on the Rhine in 58 B.C., Ariovistus told Caesar that he had not made war on the Gauls but they upon him and, as for the host of Germans he was bringing over into Gaul, his object was to protect himself, not to attack Gaul; that his warfare had been defensive not offensive. He had crossed the Rhine, he said, not of his own desire but upon the request and summons of the Gauls.

The colloquy, you see, might well have been between Hitler and Pétain seven years ago.

Things change slowly in the hearts and minds of men and we should not expect anything in the relationship of man to man to happen fast: if we do, we miscalculate. For, assuredly, they will not happen fast.

Still, things do happen. There was spoken the Sermon on the Mount, and thereafter there was some mitigation of man's inhumanity to man. Not so much as Christ hoped, but some; and even at Buchenwald they knew their inhumanity was wrong. To have made all men aware of that is no small thing.

For examples of how things happen in the relationship of man to man, I turn naturally to an example from the history of the law. The scene is France in the tenth century A.D. Men were aware of the Sermon on the Mount; the brotherhood of man, then as now, shone as an ideal before good and thinking men. Yet rapine and loot and robbery were not, could not be, quelled. There was no law powerful enough to restrain; for the right of such warfare had become the distinctive, recognized privilege of those with power enough to exercise it. But

49

The Doctor as Citizen

scholars, as we should call them now, with the ideal of the Sermon on the Mount before them, could not be content with things as they were. Legislative attempts to limit the range of the blood feud had been tried; ex-communication as a punishment for sacrilege was not new; nor was the privilege of sanctuary an innovation. Even a special care for the defenseless was not new. But none of these concepts and measures brought peace to the highways. What the scholars did, in their efforts for peace, was to make a fusion of old elements in a conscious endeavor to mark off by general definitions a sphere of peace from the surrounding sphere of feud, so that peace itself, and for its own sake, became the object to be aimed at. Thus, from the Sermon on the Mount came the powerful concept of the Peace of God. It was the work of scholars, the work of cautious scholars. As that incomparable historian Frederic W. Maitland explains it:

> The cautious particularity of the canons, resolutions, oaths, their provisos and exceptions and saving clauses . . . are the very essence of the story. Those who strive for peace are in the end successful, because they are content with small successes and will proceed from particular to particular, placing now the *villanus* and now the *femina nobilis*, now the sheep and now the olive tree, now the Saturday and now the Thursday outside the sphere of blood-feud and private war. When they are in a hurry they fail, for they are contending with mighty forces.

Not until the thirteenth century in France was the right of private warfare, on the comparatively small front of the Peace of God, destroyed: it was a gradual, snail-like process all the way, through three long and bloody centuries. We too must be content with a progression of small successes.

I have been, perhaps, over-long and over-technical in making this point, but, at any rate, I hope it now is clear that in our search for peace we too shall fail when we are in a hurry; for we too are contending with mighty forces.

In the Middle Ages the church might, and did, proclaim

the concept of the brotherhood of man as the logical corollary of the fatherhood of God, but the concept could not be made good. And the reason it could not be made good was that it was proclaimed in a society where, by and large, a man stayed where he was, in place and in station, in a minutely graded hierarchy in the social structure. It was, in short, a society in which status governed both what you did and what you were. By and large it was the land you held, or the land you tilled under another's holding, which determined your status. There was no more land to distribute, and, hence, in that society, no way to break status.

This is, I realize, much too cavalier an account of a situation that has engaged the attention of scholars for hundreds of years; but my canvas is small compared to my subject and I believe my painting to be substantially true to the subject. It was the distinctive contribution of the New World to break the lock-step of status. One example will make this clear.

The Dutch West India Company, true to the traditions of the Middle Ages, in 1629 granted to Kiliaen Van Rensselaer, a merchant of Amsterdam, a patroonship up the North River at what is now Albany, New York.

It was the intent of their High Mightinesses, the States-General of the United Netherlands, to set up in the New Netherlands, by their grants of large landholdings, a replica of their European feudal society, based on status, which in turn was based on the ownership of that land. The tillers of that soil were not to own the soil: the privileges and exemptions of the European feudal lord were to be transplanted to the New World.

Such was the plan, the European plan, formed in the council rooms of Amsterdam; and in pursuance of his part of it Van Rensselaer sent Wolphert Gerritse Van Kouwenhoven as one of his agents to the New Netherlands to acquire such title as might be had from the Indians and to establish Dutch settlers, without ownership, on his land.

51

The Doctor as Citizen

It did not take Van Kouwenhoven long, after he had fulfilled his duties to his principal, to figure out that, if he could acquire land for Van Rensselaer, he could also acquire it for himself. And that is exactly what he did, in 1636 on Long Island to be exact; and then he did the even more revolutionary thing of selling portions of his land—giving ownership of it—to his friends and neighbors from his native Amersfoort in Holland. And what Van Kouwenhoven did, thousands of others did, with the result that every man in America either became, or had the chance here to become, as good as the next; and the lockstep of Old World status found no home in the New.

But again we are mistaken if we think of this as a sudden thing. The bloody Rent Wars of the Hudson Valley are a measure of the continuing power of the Old World feudal concepts through a century and a half. And it was not until the West, beyond the Alleghenies, was opened to settlers who could own their land that the shackles of status were completely broken in the New World.

Robert B. Warren has explained the consequences of this:

> Only with the elimination of status from the conceptual structure of human society, could the way be cleared for the spiritual ideal of the brotherhood of man. This was the New World's contribution to civilization. It was not the gift of philosophers or statesmen or conquerors. It was not even the gift of the theologians. It was the gift of the New World itself, to itself, and to Europe.

Thus it was that Michel-Guillaume de Crèvecœur, writing in 1782 from Upper New York State, could say:

> This great metamorphosis has a double effect upon the settler; it extinguishes all his European prejudices; he forgets that mechanism of subordination, that servility of disposition which poverty had taught him. . . . If he is a good man, he forms schemes of future prosperity; he proposes to educate his children better than he has been educated himself; he thinks of future modes of conduct, feels an ardour to labour he never

felt before. Pride steps in, and leads him to everything that the laws do not forbid: he respects them; with a heart-felt gratitude, he looks toward that government from whose wisdom all his new felicity is derived, and under whose wings and protection he now lives. These reflections constitute him the good man and the good subject.

Ye poor Europeans, ye, who sweat and work for the great—ye, who are obliged to give so many sheaves to the church, so many to your lords, so many to your government, and have hardly any left for yourselves—ye, who are held in less estimation than favourite hunters or useless lap-dogs—ye, who only breathe the air of nature because it cannot be withheld from you; it is here that ye can conceive the possibility of those feelings I have been describing; it is here the laws of naturalization invite every one to partake of our great labours and felicity, to till unrented, untaxed lands!

But as de Crèvecœur saw the vision, he moved too fast in his conclusions. It was not to be so easy, so fast, nor so sure.

If there is anything that we—those of us who carry on researches and those of us who run foundations—should have learned, it is that no one can say from what direction, from what beginnings, great advances will come. We can, perhaps, predict the next step in a progression of steps; we cannot predict the new path leading from our little clearing, through the wilderness of the future, to the heights of the good life we want to scale, and which, being Americans, we know we can and shall scale.

But I must move my statement toward its conclusion. What I am saying is that just as no one could predict Hiroshima from Einstein's formula of 1905 and just as the methods of the Women's Christian Temperance Union may become outmoded by the work of biochemists, so also anything can happen in any field at any time—upon one condition.

That condition is, and it is a peculiarly American condition, that we give all men a chance for as much education as they can take, that they have freedom of choice as to what they will do with their education, as to the direction their education will take, and to carry on their work after they are trained to do it.

This is not, you see, a simple condition; it may not be one, but several conditions.

Reasonably, you will ask me to justify the statement. What am I really saying? Of course I am saying that we must provide a very large number of highly trained, utterly competent persons to keep the machine of civilization in working order. We need a larger proportion of the population trained to levels of high technical competence than we ever needed before.

But I am saying also that we need a great deal more. I am saying that we cannot afford to miss any of the very rare persons who pioneer the future. I am saying that suppose George Shull, who developed hybrid corn, had remained on the family farm in Ohio instead of being trained as a geneticist, what would the millions of Europe be eating now? You might say that they would never have been born. But that would not be true because commercial hybrid corn is only about fifteen years old. Suppose Thomas Jefferson had been born poor, unable to get to the College of William and Mary, unable to buy books and to afford time to think and learn. Suppose James Madison had never had a chance to study at Princeton. What would our past have been? What would our future be? These are, I submit, real questions; there are no greater questions for you and me.

I am saying, further, that all of our science and medicine and all of our technology, while not negligible in any fundamental view of us, are not to be compared in influence with the Sermon on the Mount, the Ten Commandments, the Declaration of Independence, the Constitution of the United States. It is such creative efforts of the mind and spirit, somehow diffused into our minds and spirits, which make us what we are, free men with free ideas.

Christ speaking the Sermon on the Mount, Copernicus shaking men's minds free from the theories of a fixed earth,

The Doctor as Citizen

Thomas Jefferson writing the Declaration of Independence, Leonardo da Vinci painting the Last Supper, Newton understanding the laws of motion, Bach composing, Shakespeare creating Hamlet—these are what have made us what we are—not the radio, the telephone, the motor car, nor any of our technology. All our hospitals and all our healing devices and methods can compare with one of these in importance only as expressions of the brotherhood of man.

You may now be saying to yourself: this fellow aims high, too high. We are working men, not stargazers. Where does he expect these great human beings to come from?

The answer is that I do not know. My conclusion is modest and it is this: unless we give them a chance to come they will not come. Let us give them the chance.

Thus it is that I could not approve a Selective Service Law which makes provision for assuring a supply of leaders for science and technology, medicine and agriculture and industry and for nothing else. Thus I could not approve a National Science Foundation syphoning off, by the power of allocating funds, into science and technology more than its proportionate share of the nation's ability. Thus I could not approve of any foundations deciding that this or that field is the field most necessary to advance, to the exclusion of other fields and kinds of training. I could not approve because nobody knows what is most important, and nobody can know until somebody goes ahead and does it. I am simply saying that somebody must recognize on a sufficient scale that the future will need more than science and engineering, more than medicine and food; that the needs for those who will state and provide for the higher values of American life, the values for which we always have fought, are at least as essential as the means to fight for them.

And if you want me to "go practical" with you as a final part of my statement, I will do so.

President Franklin D. Roosevelt during the war asked a

series of four questions to the end that the lessons of war might, as the President said, "be used in the days of peace ahead for the improvement of the national health, the creation of new enterprises bringing new jobs and the betterment of the national standard of living."

The President's deep concern for this question is shown in the concluding sentences of his letter to Dr. Vannevar Bush: "New frontiers of the mind are before us, and if they are pioneered with the same vision, boldness, and drive with which we have waged the war we can create a fuller and more fruitful life."

Of the answers given to these questions, the answers as respects science and technology have been listened to, but those who pleaded for a proportional share, a modest share, for the humanities and social sciences have not been heeded. The plain truth is that, as we increase the tempo of scientific advance, the more we shall need to better the quality of thought and understanding over the whole spectrum of the human mind and spirit.

But you will have gathered that I am talking not only about matters ordinarily considered within the range of practicality. I have been trying to say that in this present world of power, more power will not do for the long haul. It may serve for the short term, fighting the holding actions which may be needed at the moment—and let us pray that it will serve—but for the long term the use of power is self-defeating for the life we would consider worthy of the vision of America. Somewhere, sometime, must come men who will break through the encrustations of time and place and tradition and motive, of ignorance and greed and self-interest—who will bring the brotherhood of man appreciably closer.

They will not, they cannot, come unless, in Thomas Jefferson's saying, "worth and genius are sought out from every condition of life and completely prepared by education for defeating the competition of wealth and birth." This was a great eighteenth-century problem. Nor will they, can they, come if the prevailing thought of the twentieth century is that "civilization can be bred to greatness and splendor by science alone." If those efforts of the mind and spirit that yield results comparatively fast, if the activities that are deemed useful for present progress and power and strength, are exalted and entrenched, and if those activities which determine the character of people are denigrated, then—as a long-term proposition —the structure of freedom, the structure of liberty and order under justice, of every life, will fade. There are signs that this is a great twentieth-century problem.

Path-breaking minds, the renewers of moral and spiritual capital, will not come and develop and state our values unless we maintain in America the climate of the mind and spirit that makes this place the world's stronghold of the rights that we sum up as freedom: that sum is the essence of our strength—our internal and external strength, for both the long and the short term. This is, as Elihu Root once said, the supreme treasure of our country.

I expressed the hope, in the beginning, that in these reflections of mine, your minds and hearts would find some validity for your thinking. If so, I now shall say to The Doctor as Citizen—conscious of history and with a concern for the future—that there are no men better placed, no minds better fitted, to make the sense of these reflections effective for the long haul. I am not in a hurry: we too must be content with a progression of small successes—the successes that come through the cautious particularity, in Maitland's phrase, of those who have the vision of freedom and who know their business.

ON THE DIFFUSION OF KNOWLEDGE

AND UNDERSTANDING

THE AMERICAN PHILOSOPHICAL SOCIETY

AND THE PHILADELPHIA MUSEUM OF ART,

PHILADELPHIA, JANUARY 26, 1951

I AM writing—on assignment made by Dr. Fiske Kimball—on a proposition I believe in, the importance of the diffusion of knowledge and understanding. And in carrying out my assignment I shall follow the rule of the newsman's craft and state my "lead" at once.

You cannot for long have healthy science or any healthy scholarship, or any sound art, of any kind in any field, without effective diffusion of their products to a very general public. The reason behind that statement is, on one plane, that the possibilities of men devoting their lives to scholarship and to art do now—and will more and more in the future as income taxes make large fortunes impossible and estate taxes reduce fortunes in being—depend on public support. The rationale of that statement is most clearly seen in the public support of our great state universities which have been, to use words from our Society's title, promoting useful knowledge so long and so effectively that the taxpayers' hard-earned money is freely accorded them in ever increasing quantity for what the state legislatures do not doubt is for the public good. And so it is in fact.

Increased yields of grain and other crops, higher quality of greater quantity of food stuffs, the making of livestock into more effective protein-producing mechanisms—practically all of them the results of scholarship—could dollarwise be shown to have more than paid for the costs of the universities and their subsidiary experiment stations from the beginning. In this Society we do not scoff at corn and hogs and wheat and eggs and timber and fuel. Civilization, as the founders of the American Philosophical Society knew, rests on their supply in abundance.

But there is more to this public support of scholarship than that—important as is the abundant supply of food and housing and transportation and heat; and perhaps the old Italian word *campanilismo* will show you something more of what I have in mind. It refers to the pride of a town or village in their local campanile, the sense of destiny in their history, the uplift in their hearts for a thing of beauty which is theirs. Our state and other universities and colleges and art museums and many other cultural institutions are building this sense of *campanilismo* and those who neglect it will neglect it to their peril. Nor are the arts of the household, the arts of gracious living, being neglected by those institutions which have a proper sense of their present and future. Moreover, the diffusion of the knowledge of state and local history goes on through these cultural institutions; and the *campanilismo* that comes from the certain knowledge that we tread holy ground surely is one of the major factors in our internal and external strength, surely both for the short and the long term. George Washington and Benjamin Franklin, the voyageurs on the Mississippi—St. Anthony and Fond du Lac, St. Louis and Louisville, Natchez and New Orleans—Independence Hall, the Field House at Stagg Field, and Alamogordo, Pickett's Brigade and the First Minnesota at Gettysburg, Lewis and Clark and Professor Shull in the Hall of the Philosophical Society. We are rich in the things of the spirit! But rich only for those who have the eyes of the spirit to see the riches thereof.

Scholarship and, no less, artistic creation come first, no

On the Diffusion of Knowledge

doubt. What I am saying is that those who pay the bills, which —make no mistake, will be more and more the general public —must be made party to their secrets. Unless they are, they will not continue to pay the bills. It's as simple as that.

But the problems of sharing the secrets are not easy; they are in fact very hard. Anti-histamines whose pharmacology is largely unknown, cortisone which is in similar position and cannot yet be produced in quantity, tests for cancer which are full of holes, all have been shouted; and the shouting has led many to think that there is too much diffusion, too fast, rather than too little. And there's a lot in that point of view.

Such shouting, too fast, is, indeed, one cause of the taboo among scholars against writing for popular consumption. All scholarship worthy of the name, they say truly, is matter of tested facts, conclusions accepted by colleagues under diverse conditions of test, of explained method and mechanism, of repeatable results. And after you get all through with these necessary things, it is not "news."

But I am not talking only or even principally about diffusion of knowledge in the press. I am, rather, talking about the much slower processes of diffusion through general education, through exhibitions in museums, through the publication of books and journal articles for public consumption. Neither, again, referring to the press, am I in a hurry: I strongly suspect that prematurity of publication is the base of the scholar's principal objection to much diffusionist activity.

I shall give you an example of the debt of science to art. In the true spirit of the Philosophical Society for Promoting Useful Knowledge, my example begins with food.

As you know, with the discovery of America, great new staple foods were discovered: Indian corn (maize), potatoes, tomatoes, beans, and others. Of these the most important, as certainly it aroused the greatest scientific interest in the developing science of botany, was corn.

Beginning with Columbus's own reports, there are many

On the Diffusion of Knowledge

references to maize in the literature of early American exploration, and as early as 1526 Gonzálo Fernández de Oviedo y Valdés, in his natural history of the Indies, devoted one full chapter to maize, its description and its importance in the life of the American natives. But how to describe maize? Doing the best he could with words, Oviedo said that the breadth of the maize stalk was either the size of one's thumb or the thickness of a cavalryman's lance, depending on the fertility of the soil.[1] Its height, he said was greater than a man, and its leaves look like those of the common cane of Spain but "much longer and narrower, more flexible and greener." And he went on:

> Each stalk produces at least one ear, and some two or three. There are about two hundred or more grains, depending on the size of the ear. Each ear is wrapped in three or four rather coarse leaves or coverings, attached close to the grains, one on top of the other, and of the same texture as the leaves of the stalk.

That is pretty good verbal description, you will agree, yet it gives you a picture of corn only if you know what corn looks like before you read it, only if you have seen growing corn or have seen an accurate picture of it. Such pictures Oviedo's natural history contained, probably, in the edition of 1535.

The consequence of such pictures, and the story of how they came to be used for scientific purposes has been told by that man of acute intellect and widely ranging knowledge, William M. Ivins, Jr., Curator Emeritus of Prints in the Metropolitan Museum of Art, and you may read it at large in the *Bulletin* of the Philadelphia Museum's great sister institution.[2]

Pliny the Elder had called attention to the problem; he wrote that

> . . . some Greek writers . . . adopted a very attractive method of description, though one which has done little more than prove the remarkable difficulties which attend it. It was their

[1] John F. Finian, "Maize in the Great Herbals," *Annals of the Missouri Botanical Garden* 35 (1948): pp. 149-191.

[2] William M. Ivins, Jr., "A Neglected Aspect of Early Print-Making, *The Metropolitan Museum of Art Bulletin* 7, 2 (October, 1948): pp. 51-59.

plan to delineate the various plants in colours, and then to add in writing a description of the properties which they possessed. Pictures, however, are very apt to mislead, and more particularly where a number of tints is required for the imitation of nature with any success; in addition to which the diversity of copyists from the original paintings, and their comparative degrees of skill, add very considerably to the chances of losing the necessary degree of resemblance to the originals.

It was the print—woodcuts and engravings, invented about the middle of the Fifteenth century shortly before the discovery of America, and used to turn out cheap pictures for the laity, that solved the problem posed by Pliny. For the print provided the means by which exactly the same pictorial statement could be made any number of times.

Continues Ivins:

> If we look at these early illustrated books and watch how the techniques of representation in invariant pictorial form developed in them, and how the skills so acquired spread over the fields of knowledge, we can feel that we are in the presence of one of the most momentous movements that has ever taken place in the history of either knowledge or thought. We can see how men finally came to grips with the problem of making variant illustrations for scientific descriptive texts that had blocked the Greeks and their successors for so many centuries. Should we stretch the length of the period of our examination we could see the struggle of the scientists for scientific classification going on before our eyes in the botany books. . . .
>
> If we stop to think that the history of science consists, not in the discovery of particular, previously unknown, and isolated facts or truths by particular and isolated men, but in the continued publication of statements about observations and hypotheses in such shape that the world can, first, understand and recognize them, then test them, and finally act on them, we can get some idea of the meaning of the story. . . . Discoveries mean little unless or until they are adequately published. Many of them can only be made plain by pictorial statements. If the humanist period made no discovery that is still of importance in modern science, it resolved the intellectual road

block which (as described by Pliny) had defeated the Greeks, and it produced the method of description and record that in the following period was to revolutionize exceedingly important parts of knowledge and practice. . . .

The photograph in time largely superseded the engraving, and photography also was an invention of artists. At least Leonardo da Vinci first described the principle; and Renaissance artists constantly used the *camera obscura*, else, as one writer put it, they could not "have otherwise represented things so much to life."

Let us not, in these days when all learning defers to science, forget these things! Let not science think that it can go its own way, alone.

Our topic is diffusion. Let us not forget that the artists' methods for popular diffusion gave the scientists their first method for scientific diffusion and, no less importantly—by the print and by the photograph—gave them their best method of recording provably observed facts, and in many situations gave them their only method of observing at all. I am saying now that there are many pieces of apparatus into which you can put a camera, but you can't stick your head into them and see with your eyes; and that there are many phenomena which can be photographed but which cannot be seen with the eyes at all.

*   *   *   *   *

What are the lessons we may learn from this? Certainly from the first we may say that in some situations the necessity for diffusion is absolutely essential; and certainly from the second we may say that methods invented for popular diffusion have become essential for all scholarship that has any need for provable, repeatable pictorial statement—and there are not many fields without that need.

But many hard problems remain concerning the diffusion of knowledge to the general public. Professor Einstein touches the hardest problem in his foreword to Lincoln Barnett's excellent popular book, *The Universe and Dr. Einstein.*[3] Speaking of the popularizer of science, Einstein says:

> Either he succeeds in being intelligible by concealing the core of the problem and by offering to the reader only superficial aspects or vague allusions, thus deceiving the reader by arousing in him the deceptive illusion of comprehension; or else he gives an expert account of the problem, but in such a fashion that the untrained reader is unable to follow the exposition and becomes discouraged from reading any further.
>
> If these two categories are omitted from today's popular scientific literature, surprisingly little remains. But the little that is left is very valuable indeed. It is of great importance that the general public be given an opportunity to experience—consciously and intelligently—the efforts and results of scientific research. It is not sufficient that each result be taken up, elaborated, and applied by a few specialists in the field. . . .

As most problems do, the solution of the problem of the adequate and accurate diffusion of knowledge depends on trained persons, on training a corps of writers able to deal adequately and accurately with the materials. Such writers should be encouraged, not rebuffed; for not only are scholars materially dependent on public understanding but also, and more importantly, as Dr. Einstein concludes, "Restricting the body of knowledge to a small group deadens the philosophical spirit of a people and leads to spiritual poverty." There is mutuality of interest: scholars need the people and the people need the scholars, and neither's need is greater than the other's.

To sharpen my point, I shall turn to an example from the history of the law; for the law affords a very accurate and very long record of man's career. My example this time is that of "benefit of clergy," "pleading the clergy."

In the history of English law, the canon law made itself the

---

[3] Lincoln Barnett, *The Universe and Dr. Einstein, with a Foreword by Albert Einstein* (New York, William Sloane Associates, 1948), p. 1.

law of the only courts to which the clergy would yield obedience. The clerk in holy orders might not be accused of felonies before a temporal judge. Thus, men in holy orders could not be haled before the king's court and be accused of such crimes; and all felonies then were punished by death. If a man were brought before the king's court on a felony charge and could prove himself to be in holy orders the king's court had to release him, because that court had no jurisdiction. But how could the prisoner prove that he was in holy orders?

The answer is the, to us, startling one that if he were able to read he was deemed to be in holy orders; and, having read, he was released by the royal court. This was well established by the reign of Edward IV in the fourteenth century and the rule of law persisted, in part, into the nineteenth century to the reign of George IV. What the prisoner commonly was called upon to read to test his clerkly status and thus to establish his claims to benefit of clergy was the first verse of the 51st Psalm, which appropriately enough is as follows:

> Have mercy upon me, O God, according to thy loving kindness; according unto the multitude of thy tender mercies, blot out my transgressions.

And because it was well known that the prisoner would be called upon to read these particular words if he pleaded his clergy, a prudent, although unlettered, person might establish his claim to benefit of clergy by showing a parrot's knowledge of this so-called "neck" verse.

Why were these things so, what was the rationale, or alleged rationale, of the rule of law about pleading one's clergy? Doubtless the rule was allowed to persist into the nineteenth century because it afforded a method for the courts to mitigate the savagery of the penal law. But what was the rationale of its origin and development?

There is no doubt about that, I think. Holy orders were regarded as conferring a kind of nobility. Clerks in orders could read and, in time, some of the privileges of this clerkly nobility were acquired by those who had only book learning. In ages when the ability to read was very rare, the rule of law—legally pretty reasonable in origin—was transmogrified to create a privileged status, based solely on ability to read, or ability to pretend to be able to read a verse in the Bible. We should err if we thought of this development as unique or even unusual. It was only after the discovery of America, in America, that the lockstep of status was broken.

I shall draw no moral from this somewhat cavalier account of the nature of benefit of clergy except to say that in these days when ability to read and to understand is so widespread, the scholars' taboos against writing for popular consumption smack too much of the nature of pleading their clergy to suit my, I hope, very American ideas. The chance to become a scholar creates duties, among them the duty to communicate beyond the circle of their fellow specialists, and should not in our America be sought to be used to acquire privilege of status.

Artists can be, of course, the diffusers supreme; and they, no less than scholars, have a duty to communicate. So Leonardo did, painting "The Last Supper," and by it he made all Western men since Leonardo see Christ as Leonardo saw Him. Charles Dickens's novels were the effective cause of the Reform Acts in nineteenth-century England. William Langland's poem *The Vision of Piers the Plowman* turned Englishmen's thoughts and acts toward a new kind of society.

It is the broad diffusion of knowledge and understanding which has made a new kind of society in this, our America. It is our wide diffusion of knowledge and understanding which makes possible for us the great flow of scholars and creators from our large pool of recruits. It is the diffusion of knowledge and understanding which makes us presently strong—in the millions of young men who can read words and thus take written orders, in the hundreds of thousands who can read the blueprints, charts and diagrams of the new electronics and thus make effective their manning of the ramparts of freedom we watch.

In the processes of the diffusion of knowledge and understanding, no institutions, within the range of their materials, have had a larger share than our museums. They know and have realized their duties to communicate to the public, and so a soldier, Marshal Joffre, might say, and did say truly that if anyone wanted to know the secret of France's survival in 1914 he might read it clearly in her museums.

In America, certainly no less than in Europe, as this great Philadelphia Museum exemplifies in the juvenescence of her seventy-fifth birthday, the museum is our finest campanile. This "is a place where all that our race knows of magic allows us to see the splendor of the human past, and the way that splendor continues and evolves when aristocracy of intellect is united with democracy of opportunity."[4]

Here in America we believe in the meanings of these words and use them unafraid.

[4] Walter Pach, *The Art Museum in America* (New York, Pantheon, 1948), p. 28.

THE POWER OF FREEDOM *

THE JOHNS HOPKINS UNIVERSITY,

BALTIMORE, MARYLAND, FEBRUARY 22, 1951

BY invitation of the President, Dr. Detlev W. Bronk, and the faculties of the Johns Hopkins University, I read this paper there, as the 75th Founder's Day Address. It represents the best I could do to illustrate the power of freedom in affairs of the mind and spirit: it states my considered conclusions formed out of experience under the burden of my responsibility as the operating head of a great foundation. In its preparation I had the advice of Dr. Edwin Bidwell Wilson, retired Professor of Vital Statistics in the Harvard University School of Public Health, and Dr. Carl O. Sauer, Professor of Geography in the University of California—both, for many years, members of the Foundation's Advisory Board and of its Committee of Selection. Indeed, there is no paper in this volume which was not improved by Dr. Wilson, the most cogently wise and the most exactly learned man I ever have had the good fortune to know.

MAN'S temple of achievement has been built by individual men—men of eager, questing minds and devoted spirits—thinking and visualizing and feeling through all the ages. Most of them were journeymen, good craftsmen entitled to our honor, but here and there stands out one who exemplifies, in Bertrand Russell's words, "all the noonday brightness of human genius."

The gods in my pantheon are these individual men, the

* Reprinted by permission from *Amer. Assoc. Univ. Professors Bull.* 37, 3 (Autumn, 1951).

geniuses and the journeymen both. They have made us all that we amount to; and my purpose here today is, very simply, to insist, in a world that exalts organization, that, for you and me, and for things of the mind and spirit that principally concern you and me, individuals—individual persons only—are all that matter in our search to control our fates.

This is what I shall talk about. If I seem to claim too much in the preceding sentence, I ask you to remember that one of the difficulties about saying anything is that it cannot be said all at once. The corollaries will appear later; but, at the end, the sentence will stand. It will stand in the clear sense of Albert Einstein's statement to Abraham Flexner: "I am a horse of single harness." The Field House at Stagg Field, Oak Ridge, and Alamogordo are the evident corollaries here; and what I am saying is that without the horse of single harness, the lonely seeker Albert Einstein, these organizations would never have been, nor had any reason to be.

As I go on I want you to know that I am saying what I have said before, in the reports of the Guggenheim Memorial Foundation. I tell you this because I want you to realize that I wrote these things under the conditions that Mr. Justice Holmes laid down for statements that truly had meaning—out of experience, under the burden of responsibility. These, then, are not a theorist's but an operator's words; at least one foundation has been managed on these principles, with what success some of you may judge better than I.

"The progress of society," wrote Sir Henry Maine in one of the most brilliant of legal generalizations, "is from status to contract." The essence of contract is that one makes a choice of what one will or will not do. The greater the range of choice, the greater the rate of change, for change is dependent upon the possibilities that individual men see for the future. It is so in all researches; it is so in all human affairs.

Thus, all knowledge and all understanding in the present depend on what individual men have had a chance to think

The Power of Freedom

and do in the past; for knowledge and understanding are the results of the intellectual processes only of individuals. Whatever the results—good or evil—they all start with an individual.

For example, to Becquerel's discovery of radioactivity in 1896, and Einstein's theory of the equivalence of mass and energy announced in 1905 were added the contributions of other individual scientists and engineers to make an atomic bomb in 1945. The progression up to that result can be followed—except for the partial blank of wartime secrecy—name by name and step by step. It is known who did what, when he did it, and the material conditions under which he was able to do it.

Doubtless all developments of the human mind and spirit, had they had in the past the precise reportage of modern science, similarly could be tagged with the names of individual persons, including developments in the arts, it ought to be affirmed; for there is no distinction of kind or quality between so-called scholarship and so-called creative work in their highest exercise. The reason is, of course, and very simply, that both in their highest exercise are creative performances. John Livingston Lowes has explained it in *The Road to Xanadu*—"the imagination voyaging through chaos and reducing it to clarity and order is the symbol of all the quests which lend glory to our dust."

All the quests, be it noted; and be it noted also that "the imagination voyaging through chaos and reducing it to clarity and order" is what makes all scholarship and all art worthy of their proper pride.

To develop and bring to their highest possible exercise the capacities of individual persons to make that voyage is, quite obviously, the world's most needed result. Only thus shall we add that knowledge and understanding which is our best hope for survival and progress. All universities and all foundations should know that they miss all their best opportunities if they fail to recognize that this should be their one goal, and that it is the only goal that is within their reach.

The Power of Freedom

As said, in this day of close intellectual reporting we are likely to know by whom, when, where, and under what material conditions a thing of the mind was done; but what we do not know is in what concatenation of circumstances internal to the individual the thing was done. What made Leonardo see Christ as he painted Him in "The Last Supper"? How was it that Copernicus was able to take the intellectual step that freed men's minds from the shackles of the theory of a fixed earth?

The only possible answer is that we do not know any answers to these questions. But what can be said with confidence is that these men did what they did to affect the lives of all subsequent civilized men because they were somehow enabled to do the work they wanted to do.

This simple conclusion points the course for all foundations and all universities: they should have it as their purpose to make opportunities for the ablest persons they can find to do what they want to do. Administrators should not interpose ideas of what should be done, for while the next step in a succession of steps may sometimes be predicted, the truly path-breaking step never can be predicted by others and seldom even by those who expect to take it.

For any foundation, any university, which hopes to contribute to the survival or progress of mankind by assisting men and women to do their work of research and artistic creation, it follows that the only possible kind of aegis that should be provided is that which gives the utmost in freedom to those who are contributing to the advancement of knowledge and understanding. No other course will result in, can result in, work of the highest order; and while, even under such free aegis, obviously most of the work produced will not be of such order, still without it none of such order can be produced.

It is impossible for me to understand those who say that they are interested in work in this field and in that field and in no others; for saying that is saying that they think they

71

know where the next best developments are to come, and that is beyond any human knowing. For although it may be agreed, for example, that the next best step for mankind is not needed to be taken in atomic physics but in the understanding of man's relationship to man, it cannot be known from what place this next best step—if there be one such step—will be taken. It may be taken by a student of the anatomy and physiology of the brain; it may be taken by a biochemist, by an anthropologist synthesizing the data of his science as Copernicus did the data of his, by an atomic physicist, indeed, or by a religious seer, by a poet, or by a lonely seeker in a yet unnamed area of human endeavor.

We cannot know in advance these developments of the future, but we ought to be able to take some lessons from history to keep us on the beam. One such lesson is that all scholarship, including science and all the arts, tends to follow modes, and that it is precisely when a field has become modish and accepted, when its vested interests are at their highest, that it tends to become sterile. We can see this in the history of all human endeavor, in the histories of Greek sculpture and Greek geometry, for examples. And more recently we saw it in the judgment of America's first winner of a Nobel Prize, Professor A. A. Michelson, who predicted in the early 1890's that the future of physics would be in the refinement of measurement rather than in new discovery.

Yet the lesson of the history of all human advance is in the history of man finding new problems and then finding ways to solve them. So the physicists did in the period following Michelson's statement. Some of them, somehow, broke away from what was modish and accepted; they broke away from measurement and discovered X-rays and radioactivity. And then began a period which was one of the greatest in the development of physics that the world has ever seen.

No supporters of research—foundations, industries, private donors, government—could have predicted the discovery of these new problems and their solutions, much less dreamed of their effects upon the world. Only those givers and administrators of funds who had as their philosophy and practice that they would give able men opportunities to do what these men wanted to do, were—or could be—of any help.

Givers and administrators of funds to assist research and creative work ought to know that they have no future if their role is that of a priest of the accepted gods looking askance at the new. Certainly one of their principal tasks should be to recognize changes in value, to see men glimpsing new possibilities and new avenues for thought and expression, and to help them decide what they want to do. Likewise, there must be understanding that there are great traditionalists and great innovators both; they must clearly understand that the accepted gods often are good gods, often better than the new. But whether the good gods be old or new, there must be understanding that to be exponents and strongholds of free enterprise in things of the mind and spirit is the administrators' only possible role, if their purpose is the highest good of mankind.

Such are my principles. Such, I dare to say, is my administrative theology. It is what I believe in—cannot help believing—out of experience, under the burden of responsibility. The exponent of these principles of administration recognizes always that he is not omniscient, and thus he does not have to play the Almighty, which makes things a lot simpler. He does not try to usurp the management of people's lives and minds. He regards himself, clear-sightedly, as a gardener nurturing the high yield, high quality strains, always with an eye for the hopeful mutants, the significant hybrids. If one does not find pleasure in these things, in doing them this way, he ought, I suggest, get out of the game. For if he proceeds as a commercial florist does, to "force" his plants to early bloom to make him a commercial crop for the day, he will leave the world not better off, but weakened, as those strains that are significant for the future run out under his all-for-today manipulations.

It is not revealed to you nor me, nor to any other givers or administrators of funds, what ought to be done as most useful to the state or society, and therefore we cannot validly erect a design of inquiry. We are good operators only if we know we do not know what is the Great Design, and only if we make our institutions into strongholds of free enterprise in things of the mind and spirit.

It is clear from the record that Daniel Coit Gilman proceeded so; and Welch and Osler, Gildersleeve, Sylvester and Remsen, Rowland, Halsted and Abel are the proof that it is a good way and probably the only way to proceed. Indeed, President Gilman made it explicit that this was his way at a convocation of the University of Chicago in 1903, following his retirement from this University. He had disclaimed expertness in any branch of knowledge. "Yet," he said,

> I am an observer of the progress of science, who has had opportunities, prolonged, and in some respects unique, for watching and now and then for helping the workers, to whom appreciation and sympathy could at least be offered; often, pecuniary support; once in a while, counsel; sometimes defense; always, admiration.

"Always admiration!" Mark it well, for, at bottom, it is the administrative idea that the administrator, somehow, is better than the worker that makes him think that he, who is in fact the camel, is entitled to crowd the intellectual pilgrim out of his tent. It is only when the cultural administrator knows that his only function, like the camel's, is to bear the burdens of the intellectual pilgrim that he can be good as his task.

But I am getting ahead of my story—my sermon, if you prefer, as I do, to call it so. I have alluded to some words of Hans Zinsser that go like this: "The administrative camel has crowded the intellectual pilgrim out of his tent." This is my text. This is the sin my sermon is against. Zinsser's statement,

Christian Moe with his two sons
Henry and Thomas, 1898

Sophia Martha Gaustad Moe
Henry's mother, about 1890

Henry Allen Moe, Naval officer
World War I, 1918

Henry Allen Moe, English barrister
London, 1924

Henry Allen Moe on the left, with Wallace K. Harrison, Mrs. Simon Guggenheim, Jose Vela Zanetti, Guggenheim fellow and his wife. Trygve Lee, Secretary General, accepts Zanetti's mural for the United Nations, New York, 1953

Henry Allen Moe, standing. In his office with board members
of the New York State Council on the Arts. Portraits of Senator and Mrs. Simon
Guggenheim in background. New York, N.Y., 1962

Henry Allen Moe, seated second from right, at a meeting of the board members of the New York State Historical Association, Cooperstown, New York, 1963

Henry Allen Moe, ninth from left, at a meeting of the Council of the National Endowment for the Humanities, Washington, D.C., 1965

Henry Allen Moe, recipient of the second Cosmos Club Award, with his wife Edith, and Dr. Allen Varley Astin, president of the Cosmos Club, Washington, D.C., 1965

Sculptured Portrait

my experience tells me, is true, and this, my administrative theology tells me, is wrong. And the condition, no doubt, has worsened since Zinsser declared it in 1929.

It has worsened with the proliferation of all kinds of funds, national councils, governmental projects, professional associations, money for specified industrial research, donors intent on getting certain things done—worsened most with the multiplication of the planners, the do-gooders, and the whole kit and caboodle of those who are sure they know best.

Continuing as any Puritan divine who will not be deterred from exploiting his text, I must remind you that this sin that I am against is not only imposed upon your academic world from without but also flourishes within that world by your own making. In that world, too, are learned expositors who are untroubled by doubts, Keepers of the Seal who get the shudders if some one develops suspicions that a traditional view of the past may be in error. In your own world, I fear your little administrators, and especially your would-be administrators, your coordinators, your integrators, your setters-up of plans and charts and tables of organization and mechanisms. You are letting the smart operators get into the drivers' seats, and when they do the horses of single harness, the hopeful mutants, the significant hybrids, the essentially lonely seekers do not stand a chance.

How the administrative camel keeps himself under the university tent is a development of the sin I have to reveal, and the story, I sadly fear, goes like this:

In the big academic worlds men who enjoy the kind of work called administration normally become chairmen or directors or other administrators. Such men recognize and are drawn to their kind, with whom they are at ease, and thus, year by year, the selection of men for university posts tends to proceed in this direction. This is not the result of design, but is mainly a direction of congeniality of temperament that, consciously or unconsciously, wishes too much the result that is commonly called cooperation. But you see what the process does: it tends gradually to eliminate the significant variants, the persons who are interested in unfamiliar ideas, those who lack a definitive label, those whose interest and bent cannot be named by a word, those lonely seekers whose intellectual curiosity and creative imagination come to flower and fruition only when left alone, uncooperatively except as they themselves seek out kindred souls.

In the long run this process spells suicide, almost by definition. For civilization does not advance by treading the familiar paths, and we cannot afford to miss any of the very rare persons who will find new paths and, treading them, will pioneer the future.

Cooperation, I remind you, is only one of the littler virtues necessary for fellows like me; but its lack is of no account in fellows like some of you.

But my catalogue of the variants of the sin I am against is not yet done, and the variant I shall now expose is a joint sin of the foundations and of the universities. It arises, and it arises often, when funds are offered for particular purposes. Then the pressures are put on the scholars, by the administrators of the funds and of the recipient universities, to turn aside from the problems that interest them or to remold those interests to fit into an overall method. I have seen this happen, with the presiding officer gently urging the lonely seekers to get into this game, to learn how to play it, and perhaps even help improve it, perhaps even make it honest. But however gentle the prodding is, it is still the spinach of controlled, cooperative effort that is being offered, with the plays called by a coaching staff that gives and gets the dollars. It is still another variant of Hans Zinsser's warning against "forgetting that discovery was ever a solitary task in which cooperation must be spontaneous, asked, as the need arises, by one lonely seeker from another."

The Power of Freedom

If this sermon were being preached in a New England of the eighteenth century, instead of in less dour Baltimore in this twentieth century, my catalogue would be longer. I should, no doubt, even feel it necessary to advert unkindly to the effects that great quantities of public money made available in the effort of the Great War had in raising intellectual mediocrities to responsible positions in cultural matters, and to the time it will take them—if they ever can—to recover their sense of moral responsibility for the money they spend. I was told by one of them that the thirty million dollars of the Guggenheim Foundation would only be peanuts in the postwar scientific dish, and I think this makes clear the particular sin I am against.

But the instant that I spoke of "less dour Baltimore in the twentieth century," you and I both knew I was wrong. What makes me wrong is war and the shadow of war. In this twentieth century, few scholars can escape the fact that they may have to be called upon to contribute what they know, to do what they would not choose to do were conditions otherwise, to bring to imperfect practical results what their scholarly conscience tells them is not good enough for translation into operations. But when all that we hold dear may be at stake, the issue is not money nor who controls the money nor what we like or do not like. We must stand on high ground or we shall not stand at all.

That high ground on which you and I ought to take our stand is that we are sure that only from the products of freedom of inquiry and creation can come the salvation of the world from the ills and doubts that now beset us. Thus our first duty is to try to keep things so that individual men can reach and grasp higher than hitherto, else the complexities and ills of the world will overwhelm us. The past is obviously not good enough. We must be sure and we must act surely so that the spirit of free inquiry and creation flourishes. We must know that this spirit is a function, in the mathematicians' sense of the term, of individual freedom, and that individual freedom, in turn, is a function of constitutional government —of, by, and for the people.

One of the clarifications of the postwar years is that the condition of stable peace, in a world as interconnected as the world now is, likewise is dependent on governments predominantly of, by, and for the people. Repression—mental, moral, and physical—is the grand ingredient of tyranny; tyranny is the grand ingredient of aggression. The progression is as simple as that, as the years of clarification have shown.

And of this also we must be sure: Governments—even those of, by, and for the people—are necessarily much concerned with any present time, the time during which the governmental operations are going on. In a time such as this present, government must predominantly be concerned that the *status quo* does not deteriorate; governmental actions must be predominantly holding actions on the battle lines of civilization —important holding actions, to be sure, but nonetheless holding actions. The way to the life that interests us cannot be won except by the processes of education and creative thought, and these are slow processes. If governments of, by, and for the people can hold the line while these processes develop, they are probably doing the most they can.

The application of this kind of thinking for all educational institutions is clear in principle: just as freedom is the grand ingredient of constitutional government and of peace in the world, so also is freedom the grand ingredient of all education beyond the primary stages. It is clear that no path-breaking can take place, none of our moral and spiritual capital can be renewed, none of our values can be stated and developed unless there be maintained in America a climate of the mind and spirit and body that makes this place the stronghold of the rights that we sum up as freedom. That sum is at once the cause and the result of our strength, our internal and external strength for both the long term and the short term. "Freedom is," as Elihu Root once said, "the supreme treasure of our country."

This also, said Detlev Bronk, thinking in terms of the materials of which he is master, in his Benjamin Franklin Lectures: Freedom is the grand ingredient of the great adventures of the human mind.

But in the long run, given the present state of the development of technologies for war, repression, and aggression, our supreme treasure cannot, probably, be maintained unless the world is at peace. This is the other side of the shield, and scholars and creative workers, no less than other men, had better be aware of it. Thus it is that the governmental holding actions may be the most important things to be done in any present; may be so important that they must preclude the doing of practically anything else. But we err if we ever regard them as anything but static, holding actions.

Before I go on, I think I ought to pause to remind you again that I regard myself as an operator and not a philosopher, just as—as a lawyer—I am a case lawyer and not a jurist. Thus, the operational possibilities in any situation will always restrict any ringing declarations I might philosophically otherwise feel called to make. Nor will I make the declaration that the pressures for governmental research are ruining scholarship in the universities, but I would hasten to add that too much of it would. I will not make the declaration, for I recognize that much governmental support is well administered and is granted for pure science—whatever that may mean exactly—and not applied. And even if it were applied, I still would not make the declaration, for I recognize that many good scholars work best and do their best work when they are under some pressure, not with respect to their ways of doing things, but for what are commonly called results. Men differ, good men differ, and this is one of the ways in which they differ.

The Power of Freedom

Within the limits of my ability, or rather inability, to generalize operationally desirable propositions, I shall say that the touchstone of the desirability of acceptance of governmental funds should be the national interest, and that goes either for the long or short term interest.

But, having stated my operational proposition, I must go on to say that it does not operate itself. Those operationally responsible must know their staffs—their interests, their predilections, their desires, their bents; they must realize that quantity of governmental support is an important consideration. As those funds become proportionately larger, more and more essential becomes the catalyzing influence of free funds from foundations, private givers, and industry. Those who have the welfare of our country at heart must not leave the support of the potential pathfinders to the mercy of any one source.

But the large question is truly on what is the national interest. In the absence or even in the presence of a declaration of policy as to that interest, it seems to me to be particularly the public duty of educated men to assist in its formulation by action if not by words. We Americans have never been backward either in expressing opinions of national policy already formulated or in expressing opinions which cause policy to be formulated. I think strongly that now is the time for educated men to express opinions and do acts which cause executive policy to be made. I am thinking, of course—operator that I am —of what is particularly within our competence to think about: education, scholarship, discovery, of all those values which dignify, ennoble, and delight mankind; of his intellectual and moral wealth, the working capital of men and nations.

I am thinking of what you and I know: that never before, in recent history at any rate, has the margin between what we know and what we use been so thin. The stockpile of unused knowledge is much too low for safety.

The Power of Freedom

I am thinking that as good fruit cannot be gathered from any plant long neglected and undernourished, so new fruit cannot be called into being by wish or command, but only genetically, after long lines of breeding. So it is with a reservoir of trained minds and a stockpile of knowledge, old or new. You cannot produce either without long periods of support and training, and you certainly cannot get them either by fiat or by longing. It does no good, as is our fashion when an emergency comes, to make an appropriation and demand a miracle. We, you and I, must think and act so that the stockpile of trained ability is ready when needed. There is no higher national interest than this, no matter who forgets it now.

I am thinking, gratefully, that we are not oppressed by anything like the medievalism of the Lysenko genetics; but I worry a great deal to see the shrinking of our intellectual and cultural and material freedom. I worry about that not only for ourselves, but also for its example to the world. I worry about the ease with which a few ignorant and irresponsible men can make conditions of governmental service, including the doing of research for the common good in the universities, all but unbearable for gifted and devoted men. I worry about these things more, because until recently in this our beloved America, conditions were not so. The power of our freedom was such that here, at any rate, it seemed that the dream of the brotherhood of man need not be dreamed in vain. You and I must think and act to make the great American dream have present value, and again I declare there is no higher national interest, internally and externally, than this.

I am thinking now of what Lewis Galantière has said and said well:

When a nation . . . attains to world leadership, it retains that rank only so long as its culture, which is to say not merely its achievements in the humanities but also its manners and beliefs and civil institutions, commands respect and some degree of emulation. For though leadership is conquered by power,

81

it is maintained over a significant span of time only with the free assent of the led, and free assent is given only to moral and not to material authority.

Thinking this way, you will see that he serves best the national interest who does his best in any of the higher ranges of the mind and spirit. And Galantière continues:

These are the conditions of world leadership. Without them wealth and might lead only to hatred, conspiracy and revolt against the physically dominant power. The Romans themselves carried with them their language and its prodigious literature wherever they conquered, and when Roman arms had ceased to prevail, when Rome itself was no longer a capital, Roman law and Roman Christianity sufficed for centuries to hold the Germanic barbarians in awe of the name of Rome.

I wish I had grounds to be sure that university presidents generally understand this as well as some generals and admirals do.

TO SECURE THE BLESSINGS
OF LIBERTY*

FIFTH SEMINAR ON AMERICAN CULTURE
OF THE NEW YORK STATE
HISTORICAL ASSOCIATION, FENIMORE HOUSE,
COOPERSTOWN, NEW YORK, JULY 6, 1952

WE are all historians and students of history by right of our interest in history. And if somebody wants to apply the epithet of amateur to us, or to some of us, that is all right with me—and, indeed, is so much the better. For we are lovers of our history, else we should not be here. And amateurs, too, and amateurs in our sense of lovers of our history were those great American historians: Motley writing his *History of the Dutch Republic*; Prescott the histories of the Inca and Aztec civilizations in his *Conquest of Mexico* and *Conquest of Peru*; Parkman, he of *The Oregon Trail*; Mahan, a naval captain in his profession, author of works on the influence of sea-power on history; Emory Upton, a general, on *The Military Policy of the United States*; and in our own day the biographer of Lee, Lee's Lieutenants, and now of George Washington, Dr. Douglas Southall Freeman. Americans all and amateurs all; and assuredly there is no list of historians of greater influence.

And the great amateurs, lovers of our history, were all his-

* Reprinted by permission from *New York History*, October, 1952.

torians with a purpose—just as we are. They and we were never a prey to the objectivity theory of writing history—that you put it all down and add up the plusses in one column and the minuses in another and strike a balance to find out whether or not it is good or bad! We know that we like the United States; we know that the balance is overwhelmingly good. What we are interested to find out about is: *causes, the whys, the workings out, the details.* Our convictions remain steadfast; our purpose is patriotic. If this be not history, let those who dissent make the most of it.

Those of you who were at our West Point meeting in March, 1952, will see especially clearly what I have in mind; for it was stated explicitly by Dr. Freeman. It was Dr. Freeman's basic thesis that God has been good to us, that that goodness —manifesting itself in the character of our people, in our leadership in crises, in our natural resources—has made our beloved country what it is, all that it is, as great as it is. Assuredly, one cannot consider Dr. Freeman less the historian because he starts with that basic point of view.

If any of you should think there is anything inadequate in Dr. Freeman's point of view, just consider this statement of the greatest of American economists, Dr. Wesley Clair Mitchell:

> Our predecessors seem to have thought of the resources provided by nature as imposing a presently flexible but ultimately fixed limit upon what men can produce. We shall come to think even of natural resources as cultural products. Are they not that to all intents? The aboriginal inhabitants of this continent north of Mexico had little farm land, virtually no coal, no metal beyond bits of virgin copper, no petroleum, no electric power, no plastics. European settlers brought some of these resources with them in the form of knowledge; their descendants have invented the rest.[1]

[1] Reprinted from "Empirical Research and the Development of Economic Science," by Wesley C. Mitchell, in: *Economic Research and the Development of Economic Science and Public Policy* (National Bureau of Economic Research, Inc., 1946).

The Blessings of Liberty

The Founding Fathers had no doubt of their point of view, what they believed in. In the majestic Preamble to the Constitution of the United States, they stated it:

> We the people of the United States in order to form a more perfect union, establish justice, insure domestic tranquility, provide for the common defence, promote the general welfare, and secure the blessings of liberty to ourselves and our posterity, do ordain and establish this Constitution for the United States of America.

The Constitution was adopted in 1787; and four years later, in 1791, to secure the blessings of liberty for themselves and their posterity, there were enacted the ten first amendments to the Constitution, collectively known as A Bill of Rights. You can be very sure that the Founding Fathers, out of a maritime people as they were, used the words *to secure* not in their modern sense of *to obtain* but in the old primary sense of *to make fast*, as *to make fast* a boat by tying it up with a knot that would not slip.

I shall speak of the blessings of liberty and the means for their security in this mid-twentieth-century America; and to bring up most cogently what concerns you and me as historians, as amateurs of our history, I shall speak of the present condition of freedom of inquiry and creative thought in our beloved America.

Specifically my convictions on this subject are two: First, that as historians we are also, inseparably, citizens. That is, we must have what the Quakers call a "concern" for public policy and for what it is founded upon, the bed-rock principles of our social institutions. For only within the structure of our social institutions can we function as historians, in our search for American truth; and only within a suitable social structure can we hope to have that human freedom, that liberty, which is all that makes the search for truth and right a possible thing.

My second conviction is, as Professor C. I. Lewis of Harvard has stated it recently, that these "matters of public policy and of the principles underlying our social institutions must have some essential connection with questions of right."

That these are very American convictions I hope that no one will doubt. For, as prohibitions against curtailment of freedom of religion and of speech and of thought, of peaceable assembly and of freedom of the press, they are written into our Bill of Rights and were among the bases of our Declaration of Independence. Indeed, "we hold these truths to be self-evident. . . ."

And I will add that it is our traditional conception, the wisdom and rightness of which I do not doubt, that governmental policy should be rooted in justice and be directed to ends consonant with the Preamble to our Constitution.

To be concerned with questions of public policy and the principles underlying our social institutions, to believe that the answers to these questions must have some essential connection with questions of right are what the philosophers call imperatives. And Dr. Lewis recently expressed the sharp conclusion was this: "Anyone who asserts that there are no imperatives, and by argument seeks to oblige us to believe that there are no obligations must be either stupid or silly or perverse."

I do not doubt that there is an obligation on us as citizens and as students of our history to maintain freedom of inquiry and creative thought. This is an imperative which I do not doubt; and one who doubts it must be, in my view, either stupid, or silly, or perverse. Belief in such freedom is, for me, an imperative in this our beloved America and, no doubt, has been such from the days of our Founding Fathers.

It is my constant theme—because I have no doubt it is the theme of the greatest importance for you and me—that only from the products of freedom of inquiry and creative thought is there hope toward the salvation of the world from the ills and doubts that beset us.

The Blessings of Liberty

Year after year, it is my affirmation and my prayer, individual men must reach and grasp higher than hitherto, else the complexities of the world will overwhelm us. Nothing that has happened recently has given me ground for changing my mind about this; and, indeed, it is clearer now than ever before that the past is not good enough to lead either the present or the future—for the simple reason that much of great moment has been discovered recently and that these discoveries cannot—can never—be unlearned or ignored.

The discovery of ways to control men's minds and their applications to war and tyranny, the discovery of the facts of nuclear physics and their application at Alamogordo—these can never be unlearned nor ignored and their consequences will be with man forever.

We are just beginning to try to learn to live and deal with these discoveries. In the long perspectives of history, it will be seen that we are now only in the opening phase of learning, a phase of disturbance and of seemingly insuperable adjustments. Men will make great errors in dealing with these discoveries. It is idle to think either that they will not make them or to hope for quick and easy solutions. Solutions will come only after long trial and error; but they will not, cannot, come at all unless they come as the products of individual men's freedom and creative thought. It is my faith, and it must be yours, that *they will come*; and we know that they can come only from individual men; and this is the faith that must govern our deeds.

It is clear, beyond any possibility of doubt, that no path-breaking can take place, none of our moral and spiritual capital can be renewed, none of our values can be stated and developed, unless there be maintained in America a climate of the mind and spirit and body that makes this place the stronghold of the right that we sum up as freedom. That sum is at once the cause and the result of our strength—our internal and external strength, for both the long and the short term. Freedom is, as Elihu Root once said, the supreme treasure of our country.

Only by the products of freedom can we hope to save the present or lead the future.

It is commonly said that our form of government is responsible for the freedom we have; but it is much more true to our history to say that our freedom has determined the form of our government.

Thus it was that, in our beginnings, the role of government in the lives of Americans was minor. As our economy became industrialized and urbanized and large-scale, the interdependence of men increased, and, in consequence, it was judged that the range of operations of government had to be increased—with the consequent yielding of areas of individual freedom to government. The essential point to be noted here is that that was a *yielding*, a giving, by the people, to government. In other parts of the world the process has been otherwise: government has yielded freedom, most often forced by revolution but sometimes forced—from the example of America—by evolutionary social change.

The history of America, in its main stream, is a history of the guarding of the ramparts of freedom. Of no other part of the world can this be said with equal truth. In one aspect, the history of freedom in America is a history of the proper line dividing the functions and operations of government and of private enterprise. Every shift of that line, to enlarge the functions of government, has involved a hard-fought fight. We did not like it and we do not like it; but the judgment which now controls is that the size of internal and international social and economic problems—problems often become too great to be dealt with by private enterprise or individual or local action—sometimes has made it necessary.

There is a lawyers' maxim that "Hard cases make bad law," by which is meant that in cases of hardship, a judge, being human, is inclined to forget principles to achieve an apparently immediate just result. It is the same in all fields: we tend to yield principle to the necessities of the moment.

It certainly is true that there are hard cases now, hard cases concerned with the issue of freedom; and the answers to, the decisions on, many of those cases are not easy. But we have our courts to settle these cases; and I am one who has a faith, which I hope is childlike in its completeness, that our courts will settle them right in accordance with completely American principles and law. Nor am I one of those who, apparently, thinks that the vessel of our beloved country is so fragile that, *in any storm whatever*, we need to throw overboard our motive power, which undoubtedly is our freedom. Rather, I would affirm that the American principle of freedom —subject to any diminishment on account of deeds, or words, or conspiracies which our courts deem actionable—is precisely what we must never jettison, else we shall be wholly unworthy of our America.

For, without freedom, without the all-pervading concept of freedom which *is* the United States, there can be no creative thought in its highest exercise; and there is nothing in the world, *under God*, as important as that.

Free-wheeling ideas, man's concepts of ultimate truths and of practical operations of such quality and size that they are truly revolutionary, the aspirations and the ideals of Western man, all are the results of free creative thought in its highest exercise. If we impair that freedom, *even* by means *judged benevolent and practically necessary in any present*, we slow down not only our means for survival in the world as it is but also cripple the long term processes of making life better for ourselves.

My faith in America is that we will remain free—will continue to secure the blessings of liberty to ourselves and to our posterity. To see to it, as best I can, that this is so, is my clear obligation as a citizen and my clear duty as a principal servant of the New York State Historical Association.

FREEDOM

AND THE CREATIVE PROCESS

MUSEUM OF MODERN ART, NEW YORK

MARCH 18, 1954

MY welcome to you will consist in giving you the best thinking I am capable of on one phase of your conference topics, the creative process. On my theme, "Freedom and the Creative Process," I have not written an easy paper which one who lets his mind wander will follow. Instead, I have done you the honor of thinking hard about what might be worth your while to hear; and I invite you to think hard as you listen.

My paper will essay a comparison of the development of modern physics and modern art. The parallels are striking and, to me, they are very informative.

In the latter part of the nineteenth century there were floating around in what a layman can only call the rarefied strata of mathematics and of what later came to be called mathematical physics, a series of theoretical ideas which a half-century afterwards became immense reality. The names of Lorentz of Leyden, Minkowski of Göttingen, Poincaré of Paris weave in and out of the development of these ideas in the mathematical journals, until Albert Einstein in 1905, then a Patent Office examiner in Zurich, set down the culminating symbolism that $E = Mc^2$. This symbolism, as all know now, expresses the interconvertibility, the equivalence, of mass and energy. It grew out of the mathematics and philosophy of special relativity. It was set down in a purely speculative, yet, to some mathematicians, in an astonishingly compelling manner. It was, when set down, simply a theoretical mathematical proposition—nothing more. So far as an engineer interested in the production of power could see, it was a piece of mathematical fiction—nothing more. It remained so until 1939 when, in that fateful year, experimental procedures produced nuclear fission and proved the truth of the symbolism. Nature then, as Hermann Weyl has remarked in another connection, graciously confirmed the symbolism with as clear an *okay* as one ever can get from her.

Revolutionary in its implications though Einstein's symbolism was, wholly unproven experimentally, it was nevertheless received with respect. In time, as physicists considered the matter, it became documented with a few disconnected pieces of experimental evidence; but these were held together only by Einstein's daring symbolism of deduction and generalization. The symbolism became immense reality at Alamogordo and Hiroshima; the mathematical fiction became the engineer's El Dorado of power.

At no stage of the development from Zurich to Alamogordo was it suggested by any free scientist concerned, nor was it thought by any of them, that these developments were too revolutionary to be continued; nor was it considered that the Einstein concept was too crazy to merit attention. It is the method of free science that truth and error shall be pursued wherever their paths may lead. In science, concepts arise in the minds of free men; and are verified or not verified by experiment and observation, and out of experiment and observation arise new concepts which lead to new experiments and new observation, and so on and on, *ad infinitum*.

Yet the story is not all sweetness and light. As late as 1923 the writers on relativity theory were accused by competent and respectable mathematicians of "having laid waste a rich cultural domain." These are the words of a great mathematician and he was referring to the algebraic theory of invariants. It simply vexed him that the classic notations of that algebraic theory were ignored by the relativitists who went their new ways, into new countries of the mind where the prospects were more pleasing, although the classicists hated the sight of the new vistas.

I have often been reminded of these facets of the development of modern physics when I have heard discussed the work of modern artists. The things said about modern art, by some, are not different at all from what the classical physicists said about relativity physics. Strictures are heard to the effect that the modernists among the artists also have laid waste a rich cultural domain, and have created a country where no prospect pleases, where the laws of perspective are no more, where all is silly, and phony; because the older learning, the older disciplines are ignored.

"Art is beauty and beauty is art," they say, and the conclusion is that when there is no beauty there is no art. In the light of the premise, there is no quarrelling with the conclusion. But if the premise be changed—and who dares to say, in the light of the truly basic principle of the free world, that the channels of communication of the mind and spirit must be kept open for renewal and development, that it may not validly be changed?—the conclusion does not follow. Decidedly, it does not follow at all.

Men of pure science are content to set down what, for them, is truth, and from that truth to proceed to new truth, or to what, to them, is new truth. In the process they stumble more often than they proceed, they follow more dead-end trails than they find trails which take them to the little hilltops of tentative truth. They discuss, they publish bits of their evidence and they publish their limited visions, they use each other's shoulders, trying to gain the stature to enable them to get some glimmerings of the direction of the trail of truth to the mountain top of understanding. Such was the progress from Zurich to Alamogordo—or rather to Chicago; for it was the old field house at Stagg Field that what began as an idea of atomic energy was realized. There $E = Mc^2$ was proven as objective, experimental truth.

Progress in the arts is no different from that in the sciences, pure and applied. The difference lies fundamentally only in the circumstance that progress in the arts cannot be proven; the chain reaction that was made to occur at Stagg Field has no counterpart in artistic history.

In the arts, as in science, the process of concept and experiment and observation and then of new concept based on the older experimentation and observation goes on and on, *ad infinitum*. And it is further just as true of the arts as of the sciences that, as George Santayana said, "The only artists who can show great originality are those trained in distinct and established schools: for originality and genius must be largely fed and raised on the shoulders of some old tradition." The progression from the alchemists to plutonium is a continuous line—not straight, but continuous. The progression from Raphael to Rouault likewise is continuous.

What is generally known as modern art had its origins shortly before 1890; so had modern physics. At that time, the leaders of physics were accustomed to think that they had a wonderfully complete, well-verified and apparently all-inclusive set of laws and principles into which all physical phenomena must forever fit; and they were heard to declare that the future of physics lay in the refinement of measurement rather than in new discovery. At the same time established artists were saying approximately the same thing about the future of art.

But in 1896 Becquerel discovered radioactivity and then began a series of discoveries and developments that made physics into a new science. What had been modish and accepted had no longer sufficed for adventurous minds in physics; and they found new paths to new truth. So it was in art about the same time; the painters were dissatisfied, as were the physicists, with what was modish and accepted, and they set out to find new paths to new truth and to achieve new means for its expression. As the physicists broke into new domains never dreamed of in the older physicists' philosophy, so modern art was born when artists created something that had never existed before: painting—they hoped and tried—to reveal, "as in a flash intimate, absolute truth regarding the nature of things." Thereafter, the concept of art as the pursuit of beauty was, in their book, inadequate. To them it was just as inadequate as the old Newtonian mechanics were to Lorentz and Minkowski and Poincaré and Einstein—and in just the same sense.

Whether they were right or wrong is not the issue. That question is the wrong question, to which there can be no right answer.

The essence of art, as the essence of science, is the pursuit of truth and its expression. The difference between them, is, as I said before, fundamentally only in that the hypotheses of science may, sometimes but not always, in time be proven or disproven experimentally; the "truths" of art are not susceptible of such demonstration. Yet it must be noted, when using the word truth, that the criterion of advance in mathematics is, among mathematicians, not truth but elegance. That is to say, a demonstration in mathematics is not judged by concepts of truth or falsity but by its elegance or lack of this quality, and thus its value is a matter of judgment, not of objective proof, exactly as in the arts.

And this is as it must be. For, from one point of view, science, viewed at any given time, is only a series of hypotheses held for the sake of convenience. When the holding of a hypothesis ceases to be convenient, it is succeeded by another that is more convenient. Thus it was that Planck, having developed his quantum theory out of Maxwell's equations, no doubt took a long stride forward in modern physics; but Poincaré was able to show that such a development as Planck had made was mathematically not possible out of Maxwell's equations! Yet Poincaré's proof in no way, it seems, affected the convenience of Planck's hypothesis for the advance of physics.

So it is, or ought to have a chance to be, in the domain of art. Those who may be called originators of modern art—in the same sense as the originators of modern physics—felt a terrible need and urgent necessity to paint what to them was the true inwardness of things, their lasting significance; to paint a person as the vessel of an idea, indestructible as a symbol; to put on canvas, as Van Gogh did successfully, a sense of cosmic terror.

These modern artists took as their purpose what John Livingston Lowes says in *The Road to Xanadu* is the only true purpose of all scholarship and all art ". . . the imagination voyaging through chaos and reducing it to clarity and order is the symbol of all the quests that lend glory to our dust." "All the quests!" The painter's imagination, and the physicist's, is not differently employed, should not be differently employed: the imagination of both should voyage through chaos and reduce it to clarity and order. It is the only quest that lends glory to our dust.

I have been talking, you see, about a particular illustration of the general proposition that the channels of communication must be kept open, that freedom can live and man can develop in the American sense only when nature and man and life as a whole and in its various forms and aspects can be examined freely and constantly, when no censor, neither the censor with a blue pencil nor the censorious majority or minority—invoking fears or applying pressures of hatred, contempt, or ridicule—is in position to tell men how far or in what direction their thoughts, their statements, their inquiries may go within the law of the land.

The Creative Process

All right, you say; but what is the touchstone for decision in the particular case?

In the first place, you can decide nothing worth deciding if your point of view is that of a priest of the accepted gods looking askance at the new. There could have been no Alamogordo if the priests of the accepted gods of physics had ruled. Certainly one must recognize changes in value, must give a chance to men glimpsing new possibilities and new avenues for thought and expression. Likewise, there must be understanding that there are great traditionalists and great innovators both. You must clearly understand that the accepted gods often are good gods, often better than the new. But whether the good gods be old or new, there must be understanding that you get nowhere unless you are a believer in free enterprise in things of the mind and spirit. Only by this way of looking at things is the highest good of mankind a possibility.

And in particular in this place, there can be no better touchstone than this: The channels of the mind and spirit must be kept open for renewal and development. Liberty and freedom must be shaped to the needs, not of the hour, but of all time. Conformity does not produce freedom and liberty in the American sense. We were born in revolution and the American system *is* revolution. We shall not remain the land of the free, if we are not also the home of the brave.

You have it all there, ladies and gentlemen—the important things that one needs to know in the world as it is.

This place is a stronghold of American free enterprise in things of the mind and spirit; and here there are no other principles. These principles are at once the result and the source of our American greatness and of our American strength.

In this spirit, I welcome you, on behalf of the Museum of Modern Art, to your conference here.

THAT BLESSED WORD MESOPOTAMIA:

A LAWYER'S REFLECTIONS

PHI BETA KAPPA SOCIETY,

UNIVERSITY OF FLORIDA, GAINESVILLE,

FLORIDA, MAY 11, 1956

THE two and a half billion, or so, people in the world come in only two shapes and in what we usually call five colors that gradually fade into one another, although in varying sizes depending chiefly, but not exclusively, on age. This is indeed something to contemplate; the miracle is not that any two and a half billion separate items each are a little different but that all are so much alike.

There is no evidence that, at any rate in historic times, these broad physiologic facts have changed. Nor is there any evidence that the fundamental needs, desires, and hopes of men, since the dawn of recorded history, have changed: I refer now to men's needs, desires, and hopes for food, shelter, family, safety from harm and disease, and for some of the things we commonly include under the term "good life." What constituted a good life along the Tigris and Euphrates Rivers, in 3500 B.C., of course, differed a good deal from the meaning we put into the term; but you can be sure that, within their lights, the Mesopotamians had the desire for it. They didn't like to be killed or wounded, have their goods and chattels stolen, be defrauded in a business deal or be pushed around any more than we do, although I think it fair to say that the terms murder, mayhem, arson, theft, fraud, and—in the realm of what we call civil liberties—being pushed around, have received certain refinements of definition since 3500 B.C.

To look at it from another perspective, as Sir Winston Churchill does in his *A History of the English-Speaking Peoples*: "There is no reason to suppose that this remote Paleolithic ancestor was not capable of all the crimes, follies, and infirmities definitely associated with mankind." In short, we have here some constants—constants for five thousand years or so—but, of course, there has been change.

The acceptance of things as they are can preclude progress, and usually does. But when change is desired, there must be freedom to make the change. And the essence of that freedom is that one may make a choice of what one will or will not do. The greater the range of choice, the greater the rate of change. For change is dependent upon the possibilities that individual men see for the future. Thus, all knowledge and all understanding in the present depend on what individual men have had a chance to think and do in the past; for knowledge and understanding are the results of the intellectual processes only of individuals. Whatever the results—good or evil—they all start with individuals.

I have explained and developed this theme in the paper called "The Power of Freedom," which was the Johns Hopkins University's Seventy-Fifth Founder's Day address in 1951. I said that, for example, to Becquerel's discovery of radioactivity in 1896, and Einstein's theory of the equivalence of mass and energy proclaimed in 1905, were added the contributions of other individual scientists and engineers to make an atomic bomb in 1945. This result can be followed name by name and step by step. We know who did what and when he did it, and the conditions under which he was able to do it.

It is clear that all developments of the human mind and spirit, had they had in the past the precise reporting practiced by modern science, would have given us the names of the individual people responsible for the small and great changes, in the arts, indeed, as well as in the sciences. It is important that we understand that there is no distinction, nor should there be, of kind or quality between so-called scholarship and so-called creative work in their highest exercise. The reason is that both, in their highest exercise, are creative performances. Always in my thoughts on this subject are John Livingston Lowes's words in *The Road to Xanadu*, "The imagination voyaging through chaos and reducing it to clarity and order is the symbol of all the quests which lend glory to our dust."

In all the quests of individuals, the imagination "voyaging through chaos and reducing it to clarity and order" is what makes all scholarship and all art worthy of their proper pride.

What the world needs most at all times and in all places is the freedom to develop and bring to their highest possible exercise the capacities of individual people to make that voyage. Knowledge and understanding have always been, and will always be, the hope for progress and survival. All universities and all colleges should know that this should be their one goal, and that this is the only goal within their reach.

We do not know what conditions internal to the individual enable him to make works of art or scientific discoveries, but we do know what conditions external to individuals allowed them to do what they did and to affect the lives of all subsequent civilized men. They were somehow enabled to do the work that they wanted to do. Freedom and liberty were present; there was no book of rules to tell them how and in what direction they might and might not move. It cannot be said too often that the increase and diffusion of knowledge and understanding depend utterly on freedom; freedom to worship, to seek, to experiment, to criticize, to argue, to proclaim, to think—indeed, freedom to be wrong—but the greatest of these is freedom of thought.

During some of the unhappy events in our country since

1951, I have been taunted by the pessimists and the doubting Thomases that I ought to make another address, entitled "But Freedom is not Enough." I thought then, during the taunts, and I still think that the doctrine of "The Power of Freedom" is sound doctrine, requiring no corrective speech, no glosses, and no explanations for complete validity. Thus I stand exactly where stood our Founding Fathers, who believed that freedom is the indispensable ingredient of all progress, to which concept they pledged their lives, their fortunes, and their sacred honor. The true faith is Thomas Jefferson's: "I have sworn, upon the altar of God, eternal hostility against every form of tyranny over the mind of man."

Still, despite my lack of doubt about the faith of our Founding Fathers, as a lawyer I kept wishing for further evidence that freedom is the open door; and that, if the door is not open, everything stagnates and nothing progresses. Hence I went searching in the facts of human history for evidence either *pro* or *con*. The evidence came, very surprisingly to me, during a recent visit to the Middle East. I do not apologize for bringing in this personal evidence, for I hold that no man is capable of dealing with facts and with evidence unless it is somehow experienced, somehow made real to him. And in the Middle East human history is everywhere before one's eyes, experienced every day.

For me, the significance of history lies not so much in the rise and fall of civilizations as in the enduring tradition of values created by past men in millions of situations and carried into the future in the collective memory of peoples, often as their guide and inspiration. For cultural values can be and have been carried on from one civilization to another and live on as adapted by the inheritors. It is ordinarily reckoned to be almost an unreal use of words to say that the soul of the Greeks lives on in us; but whether seemingly unreal or not, it is true. And it is equally true that for us, as Western men, the peoples of the Mediterranean, as far eastward as the Persian Gulf, live on in us and that we live on some parts of the treasury of the merits of these peoples. From there common memories make a tradition continuous with ours; and from there has come real change as contrasted with the almost static spiritual history of the East.

One of the difficulties of saying anything in words is that it cannot be said all at once, as, for example, a painting says its say. Hence, I must ask you to bear with me for a while as I bring in, for you to look at, my evidence from the Middle East. The greater part of this evidence I got from reading, but some parts I got from looking; and the importance of the looking was that it made credible what I read.

Recorded history goes back, at most, 5,000 years; that was when writing was developed and, by definition, recorded history begins with writing. For the period before that—perhaps for a half million, perhaps for a million years—there is plenty of evidence of living human beings; but this is evidence derived from cave deposits, remains of agricultural and village settlements, stone tools, broken pots, and, more latterly, evidences from radiocarbon dating. But with the evidence of writing—on baked clay tablets, on carved stone, and on leaves that have come down to us from 5,000 years ago—historic communication begins. It could not begin earlier, for quite obviously communication across the ages depends largely on writing. For it is through writing that we know best what men did and what they thought across the ages. Oral tradition and oral memory no doubt played its role, but it was a minor role compared to writing, for the destruction of whole peoples by pestilence, war, and mass slaughter—all not uncommon in those days, nor, alas, in our own—would obviously break the memory of what was not undestructibly committed to writing.

All the evidence there is tends to show that writing began in the Middle East, and the Middle East in this context means the land near and between the Tigris and Euphrates Rivers —in short, in Mesopotamia, which word means "land between the rivers."

There was another place, too, where recorded history began early, although not quite so early as in Mesopotamia; and that place was Egypt. But while Egypt, at the height of its military power, made forays and conquests into Mesopotamia, always, up to now, it has remained isolated. I do not say that there were not cultural borrowings, great and small, from Egypt; for there were. Egyptian architecture, sculpture, painting, agricultural methods, were noted by travelers—early men were surprisingly constant and untiring travelers—and these borrowings duly lived on in other lesser and later peoples.

But, despite the borrowings from Egypt, the statement stands that Egypt remained Egypt and Mesopotamia became us. I propose now to take my courage in both hands and tell you why, in my opinion.

If you will think about it, it will be clear to you that all developing societies are faced with two basic problems, whose solutions determine the character of their resulting civilizations. One of these great problems is the relation of the individual to his society, the relation of man to man—in short, law. The other great problem is the relation of man to the universe —in short, religion.

We are now, in our exposition, at the dawn of recorded history, which began with writing; and we are in Mesopotamia. There were villages, but no great cities. There were gods, but no one god. There were customs on the way to becoming law. The boundaries between what we would call law and what we would call theology were indistinct, with theology in the ascendant at the beginnings of recorded history, so let us first look at the gods.

In Mesopotamia there were many gods, and they varied as to names in time and place, but regardless of the exact place and regardless of their names or functions—that is, the jobs of work they were supposed to do, their position in the hierarchy of gods did not vary. But most important of all was the fact that, although the gods had rank in the order of their importance, none of them, not even the top god in the pantheon, was omnipotent. Ultimate authority was vested not in a single chief god but in the community of the gods. The Mesopotamian cosmos was a state whose chief god did not command absolute power.

The Mesopotamian view also included this further fundamental basis: human society was thought of as a replica of the society of the gods. It followed from this view that no mortal ruler could be endowed with absolute authority; for the gods, either separately or all together, themselves did not have it. The power of the king, the ruler, was thus doubly circumscribed. On the one hand, his power was derived from the gods, to whom he was responsible for everything he did: on the other, the king was subject to the will of the community, just as was the head of the pantheon. This will was expressed through the assembly of the elders.

The assembly of the elders, whose existence is proved by many documents, from the earliest of recorded history onwards, constituted an effective check on power in any hands, and this check on power led inevitably to the protection of the rights of the individual. The instrument by which these individual rights were safeguarded was the *law*. The king emerged as the servant of the law, to whom the gods had entrusted the law's just enactment and enforcement. The existence of writing—as distinct from, say, oral tradition, for the head of the possessor of oral tradition is easily chopped off—was a further guarantee against abuses of power by the king. For the law, at the very dawn of history in Mesopotamia, was written down where all who could read might read it, and thus know what their rights were. Written compilations of law—long before the famous code of Hammurabi of about 2100 B.C.—date from almost 3000 B.C.

Blessed Word Mesopotamia

It would not do, because it would not be true, to let you think that the Mesopotamian law rose full-grown and beautiful, like Venus from the sea, out of the mud-walled villages of the Euphrates. This law was, of course, rudimentary, hardly more than an embryo of what was to come; and it was not yet beautiful. For the Assyrian, you will remember if you remember your Byron, came down like a wolf on the fold and so did Hurrians, Hittites, Elamites, Syrians, and many other conquerors, burning and slaying and destroying, for century after century after century. One wonders how it could be that the human race in Mesopotamia was not exterminated.

Yet do not doubt that this was the embryonic state of the law, as respects personal rights, in ancient Mesopotamia. This law is the basic feature of ancient Mesopotamian society and, as such, is attested overwhelmingly in the cuneiform legal tablets. In the last analysis, as said, that law rests on individual rights. Such as it was, the law applied to ruler and subjects alike. The king was no more than a great man. He may have been the administrator of a great empire with worse than autocratic powers; but even so he was still the servant, not the source of the law, and he was responsible to the gods for its enactment and enforcement.

To sum up, in ancient Mesopotamia there existed an intimate relation between intellectual progress and the mainstay of its civilization which was law. Underlying all progress was a social order resting on the rights of the individual, embodied in a competitive economy, and protected by the supreme authority of the law.

The Mesopotamian way of the law, with its emphasis on the rights of the individual and the responsibilities of the ruler, spread fast and widely as might be expected, for the people as people, as I said in the beginning, had just about the same wishes, hopes, and yearnings that we have now. They are constants through all recorded history. It did not seem to matter much to this law if Mesopotamia were conquered and reconquered, as she was, for the people of the conquerors had all the hopes and desires which made them want to adopt the law of the conquered. Thus, and there, began the long struggle upward of the people for freedom based on law. It is a struggle which, as you all have seen, continues still.

One could follow the dynamism of the Mesopotamian civilization based on law as it spread, chiefly westward; but there is not time this evening to follow it. One may be sure of one thing and that is that its appeal, in the final analysis, was in the fact that the Mesopotamian law started the procedures for guarding the rights of the individual. The people, all peoples, in all times, are as wise as a treeful of owls.

My wife—who, like you, is a real member of the Phi Beta Kappa Society and thus may be presumed to be able to think, as indeed she can, and as you can—was with me on our trip to the Middle East. But she is not a lawyer and, as I began to develop my thesis through materials derived from a lawyer's way of looking at the facts of history, and with what I hope is a sensitivity to the ways men have used in their struggle to achieve liberty, she assumed a wife's most skeptical look. And I assure you that nothing can be more skeptical than that.

But there was one set of facts which finally convinced her of the validity of the two main points of my thesis, which are, first, that the Mesopotamian law protecting the rights of the individual was what I say it was, and second, that it caught on among and thereafter dominated the ways of life of even alien conquerors of Mesopotamia. The persuading set of facts was this:

The law code of Hammurabi—of 2100 B.C., you will remember—was not found in Mesopotamia, nor in its capital, Babylon. It was found in Susa, the capital of the Elamite conquerors of Mesopotamia, about 225 miles to the northeast of Babylon. That code was engraved on a stone slab of diorite, and it weighed close to a ton. Yet this stone was transported from Babylon to Susa over the most difficult terrain; and one can only presume, I submit—because the stone had no intrinsic value, like gold—that the Elamites went to all the trouble of stealing, transporting, and cherishing it because Hammurabi's code was something that they felt they had to have for themselves.

I have spoken repeatedly of Mesopotamia, although the word represents no ethnic, linguistic, or political unit. On the contrary; for the Biblical story of the Tower of Babel and the confusion of tongues is good history. The Elamites were not Mesopotamians, and thus spoke a different language. So were, and so did, the Hurrians and the Hittites. Nor were the various states of Syria and Palestine in the Mesopotamian orbit. Yet all of these diverse elements, in spite of their great differences, were drawn under the spell of Mesopotamian law and the way of life that resulted from it. How did this come about?

Quite clearly it was because the Mesopotamian law was designed to achieve—and now I quote Hammurabi's own description of his legal effort—"impersonal and immutable order tempered with equity and fairness."

Thomas Jefferson himself could not have done better; and, as Mr. Jefferson said clearly, the people—once they had tasted the benefits of Hammurabi's "impersonal and immutable order tempered with equity and fairness"—would be satisfied with nothing less. And so the Mesopotamian concept spread.

While there is not time tonight to follow the dynamism of the Mesopotamian law westward, we must also take a look at Egypt. For Egypt and Mesopotamia represent two sharply contrasted societies. Indeed, whereas Mesopotamia solved the problem of the relation of individual men to society as I have indicated, Egypt arrived at the other possible solution: the state with a head who had all the rights, the individual none.

In the Egyptian solution, the creator continued his absolute

rule on earth through a king in whom the creator was per-
petually incarnate. The king was thus himself a god and it
flowed from that that he was the sole source of the law and the
absolute owner of all he controlled.

In the final analysis, therefore, it is clear that the Egyptian
was given a set of rules to live by; he was not allowed to think;
he did not live in a competitive economy. One can associate,
as some historians have done, the Egyptian's acceptance of a
divinely compiled rule book and his resignation to it, with the
immutable rhythm of the Nile, overflowing its banks and fer-
tilizing the fields each year, as regularly as the sun comes up
each morning. Similarly one can associate, as some historians
also have done, the Mesopotamia solution with the dramatic,
unrhythmic, and difficult conditions of life in Mesopotamia.

But whatever the association, the facts are clear: Egypt's
answer to the problem of the relation of the individual to society was a supposedly heaven-sent autocracy: Mesopotamia's
solution was a form of constitutional government, fumbling
and fitful and only embryonic, but still containing the elements of representative government. Why?

To me, the answer is plain. In Mesopotamia, in the conditions described, there was room for the human mind to take
flights; in Egypt there was not. The answer is as simple as
that.

We may reinforce the answer by reference to the early days
of Islam, contrasted with its later days: As long as Islam,
viewed both as a religion and as a guide—which it was—to the
Arabs' daily life, preserved the freshness of its original inspiration, it opened to the people ever new and ever wider hori-
zons in the realms both of action and of contemplation.
When, however, Islam became a set of rules to be taken on
credence, and became a code of law to be applied without
reflection, it became—as all religions become if and when they
reach that situation—a burden rather than an inspiration and

a shackle instead of a force for freedom. Indeed, in such state, the letter killeth all progress; and so it turned out in the later Islam.

Egypt's solution of the problem stated led to collapse and sterility. Mesopotamia's solution, and the way of life that it led to, was to prove indestructible to our own day. It led, please believe me, to Christ speaking the Sermon on the Mount. It also led to Thomas Jefferson writing the Declaration of Independence, Newton understanding the laws of nature, and so on through all Western man's most marvelous accomplishments.

And so it has gone and so it goes: As one follows the great developments of man's mind and spirit, it is clear that they always have come from places where there was freedom for the human mind to take flights. Such were the conditions in ancient Palestine where the principle of the rule of law, as begun in the earlier Mesopotamia, underwent a notable transformation.

Indeed, Palestine took up where Mesopotamia left off, adding noble ethical standards. For the great, the overwhelming contribution of Palestine was in answering the question of man's relation to the universe. This, as pointed out earlier, is one of the two great questions faced by any developing society. Thus the Mesopotamian answer to the great problems of life was in effect only a half-truth. The Palestinian part of the answer is contained in the Bible; and indeed the whole Bible is dedicated to the theme of man's relation to the universe—in short, religion.

The conditions of freedom prevailed also in ancient Greece, and thus there the mind of man also soared as the eagle flies. Such were also the conditions in ancient Rome when the rule of law achieved a firm expression and the concepts of equity and justice were both developed and applied to be every man's due. Such were not the conditions of the Middle Ages when, for many centuries, the letter—the rule book of life, in modern terms—killed inspiration and progress. It was then that the world of Europe, mistrusting reason, weary of argument and devoid of wonder, stamped free inquiry as a sin. And until the stagnation of the Middle Ages went by the boards in the re-found freedom of the Renaissance, the search for truth was hopeless. But again the conditions were right in Tudor and revolutionary England; and such again, and most decidedly, were the conditions here in eighteenth-century North America.

The contrary condition, it seems worth pointing out, infects parts of the world today and I think the answer *why* is plain. It is this:

This growth of freedom of which I have spoken, as developed out of Mesopotamia, which moved westward by the way of the Grecian Isles, Greece itself, Rome, and Western Europe, did not move north of the Black Sea and of the Danube in that early period. For the frontiers and the freedoms that were Rome were there blocked by Eastern peoples come out of the Steppes of Asia—peoples untouched by the basic law of Mesopotamia that started safeguarding the rights of the individual. It was in Dacia, on the Danube, you may remember, that Hadrian, before he was Emperor of Rome, leading the first Legion Minervia, captured the citadel of Sarmizegethusa and there was treated to the macabre sight of the tyrant King Decebalus and all his counselors dead at table in their underground hide-out. They had ended their last banquet by swallowing poison—just as certain other despots, almost two millennia later, in our life time, took the same way out in a bunker underground. And for the same reason: neither Decebalus nor Hitler had any understanding of the power of freedom.

If there ever were one place entitled to be called the hinge of fate, that place is Dacia on the Danube. For if the Roman legions there had been able to swing northward, taking Hammurabi's developed concepts of equity and fairness with them, one can better imagine than express the consequences to our own days that would have followed upon that breakthrough.

Do you wonder, then, that I deny the implications of the taunts which said that freedom is not enough? By all men's history, freedom—opening the doors—is enough, freedom in which the mind of man shall be free to take flights. Given freedom to soar, I have concluded, the mind of man has no limits to its ability to soar.

Lest anyone say that I think, or say, that freedom need not be consonant with responsibility, I call to witness that I know that ancient Rome's great contribution was in fashioning a system of law that ensured equity and justice for the individual and, no less, security for and responsibility to the state. And, likewise, I know that here in our country the mind took flights, and practical flights, to safeguard the general welfare while creating the Bill of Rights for men.

The Mesopotamians, the Israelites, the Greeks, the Romans, the European men of the Middle Ages, and, no less, our eighteenth-century selves were religious peoples—each within their own eternal lights of time and place. It was only when the religion—whether of Amun-Ra the sun god in Egypt, of Islam in the Middle East, or of Christianity in the Europe of the Middle Ages—became a code of morals and law to be applied rigidly, became a set of doctrines to be taken on credence, that it became a paralyzing shackle instead of the liberating force it had been in earlier and better days and in some later days, too.

Let us make no mistake of easy thinking; the Founding Fathers had this in mind and what they had in mind is clearly set forth in the Constitution of the United States of America in the provision that Congress shall make no law respecting an establishment of religion, or prohibiting the free exercise thereof. They knew, even if some later comers forgot it, that freedom is the open door and the indispensable ingredient of all progress, the door to all developing goodness and to all the flights of the human mind and spirit.

Here I shall give you only one set of examples of the door that freedom opens to progress.

The American Indians had as much land as we have, as much coal and oil as we have, as much air and water, as much metal in the ore; but they could hardly feed themselves, much less a hungry world. They had water, but no water power and no electric power. They had petroleum, but they could not fly; they warred among themselves, where now all men live at peace with their neighbors. Even the love of man for woman they had not in our sense. All these—things, ideas, concepts—were inventions of individual men, built upon, developed, and adopted, almost *ad infinitum*, by other men to make us, slowly, what we are. In short, we must think, if we are to think straight, even of natural resources as cultural products if they are to amount to anything. They are certainly so to all intents, and they certainly would never have become cultural products except through the open door of man's freedom to think, freedom to let his mind soar. In the United States, in our condition of freedom, man has invented a new and best form of government, invented secular education, developed science; and I myself should say has both invented and developed the distinctive, disinterested goodness that is the United States.

There are, as I am aware, those who say that it is our economic abundance that has made us what we are, that this economic abundance has been the force for the distinctive formation of American ideals, American generosity of character, and American institutions. But I hold it evident, even if this thesis be true, that our economic abundance is a function—in the mathematician's sense of that term—of our all-pervading freedom to think.

To sum up. Perhaps I can do it best in this simple way: The Reverend Ebenezer Brewer, in his *Dictionary of Phrase and Fable*, tells of a little old seventeenth-century lady who used to say to her pastor that she "had found great support in that blessed word Mesopotamia." It seems that her pastor thought of her as a simple old lady fascinated by a mellifluous word, and perhaps she was. But I am not sure she was; and if she was, she said better than she knew. For Mesopotamia is a word in which I, too, find great support, in the blessed freedom which is ours. It is a freedom which, if man had taken the way of ancient Egypt, none of us would now enjoy. And the power of freedom, as we have seen, is such, is so all-pervading, as to permit us to have become all that we are.

And so, ladies and gentlemen, I give you—to cherish all your lives—that blessed word Mesopotamia.

SCIENCE AND WISDOM

CALIFORNIA INSTITUTE OF TECHNOLOGY,

PASADENA, CALIFORNIA, JUNE 8, 1956

AT least to the layman like myself, today the scientist, as scientist, seems to be stepping high, wide, and handsome. Like the artists of the Italian Renaissance, when art flourished under the twin stimuli of popular enthusiasm and princely financial support, you, the scientists of today, have caught the popular imagination, and, no less, make appeal to the benevolent impulses of the rich and the urgent necessities of government. This is fine, for you and for everybody. You deserve it; for in your science, in your important—important for everybody—search for new scientific truth, things are going well for you, and you are moving forward. Science has its method for going forward and you know the method. You do not know all the methods, but the larger aspects of the method of science you do know.

Once outside your science, however—outside in the world, where, if you proceed at all, you proceed by value judgments and where you, like the rest of us, live most of your lives—you are like the rest of us. There are those who say that, in the present day, you affect the course of the world more than do the rest of us. There are those who say—and some say it without approval—that, as scientists citizens, you have a preponderantly greater weight *per capita* than the rest of us. But I do not disapprove, *provided that* you have wisdom and do not think that the sciences will give you all the answers, or even the most important parts of them. They will not, for the simple reason that in most areas in which you live your lives, there is no applicable science, and there may never be.

Perhaps, therefore, a person like myself with a training and a long experience so different from most of yours, may have something to say with enough validity to go into your thinking. I ask you to believe that this is said very modestly: it may or may not be so. Of that, you will judge when I have done.

At this point perhaps I ought to say something to reassure you: I am not going to say that, for wisdom, humanistic education is the only answer. Nor am I going to raise what has become the usual hue and cry, that science is the devil and humanistic learning the savior.

What then will I say about science and the road to wisdom? Assuredly, I will not say that science is not the road. Assuredly, I shall not say that science may not be as much a part of humanistic learning as, for example, literary criticism may be. Assuredly, I shall not say that there is any conflict between the learning of science and the learning of the so-called humane and liberal studies. In the world of value where we all live most of our lives, the humanities are not the only teachers of values, nor the principal teachers, as often is claimed.

Assuredly, I do say that the study of science, any science, can be humanistic, and be as liberal as the study of, say, Greek sculpture of the age of Pericles, and can teach us just as much about the world of value. Assuredly, I do say that study of Greek sculpture of the age of Pericles can be as narrowing, can be as nonhumanistic, as the study of the properties of prime numbers can be—but neither study is necessarily narrowing in either instance. The main point is that the pursuit of any study into and for itself alone makes a situation from which no great things come—nor, I add, can come.

The humanities relate only to a part of the life of man, only to a part. Like the humanities, science relates only to a part of the life of man, only to a part. To think any other way is nonsense. To think that science and the humanities are separate is equal nonsense. To think that they are naturally at war with each other is the way to more nonsense. Science is not isolated in the lives of men, nor is it isolatable. Like everything else experienced—everything else—it is only a part of the matrix in which we live our lives.

John Livingston Lowes explained this in *The Road to Xanadu*: "the imagination voyaging through chaos and reducing it to clarity and order is the symbol of all the quests which lend glory to our dust." "All the quests," be it noted, for it is imagination that makes all scholarship and all art worthy of the best in men.

This is what Dr. Einstein did when, by a few deductions out of scientific observation, he saw the universe anew—a few deductions out of scientific observation *plus* a feeling, that I can only describe as aesthetic, for symmetry. He reduced to clarity and order a large segment of the matrix in which we live our lives. It was scientific, *yes*; it was humanistic, equally *yes*. No thinking men's lives, not even—if I may fragment my statement this way—their nonscientific, humanistic lives can ever be the same after Einstein's daring symbolism of observation, deduction, and generalization.

The trouble is not with Einstein's science; the trouble is with the humanists who do not see the humanistic values in the imaginative Einsteinian voyage through a segment of chaos, a voyage which reduced that segment to clarity and order. They do not see because they do not understand that, in the post-Einstein world, their aesthetics, their philosophy, even some of their values, never can be the same.

The new knowledge exposed the limitations of their values, as path-breaking new knowledge always has done, and, what philosophers ought always to know, the extent of the contingent nature of their values. I say "contingent," for what ought to be the queen of the humanities, philosophy, is viable, has present-day life, only if it encompasses the new knowledge and the new understanding of the physical world, as of all worlds. Philosophy is contingent upon mastery of knowledge: if it has not that mastery, reasonably up-to-date, it can only be a re-hash of the old or a battle of words.

The classical antiquity of Greece and Rome, added to the patrimony of Palestine, has long supplied us with a moral and intellectual heritage—and a great and still viable heritage it is. But as far back as in the city of Alexandria in Egypt, under the Ptolemies, that inheritance was worked over, largely mechanically one must say, into a series of erudite and complex commentaries contributing practically nothing to that besetting question of the mind: Where do we go from here?

Thus it is that the adjective Alexandrine, even in the ancient world, was applied to narrow erudition for the sake of such erudition, learning for the sake of being learned in a field; and it was applied, we ought to remember, not to scientists but to humanists. And I shall say that, viewed from where I sit in a foundation office, the term Alexandrine has much more general application now to nonscientists in the twentieth-century United States than it has to scientists of the twentieth century. The reason may be that, whereas the scientist generally has some education other than scientific, and generally can understand the humanist, the nonscientist rarely has any knowledge of science beyond the fragmented, headlined bits he dimly is aware of from the popular periodical press. He simply does not have the intellectual tools to open for him any vistas of what science has done, does, and will do to his Alexandrine learning. What Galileo said of philosophy still relates to all branches of knowledge: "True philosophy expounds nature to us; but she can be understood only by him who has learned the speech and the symbols in which she speaks to us."

But neither is all well with the scientists. From where I sit again, it sometimes looks as if a seemingly so-thought scientific prudence—that is, the thought that the narrower the problem the more safely scientific it will be—coupled with what seems like indifference, leads to choice of narrow problems in which there is no risk and, indeed, which do not demand much ability, nor much work, for solution. But having said this I must go on to say that, while this is a besetting sin not only of the scientists, still it comes home to me the more because at least you know what some of your big problems are.

Alexander Pope was inclined to think that "the proper study of mankind is man." There is much to be said for his aphorism, and certainly there are no "outs" to it if it be understood to refer to the great questions of man's mind. To the extent that you do not tackle them, you, too, are Alexandrine. To the extent, also, that you limit yourself only to what you can prove by demonstration, experiment, and observation, you are doing less than your best to bring order out of chaos. For, if I mistake not, the best of you are usually a bit ahead of your data. But this statement, like most statements, needs qualification to make complete sense; and the needed qualification is that the best of you are—as you ought to be—undogmatic about those matters where you are ahead of your data, and regard them, at best, as hypotheses to test with additional data.

This is what I did not understand when, long ago, I sailed from Norfolk, Virginia, for Europe with a cargo of steel rails under a magnetic compass. As we cleared the Virginia Capes the fog closed in so thickly that no sight of any celestial body could be had to check our compass error. In these circumstances I retired to my room to calculate, mathematically, what that probable compass error was; and I gave a compass course to the captain in accordance with my calculations. He, knowing little mathematics, could only approve, for this was before the days of radio bearings; and on my calculated course we steamed for six days without a sight of anything celestial or terrestrial. At the end of the sixth day, when confidently, even dogmatically, I thought we were comfortably on the modified great circle course, the captain ordered soundings and in an hour it was clear that we were not where I thought we were, but a few miles off the tip of Cape Race, Newfoundland. I had conceived the problem narrowly and had thought I could solve it from the point of view of one discipline; but the captain had the wisdom of the sea, and solved it with all he had—my calculations, his knowledge of the set of the Gulf Stream, the feel of the breeze, the temperature of the water, the chop of the sea, and I do not know what else besides. It gave me a lesson I never have forgotten, nor should you.

I am, you see, talking about, pleading for, wisdom added to specialization, and, in this place, specifically for wisdom and science, wisdom added to science. There are, alas, no method and no formula for the acquisition of wisdom. But while there are no sure-fire methods for the acquisition of wisdom, there are sure-fire methods for its nonacquisition.

One of these is narrow specialization in education. I know, I know well, that you, like the rest of us, have to specialize and acquire detailed knowledge. Still, somehow, for wisdom, you like the rest of us also have to acquire the capacity for coordinating, for seeing relationships; and you can neither coordinate nor see relationships if you have nothing, or too little, else, to coordinate and see relationships with. For assuredly, without a certain inclusiveness of vision, path-breaking steps seldom, if ever, are taken. Without a certain inclusiveness of vision, the road ahead appears to be the only road worth traveling. But this, all history shows, is not so. For if you cannot see the territory contiguous to yours, you cannot know what it may contain of value for you or anybody else.

So far as known to me, none of the world's great men—

great, that is, in things of the mind and spirit—were specialists solely at the times they achieved greatness, although they might well have had to have been specialized when young. And I freely concede that the conditions seeming to require early specialization today look more persuasive than they seem to have been in earlier and perhaps simpler days. Never-·theless, it should not be forgotten that Copernicus was lawyer, theologian, and astronomer; Maimonides was jewel trader, physician, rabbinical scholar, and philosopher; Voltaire was poet, historiographer, and political thinker; Jefferson was farmer, botanist, architect, natural philosopher, political thinker, and politician. Benjamin Franklin was practically everything! Churchill was journalist, man of letters, statesman, and somewhat of an artist and bricklayer. Leonardo was engineer, painter, sculptor, musician, and poet. Thomas Aquinas was a pupil of Albertus Magnus, known as *doctor universalis*—theologian, ancient historian, mineralogist. Newton was mathematician, physicist, theologian, and a first-rate Warden of the Mint. Darwin studied theology and medicine, was entomologist, geologist, and from this varied background became the author of his great work *On the Origin of Species.*

These are all individuals, and I think it needs no argument in this place to sustain the thesis that all knowledge and all understanding are the results of the intellectual processes *only* of individual persons. Whatever the results—good or evil —they all start with an individual. I think this needs no argument, despite the recognition that, nowadays especially, some work of the mind—but by no means all—has to be done by teams. For I am not saying that a path-breaking work of the mind is necessarily one mind's work. Ever since creative work of the mind began, it has always been so that no mind, great or small, has gone it alone. Shakespeare doubtless was a good listener to other men's ideas and, according to some, was a very skillful plagiarist, or at least was a fine adapter to his own purposes of others' work. And, more likely than not, the most original men are both—a thought I think I had better not develop any further.

It also, I think, needs no argument to sustain the thesis that such individual development can only take place where the mind of man is free. We see this through all history. We see it in the history of Babylonian mathematics and astronomy under the earliest codes of law that safeguarded the rights of the individual to think. We see it in the history of Arabic medicine and algebra, before Islam became a set of doctrines to be taken on credence and a code of law to be applied rigidly and blindly. Conditions of freedom prevailed in ancient Greece and in ancient Palestine. Also the conditions in ancient Rome were such that concepts of equity and justice and freedom of thought were developed and considered to be every free man's due. However, these were *not* the conditions in the Middle Ages in Europe. It was then that the world of Europe was mistrustful of reason, trustful of revelation, weary of argument, and apathetic to the wonder of the capacity of men's minds. Until the Middle Ages were past, and men moved into the re-found freedom of the Renaissance, the search for truth languished. But again the conditions were right in Tudor and revolutionary England; and so, most decidedly, were the conditions here in eighteenth-century North America.

I have the Middle East and the old Arabic learning very much on my mind these days; for I have recently come home from there. I had been given what the Navy calls a roving commission to find out what I could about the present state of higher education in the Middle East. After I got there, it came to me that I was not as ignorant, nor as unqualified for the assignment, as I had thought—and that was because, in a very modest sense, I am a historian of the law of Rome. The writ of the ancient Roman Law, I should explain, ran all through the Mediterranean littoral, longer in time in some places than in others, but here and there certainly for a millennium. During some periods the writ of the Roman Law ran as far eastward as the Persian Gulf; in short, through all the territory that we now call the Middle East.

It was not that I studied or learned, last autumn in the Middle East, anything that I had not known in the way of a lawyer's specialized learning about the law of the sale of goods or of commercial practice, or of any other branch of the law, in ancient Egypt or Phoenicia. It was rather that as a historian of the Roman Law I could not help becoming aware, out there, of the intellectual scope of the men who made the Roman Law the force for civilization that it was in the ancient world.

History is always before one's eyes in the Middle East—but, I suppose, only if one has a specialist's eyes to see, in detail, some facet of it. I do not mean only physical evidence, I mean also remembered evidence. I remembered that Beirut in the Lebanon—the Berytus of ancient Roman Phoenicia—had had a law school which was accredited along with those of Rome and Constantinople as one of the Roman Empire's three schools of law.

Such standards of teaching are hardly to be found there now; but just the same, I learned that those standards live on in modern Beiruti lawyers, often for their guide and almost always for their inspiration. They do not allow one to forget that Tribonian, head of Justinian's Commission for the Codification of the Roman Law, was a teacher in the Berytus Law School, as were three others of Justinian's Commission. Justinian's code, I should perhaps explain, was the greatest triumph of lawgiving, with the most lasting effects throughout the whole of the ancient and, no less, the modern world that the world ever has known. And the modern Beiruti lawyers do not ever forget that Ulpian, by reason of his scope and by common consent one of the two greatest of Roman jurisconsults of all Roman times, was a Phoenician.

Science and Wisdom

History, recorded history, is long in the Middle East—five thousand years or so; and the sensing of past values of past civilizations gives a man a certain perspective on his own.

Contrasting the present with the great Middle Eastern past, I asked myself *why*. In the Middle East, I stress again, the present has deep roots. What happened to the deep roots of the law? And lest I seem legally parochial, I call to witness that one cannot look at a clock without being in debt to the method developed in ancient Babylon for reckoning time; one cannot read or write a Western language without being in debt to what went on in Byblos in ancient Phoenicia; for it was there that our Western alphabet, if not invented, was certainly developed to be the sharp intellectual tool we know. When, at the site of ancient Babylon, I was viewing the old irrigation ditches, dating from at least the time of Daniel— he of the lions' den—I asked an American reclamation engineer how far off his modern surveys showed them to be. He said they were off, in vertical distance, at most only fractions of an inch over hundreds of miles of extent.

And again I asked *why*: I asked why they could do it and did it then, and why not now?

I could not find complete answers out there, nor have I been able to find them in scholarly works since my return. But one thing is clear and it is this:

Just as in our Western world the path-breaking steps have always been taken by men who were free to think and by nobody else; and, just as in our Western world the path-breaking steps have not been taken by men who wore the blinders of one discipline, so it was in the great periods of the historic Middle East.

Omar Khayyám, he of the Rubáiyát—in FitzGerald's translation, he of "a loaf of bread, a jug of wine and thou"—was also and perhaps principally a mathematician. His *Algebra* is a first-rate path-breaking work, including a kind of analytical geometry as it was conceived before Descartes, at a period

122

when the systems of coordinates and mathematical notations were not established. He was also a superior political thinker and astronomer.

The great jurists of the Roman Law were rhetoricians in the ancient and honorable sense of that word, sometimes governors of provinces, sometimes quaestors—that is, secretaries of the Roman Treasury in our terms—as well as lawyers. All of them, as Mr. Justice Holmes was fond of saying of men for whose judgments he had respect, had formed their inductions as jurists out of experience in other fields, under the burden of responsibility.

So it was in the great and historic past of the Mediterranean, so it is in our own era, and so therefore I expect it to continue to be. The path-breaking steps of the human mind are not taken by specialists who are specialists only. They are taken, always, by specialists who have a wideness of vision, who see relationships, who can coordinate the observations and deductions of fields besides their own. If to this capacity to see relationships, there be added precision of expression, purity of diction, fine wit, concern for the spirit of man, then the labor of those who have those abilities, in the difficult and obscure field of final principles, surely will rise to heights otherwise impossible. Then they, like Omar Khayyám, will not only advance knowledge but also will have attained to wisdom; and they, and only they, will place their intellectual and spiritual signatures on their days.

There is another facet to the lesson that specialization is not enough which I learned in the perspective of the history of the Middle East. It is this:

Beginning in the eighteenth century, the Middle East eagerly took to Western inventions; but those inventions, it now is clear, did not produce for them the good things they seemed to produce for the West. By Western inventions I mean not only the tractor, the bulldozer and the motor car, but also, for example, secular education, technical education, and the ballot box. And the reason that the Western inventions did not produce for the Middle East what they seemed, to some, to produce for the West is clear; and some men of the Middle East said it to me clearly: "We know we could not achieve your material position—let alone your other positions —without the breadth of your education which you have and which we used to have and have no more." That is, ladies and gentlemen, a message from the cradle of our civilization.

THE VISION OF PIERS THE PLOWMAN

AND THE LAW OF FOUNDATIONS*

THE AMERICAN PHILOSOPHICAL SOCIETY,

PHILADELPHIA, APRIL 24, 1958

SIR Philip Sidney in his *An Apologie for Poetry*, first published in 1595, wrote my text:

> And, first, truly, to all them that, professing learning, inveigh against poetry, may justly be objected that they goe very neer to ungratefulness, to seek to deface that which, in the noblest nations & languages that are known, hath been the first light-giver to ignorance and first Nurse, whose milk by little and little enabled them to feed afterwards on tougher knowledges.

I shall seek to illumine a particular case within Sir Philip Sidney's generalization; and my particular case is that William Langland's *The Vision of Piers the Plowman*, written in its several forms between the years 1332 and 1377, was a "light-giver to ignorance" in defining what are and what are not valid purposes for foundations.

By "foundation" I mean all that host of organizations set up for charitable, educational, religious, and eleemosynary purposes—of which the law says two things: the first that they may go on forever and the second that they need not pay taxes.

* Reprinted by permission from *Proc. Amer. Philos. Soc. 102*, 4 (1958): pp. 371-375.

125

The Law of Foundations

This is, indeed, the only possible definition of a foundation: that they are all those organizations which are touched neither by death nor by taxes. There is no other form of organization except government of which this statement can, even theoretically, be made. And all organizations of which the statement can truly be made are foundations, including the American Philosophical Society.

But this definition leaves open the question why the organizations called foundations are accorded the privileges of freedom from death and taxes. The present-day answer is that the foundations do things that the law deems to be in the public interest. But, of course, most businesses, too, do things that the law deems to be in the public interest, and so do banks; and banks and businesses, too, may go on forever. But these are not foundations. The distinction can be explained only by recourse to history.

"There is a supernatural element in the story. Great changes take place behind a mystic veil," as Pollock and Maitland wrote in their incomparable *History of English Law*[1] where the story may be read at large.

The supernatural element in the story begins with the first recorded words of English law. These are in the laws of Aethelbert, King of the Kentish men, baptized by St. Augustine himself, at Canterbury, about A.D. 600. These first words of recorded English law—the very first words of the laws of England ever set down—are: "God's property." God is the owner of property, and so, as we shall see, are His saints, though dead.

For example, in the oldest existing English landbook, it is recorded that the newly converted Aethelbert says: "To thee Saint Andrew and to thy church at Rochester where Justus the bishop presides, do I give a portion of my land." A saint is,

---

[1] Sir Frederick Pollock and Frederic W. Maitland, *The History of English Law before the Time of Edward I* (Cambridge, 1911) 1: p. 499.

126

The Law of Foundations

very often in Domesday Book, a landowner: it is there recorded that Saint Paul holds land, Saint Constantine holds land. Likewise, other saints, the martyrs of the Church, the prophets, the archangels are listed as landowners; and when someone alleges that the saint is not the owner of the piece of land in question, we are treated to the spectacle—as is set forth in Domesday Book, for example—that Saint Paul is charged with an invasion of land that is said not to be his own.[2]

Of course, this kind of thinking inevitably leads to complications of theory, some of which are insoluble, and proved to be insoluble even to the medieval mind. But most of these complications need not concern us. What does concern us is this: Why were these parcels of land given to God, the saints, the archangels? To that question the answer is clear: they were given as the price of salvation, to make peace with Heaven. Salvation at a price is, indeed, the theme of practically all medieval wills and of many other conveyances. In the legal Latin of the day, such gifts were made *pro anima mea, pro salute animae meae*—for the repose of the donors' souls. These gifts to God, the holy saints, martyrs, archangels, and others of the Lord's hierarchy, specified, often in great detail, what should be done with the income from the land and other property so conveyed: the saying of masses and of prayers for the dead, the maintenance of lamps and tapers before altars, alms for the poor, the building and endowments of churches, abbeys, monasteries, and cathedrals—indeed, anything of a holy nature to keep away the devils which were supposed to surround the dying and the dead.

Even so acute and learned a lawyer as Sir Thomas Littleton (1402-1481) made provision by his will for the sale of his "great English book"—that is, his work on land tenures—and that the proceeds of the sale should be applied for the benefit

[2] *Ibid.* 1: p. 500.

of his soul, for which he made liberal provision of trentals and masses.[3]

Because these gifts, whether of land or of personal property, concerned men's souls, were given for the repose of men's souls, their endorsement was matter for the ecclesiastical courts. And the ecclesiastical courts did enforce them, according to the donors' language and intent. These gifts often were large and they were numerous throughout all the Middle Ages; and because God and the holy angels, the prophets, the martyrs, the archangels—and the churches, abbeys and cathedrals which administered these properties for God—were not subject to any temporal end, the accumulations of these properties became ever and ever larger, and threatened in time to include all property. Because all this property devoted to pious uses was under the control of the ecclesiastical courts, and thus was taken out of effective governmental control through the king's courts, the question of the jurisdiction over it became the major political issue of the time, and it constituted, indeed, the greatest social problem of the time.

Such, in the large, was the state of the law in fourteenth-century England on the subject of gifts to pious uses. Let us have no doubt about it: all these gifts were made as payment for the repose of some donor's soul, and on this basis they were enforced. Lord Chief Justice Wilmot in 1768 summed up the early reason of the law in this type of case:

> The donation was considered as proceeding from a general principle of piety in the testator. Charity was an expiation of sin and to be rewarded in another state. . . . The Court thought that one kind of charity would embalm his [the testator's] memory as well as another, and being equally meritorious, would entitle him to the same reward[4]

—which was, as explained, salvation.

[3] *Dict. Nat'l. Biog. s.v.* "Littleton, Sir Thomas."

[4] Attorney General *vs.* Downing, *Notes and Judgments Delivered in Different Courts by the Right Honourable Sir John Eardly Wilmot*, Knt. (London, 1802).

The Law of Foundations

Then something happened to change the emphasis of the law, and it seemed to happen pretty abruptly in England. It had begun to happen about A.D. 1100 in Italy when Irnerius was teaching the law of ancient Rome at Bologna, and thereafter "The monarchy of theology over the intellectual world was disputed. A lay science claimed its rights, its share of men's attention. It was a science of civil life to be found in the human, heathen Digest"[5] (which was the Emperor Justinian's compilation of the law of ancient Rome). "A new force had begun to play and sooner or later every body of law in western Europe felt it."

In the sphere of this paper, Thomas Aquinas, a century after Irnerius, enlarged the range of valid purposes for gifts to pious uses. Before Aquinas, in Christendom, they had been summed up in the seven spiritual acts: to counsel, to sustain, to teach, to console, to save, to pardon, and to pray. After Aquinas, "good works," which also would avail to ensure the after-life, were held to include seven corporal acts: to clothe, to give drink to, to feed, to free from prison, to shelter, to assist in sickness, to bury. But no emphasis whatever was placed on the social utility of such gifts in St. Thomas's enlarged valid categories: they were still *pro salute animae meae*, for the repose of the donor's soul. As set forth "in the human, heathen Digest," it had been otherwise under the law of ancient Rome, and sooner or later every concept of what we now call the law of charities in Western Europe would feel the still-living breath of the greatest lawgiver of all times.

In England the monarchy of medieval theology over the intellectual world was disputed by William Langland, who, in the latter part of the fourteenth century, wrote what is commonly called *The Vision of Piers the Plowman*. Some think it was written by one, others by several; but, individually or collectively, the author is called William Langland. *The Vision* is probably the most completely national work in all

[5] Pollock and Maitland, *1*: pp. 23-24.

The Law of Foundations

English literature, and it certainly is one of the richest mines for the social history of the period. The poem was in its day, and for centuries afterwards, of the greatest intellectual and practical significance. It is said that Langland's poetry was as powerful as Holy Writ; and it was. As that great French scholar, Jules Jusserand, has said of Langland, "His book had a prodigious success. . . . So great was his influence that, from out of his writings, were taken watchwords of the great uprising of the peasants."[6] Wat Tyler's Rebellion occurred in 1381; the first version of Langland's *Vision* appears to have been written in 1362, less than twenty years before.

The author of *The Vision* painted on the largest possible large canvas, and among the many things he pictured on his huge canvas were gifts to pious uses. In Passus VII, called "The Plowman's Pardon," he considered the case of merchants who had many years of remission from purgatory but could not be granted the full *a pena et a culpa*—that is, remission from both temporal and eternal punishment—because they did not keep their holy days as the Church taught and because they swore "by their soul" and "so help me God" against good conscience for the purpose of selling their wares.

But, as *The Vision of Piers the Plowman* says, Truth sent them a letter that they should take their profits—and this is the point of my exposition—

> and therewith repair hospitals,
> help sick people,
> mend bad roads,
> build up bridges that had been broken down,
> help maidens to marry or to make them nuns,
> find food for prisoners and poor people,
> put scholars to school or to some other crafts,
> help religious orders, and
> ameliorate rents or taxes[7]

[6] *Piers Plowman: A Contribution to the History of English Mysticism* (London, 1894), p. 23.

[7] A modern English version of the "B" text. The "B" text is published in *The vision of William concerning Piers the Plowman in three parallel texts*

—and if they did these things, Truth assured them that the Lord would send Michael His Archangel to ensure that no devil should injure them or frighten them when dying; would guard them from despair and would send their souls safely to His saints in joy.

Langland's poem did not mention, as payments that would be effective for salvation, any of the most usual gifts designed, in his day, to provide for the repose of the donors' souls. In wholly Catholic England, he did not specify that prayers for the dead, the saying of masses, the maintenance of lamps and tapers before altars would be effective to send the donors' souls to the saints in joy. And Langland himself, be it noted, "had received the clerical tonsure . . . and earned a precarious living by singing the *placebo, dirige* and seven psalms for the good of men's souls."[8]

Now let us jump our historical account forward two and a half centuries, from Langland to the reign of the first Elizabeth. Her father, Henry VIII, had dissolved the monasteries, had abolished the papal jurisdiction in England, had taken over the religious foundations, and had things pretty much under the control of the royal courts. What then was the position of donations formerly made to pious uses? What gifts then would as we would put it now, by our criteria, be good in law as gifts for charitable, philanthropic purposes? The answer was given in a statute of the forty-third year of the reign of Elizabeth, Chapter 4, which codified the law of chari-

---

by William Langland: Edited from numerous manuscripts . . . by the Rev. Walter W. Skeat (Oxford, 1886) 1: p. 228. The relevant "B" text follows:

> "And amende *mesondieux* there-myde and mysese folke helpe,
> And wikked wayes witlich hem amende;
> And do bote to brugges that to-broke were,
> Marien maydenes or maken hem nonnes;
> Pore peple and prisounes fynden hem here fode,
> And sette scoleres to schole or to somme other craftes;
> Releue religioun and renten hem bettere. . . ."

[8] Walter W. Skeat, quoted in *The Encyclopaedia Britannica*, 11th ed., s.v. "Langland, William."

ties and enumerated the purposes of gifts which were good as gifts to charitable uses. This law is still basic, in all Anglo-American jurisdictions, including the United States, for legal thinking on the subject of charitable gifts.

The Statute of Elizabeth is entitled "An Act to redress the mis-employment of lands, goods and stocks of money heretofore given to certain charitable uses." It did not make new law, but rather enacted that certain commissioners of the Crown should be empowered to see to it that lands, goods, and money theretofore given for certain charitable purposes were, in fact, then—and henceforth should be—used for the specified charitable purposes.

I am not writing a legal treatise, and I shall not quote the language of the statute; but I shall say simply that the Elizabethan parliamentary draftsman included Langland's complete list of charitable objects with the exceptions that the draftsman cut down the "releve religioun" of the poem to the "repair of churches" and that one of Langland's enumerated purposes, to help maidens to marry or to make them nuns— "marien maydenes or maken hem nonnes"—is, in the Act of 43 Elizabeth, minus the last clause, which obviously could not, in then Protestant England, have been included. This completeness is remarkable; but when I tell you that the legal draftsman included essentially nothing that was not in Langland's categories of two and a half centuries earlier—considering that Langland, by the legal precedent of his day, could have included a great many other categories—it seems to me very remarkable indeed. In short, the parliamentary draftsman took Langland net, and did not bother about anything Langland had not included!

Let me digress a moment to tell you what the fate of *The Vision of Piers the Plowman* had been between the time it was written in the fourteenth century and 1601, which was the date of the enactment of the statute of 43 Elizabeth, Chapter 4. Many manuscripts of it doubtless were in circulation during the intervening 250 years; but *The Vision* was first printed by Thomas Cowley, in London, in 1550; and it ran through three editions in that year.

In more modern times, forty-eight manuscripts of *The Vision of Piers the Plowman* have turned up; and they have been classified by modern scholars into "A" texts, "B" texts, and "C" texts. Thomas Cowley printed from what is now called the "B" text; and this is the point of my digression: The "B" text—which is presumably the text that it would have been easiest for the parliamentary draftsman to have available to him in the book printed by Thomas Cowley—is closer to the Statute of 43 Elizabeth than either the "A" or "C" texts.[9]

I would not press my data to any but reasonable conclusions, and I shall state them very modestly. One is wise to remember what Pollock and Maitland cautioned: "that inquirer is fortunate who is not beguiled into positive error by the desire of making his statements less imperfect."[10]

There had been more than a thousand years of complex legal development on the subject of gifts to pious uses, from the doctrine of the sacred things, the *res sacra* of the Roman Law, through the decretals of Gratian and others, the incredible learning on the subject of frankalmoign,[11] in hundreds of thousands of pages of wills, deeds, capitularies, opinions, decrees. The keenest minds of a millennium had developed the canon law on the subject of gifts to pious uses from humble beginnings into a mighty system.[12]

All this, as respects gifts to pious uses, was understood, winnowed, and stated simply in the language of the people, in *The Vision of Piers the Plowman*. Perhaps Langland was only the mouthpiece of what was in the air; but certainly he made it known, and certainly he made it effective.

[9] For the relevant "A," "B," and "C" texts, see Skeat, *1*: pp. 228-229.
[10] Pollock and Maitland, *1*: p. 25.
[11] Frankalmoign was the tenure by which religious corporations held lands, on condition of praying for the souls of donors and their heirs or of performing other religious services.
[12] Pollock and Maitland, *1*: p. 112.

The Law of Foundations

I do not say, what I do not know, that the Elizabethan parliamentary draftsman had a copy of *The Vision* on his table when he wrote the Statute of 43 Elizabeth. But, on the other hand, I do not think it possible that the Elizabethan Parliamentary draftsman never had read *The Vision*. However, suppose he had not; suppose he only wrote down the consensus of the social thinking of his day. And if we suppose that, we must go on to say—what we know—that the social thinking of the day was strongly influenced by *The Vision of Piers the Plowman*. And so it is clear that somebody, writing as popular poet—not a canonist and not a scholar, Langland singular or Langland plural—simplified, stated persuasively, and made effective what had previously been a closed book to all but the most learned canon lawyers for more than a thousand years.

But Langland, or somebody else, did more than this: he took the purposes of gifts made *pro anima mea, pro salute animae meae* predominantly out of the class of gifts for the repose of the donor's soul and put them predominantly into the class of gifts for the general public good—gifts for the repair of bridges and roads, for the building and endowment of hospitals, for the relief of the poor, for the support of churches, for the training of scholars and craftsmen, for the endowment of learning in all its forms of scholarships, fellowships, professorships, and for the support of educational institutions generally.

Thus it is, and I think it is clear, that a poem set the salient characteristics of all the institutions of education and learning that have had an effect—unweighable, because so large—in making all of us what we are. For certainly all these institutions, with all that they do, are in the mainstream of the codification which began with Langland's poem and had its most complete legal expression with the parliamentary draftsman in the forty-third year of the reign of Tudor Elizabeth.[13]

[13] It is, of course, true that Chapter vi of the Laws of 39 Elizabeth took an important step along these lines, but not as complete as 43 Elizabeth, Chapter iv.

The Law of Foundations

This is the greatest and clearest example known to me of creating understanding by simplification to essentials—a simplification which also shifted emphasis to meet social needs and in that form lived and moved through the centuries until the popular view became embodied in the legislation which yet endures. For *The Vision of Piers the Plowman* and the Act of 43 Elizabeth, Chapter IV, determine the forms, the functions, and the purposes of all those institutions for the common good which we call foundations.

This was the vision of Piers the Plowman; and, as in his vision, the motivating force of philanthropic gifts through all the ages, then and now, has been a religious one in its essence—to do good in the world, to help one's fellowmen who need help and the function and motivating force of tax-exempt, perpetual-living philanthropic and educational foundations in society today is no different from what it has been for at least a millennium and a half.

Thanks to *The Vision*, we who are managers and members of foundations are numerous; we are a whole host; we are a host that stands at Armageddon and battles for the Lord.

We are a host, battling for the Lord, not only because we are numerous but also because we decide to do good works, the Lord's work, in the religious spirit of our history.

Thus, some foundations decided, long before there were laws on the subject, to prevent cruelty to children and animals. Some decided, long before there were state-supported schools, to provide education. There were societies for the prevention of tuberculosis, for the control of cancer, to provide relief from disaster, long before governments took action in these fields. Some societies, long ago and now, decided to foster religious teaching; we call these churches. Some decided to foster the propagation of the faith, whatever the particular religious faith might be; and these we call missionary societies.

The number of such voluntary organizations is legion, their

purposes almost infinitely various. All of them are what the law calls foundations. Life, as we know it, would be unthinkable without them; and the good life, to which we aspire, would have much less effective bases for aspiration without them.

Government could not do what these foundations do—at least could not do what they did when they began to do it. But much that the foundations did in their beginnings has later been taken over by government to do, for the people would not stand for getting along without it—of which free public education is but one example.

In a world of awful instruments and sluggish consciences, we should thank the Lord for William Langland and for his poem. What we call a foundation provides one of the best means ever invented, possibly the best instrument ever invented, by man to control his fate.

The argument of Horace Binney in one of the Girard Will cases, before the Supreme Court of the United States in February, 1844, states the simple truth concerning the scope and power of gifts to charitable uses. "They are instruments," said Mr. Binney, "in the sustenance of the poor, the instruction of the young, and the succour of the afflicted, under the vicissitudes that man is everywhere subject to—in the cultivation of learning, and the advancement of knowledge—in their tendency to consolidate and to adorn society in its progress"—and because they are "moreover, under every shape and form, an acknowledgement, express and implied of our duty to God, and to our neighbor, and directly or indirectly, acts of religious worship and gratitude."

In charity, relief, and education, in the cultivation of learning, the advancement of knowledge, and the progress in culture of society, gifts to what the law calls charitable uses have been, under God, decisive.

Henry Allen Moe, Doctor of Civil Law, Oxford, 1960

THE FUNCTION OF THE SCHOLAR

IN SOCIETY TODAY

THE ROCKEFELLER INSTITUTE,

NEW YORK, MAY 21, 1959

IT is now clear to me, the fourth speaker, that all of us had our sailing orders from Dr. Bronk. Certainly I had; and mine read that I should take the frail craft of my mind into uncharted seas and shoal waters to determine the function of the scholar in society today. But, old Navy hand that I am, I know that sailing orders are subject to the overriding consideration that I do not take my vessel into waters where she cannot go, and that wrecks are like unto the sins against the Holy Ghost: those are the sins, you will remember, that are not forgiven.

Hence, I do not propose to go where I am likely to get wrecked.

Still, it seems to me that Dr. Bronk's sailing orders do not present too great dangers; for the seas of his evocative imagination have had a reconnaissance. And Ralph Waldo Emerson, who made it, declared that a scholar's first duty in society is not to quit his belief that a popgun is a popgun, although the ancient and honorable of the earth affirm it to be the crack of doom.

It is all there, ladies and gentlemen, all that anyone needs to know about the function of the scholar in society in these days, or in any days: you go where your evidence takes you; and there you stand, even though the ancient and honorable of the earth are sure that you should be standing somewhere else.

But in this modern world—the world in which the Newtonian mechanics, to cite but one example, have been shown to have less than the divinity which hedged them about for centuries—I conceive that the Emersonian declaration needs a Moeian recension, which is this: Neither shall the scholar quit his belief that the crack of doom is the crack of doom, although the ancient and honorable of the earth affirm it to be a popgun.

Of the need for this recension, there are many examples. And in view of the fact that this is the centenary of the publication of Charles Darwin's *On the Origin of Species*, I shall refer first to that crack of doom for much of theology and more of biology. The first edition of that book, all 1,200 copies, was sold out, it is true, in less than a day. But then the wielders of the popguns began to pop.

The *Spectator* accused Darwin of collecting a mass of facts to substantiate a false principle. An article in the *Quarterly Review* said that Darwin was attempting in his book "to prop up his utterly rotten fabric of guess and speculation" and declared that it was all "utterly dishonourable to science." Darwin's own college would not permit a copy of the *Origin* in its library; and this college, I hesitate to mention in Lord Adrian's presence, was Trinity in Cambridge.

Darwin's old geology professor at Cambridge, Sedgwick, wrote him that the book was "false and mischievous" and added that when he read it he had "laughed till his sides ached." Sir John Herschel, the astronomer, described Darwinism as "the law of higgledy-piggledy."

There were defenders too: Thomas Henry Huxley, Charles Lyell, geologist, and Asa Gray, American botanist, contradicting his colleague Agassiz at Harvard. The end of the *pros* and *cons* is not yet; but, undoubtedly, it was not a popgun that Darwin fired off, although many of the ancient and honorable of the earth were violently of that opinion.

And, for another example, there was Dante of the thirteenth and fourteenth centuries—in some ways the greatest mind of all times—who, as Oliver Goldsmith put it clearly and accurately, "first followed nature and was persecuted by his critics as long as he lived," in and out of exile and in and out of prison. Sick with petty quarrels and dissensions, Dante strained the eyes of his mind for the appearance of a universal monarch who should be raised above the flaws of faction and the spur of political ambition, under whom each country and each city, might—under the institutions best suited to it—lead the life and do the work for which it was best fitted. United in spiritual harmony, Dante showed to the world for the first time a plan of a government where the strongest force and the highest wisdom were interpenetrated by all that God had given to the world of piety and justice. And it is not possible to say that Dante's dream did not work its own realization nor to deny that the high ideal of the poet had its effect. For, five centuries later, it became embodied in the constitution of the Italian state which still has no stronger bond of union than a common worship of the exiled and imprisoned poet's indignant and impassioned verse.[1]

But I need not multiply my examples. All of you will have those that are better and clearer for yourselves, because they flow from your own fields of interest.

For me, nevertheless, there still remains to relate the poignant example of Edward FitzGerald's translation—which is more than a translation—of *The Rubáiyát* of Omar Khayyám. The centenary of its publication—so far as I know—has gone unobserved. It appeared in April, 1859, for sale at a

---

[1] Quoted from *Encyclopaedia Britannica*, 11th edition: article "Dante."

shilling a copy. But it found not one buyer at that price; and all 250 copies of the first edition were remaindered at a penny each.

Omar Khayyám of Nishapur on the Iranian plateau, son of a tentmaker, was renowned and respected, in his lifetime, as astronomer and mathematician. He was one of the eight astronomers appointed by the eleventh-century Persian Malik Shah to reform the calendar; and as FitzGerald has him say in his verses—for *Rubáiyát* simply means verses:

> Ah, but my Computations, People say
> Reduced the Year to better reckoning? Nay,
> 'Twas only striking from the Calendar
> Unborn Tomorrow and dead Yesterday.

Let me not attempt to be philosopher nor to assay Omar's philosophy. I shall but relate the facts:

Omar's contemporaries honored him for his mathematical and astronomical computations; but, for his verses, they denounced him as a freethinker. The *Rubáiyát*, in essence, is a plea for tolerance. In it, everything is tolerated except intolerance, and this point of view was offensive to orthodox Moslems. This was said explicitly in *The Book of Learned Men*, an Arabic biographical work of the thirteenth century: "The inner meanings (of Omar's verses) are as stinging serpents to the Mussulman law: hence, the men of his day hated him. . . ."

Being disapproved in contemporary eleventh-century Islam, the verses lay in obscurity on through the ages. So small was their interest that only two manuscripts have survived—one in the Bodleian Library of the University of Oxford, and one in the Library of the Bengal Asiatic Society in Calcutta.

And the resistances which the eleventh-century Omar's verses met in Islam were no different in kind from the resistances which the FitzGerald translation met in nineteenth-century Christendom. So it was that Edward Cowell, the Persian scholar who had introduced FitzGerald to the *Rubáiyát* manuscripts, wrote that he would not permit a book on the Omar verses to be dedicated to him. "I unwittingly incurred," he said, "a grave responsibility when I introduced his poems to my old friend. . . . I admire Omar but I cannot take him as a guide."[2]

In the pre-Darwinian Western World, when things were known or could be known by revelation—especially about human affairs—words such as these by Omar had no takers:

> There was the Door to which I found no Key;
> There was a Veil through which I might not see. . . .

But Omar had seen clearly that the great questions always stand—*all* the great questions of literature and history and philosophy and science—stand outside the limits of finality. It is a lesson we have not learned to this day.

To cite an example, from a field in which many of you must tread more familiarly than I—an example which I have from that very great mathematician, Hermann Weyl—as late as 1923 the writers on relativity theory and tensor calculus were accused by some of the ancient and honorable mathematicians of the earth of having laid waste a rich cultural domain. That rich cultural domain was the algebraic theory of invariants.

Clearly—if I may put it so—to denigrate the relativity theory this way was the underestimation of the century. This time what was called a popgun almost literally became the crack of doom.

A new key, which the ancient and honorable of the earth had not found, was found in the theory of representations of continuous Lie groups. And by these new means, the old problems which, according to the complaint, the relativists had to let go by the board have been attacked on a much deeper level than was possible by the algebraic theory of invariants.[3]

[2] Alfred McKinley Terhune, *The Life of Edward FitzGerald* (1947), pp. 218-219.

[3] Hermann Weyl, "Relativity Theory as a Stimulus in Mathematical Research," *Proc. Amer. Philos. Soc.* 93, 7 (1949): pp. 543-545.

The Scholar Today

There yet is a "Veil through which I might not see" still a "Door to which I found no Key"; but the Veil and the Door are different veils and different doors, placed further down the corridor of men's eternal quest for Truth. "Of all sad words of tongue or pen," wrote our own Whittier, "The saddest are these, it might have been."

One is tempted to wonder—in the most futile of wonderment, as I know—what might have happened in Islam as well as in Christendom, in the Middle East as well as in the West, if the freedom-giving intellection behind Omar Khayyám's *Rubáiyát* had become as well understood as Charles Darwin's intellection *On the Origin of Species*.

But let me not engage in speculative futility on this occasion. Rather, let me hope with Omar, for each one of us, that:

Of my base metal may be filed a Key
That shall unlock the Door he (the Dervish) howls without.

"A Hair, perhaps, divides the False and True," wrote Omar in the eleventh century. A hair, perhaps, divides the popgun from the crack of doom, the crack of doom from the popgun. The function of the scholar in any society, is to make that division for himself, and then to stand firmly on the side of the divide that represents Truth for him.

142

SOME CLUES TO THE OPEN,

BUT NOT GULLIBLE, MIND

BROWN UNIVERSITY, OCTOBER 27, 1960

IN the latter part of the nineteenth century, there were floating around in what a layman, like me, can only call the rarefied strata of mathematics and of what later came to be called mathematical physics, a series of theoretical ideas which a half-century afterwards became immense reality. The names of Lorentz of Leyden, Minkowski of Göttingen, Poincaré of Paris, wove in and out of the development of these ideas in the journals—until Albert Einstein in 1905, then a Patent Office examiner in Berne, set down the culminating symbolism that $E = Mc^2$. This symbolism, as all know now, expresses the interconvertibility, the equivalence, of mass and energy. It grew out of the mathematics and philosophy of special relativity. It was set down in a purely speculative, yet to some— but not all—mathematicians, in an astonishingly compelling manner. It was, when set down, simply a theoretical mathematical proposition—nothing more. So far as an engineer interested in the production of power could see, if he saw it at all, it was a piece of mathematical fiction—nothing more. It remained so until 1939 when, in that year, experimental procedures produced nuclear fission and proved the truth of the symbolism. Nature then, as Hermann Weyl—another very great mathematician—remarked in another connection, gra-

143

ciously confirmed the symbolism with as clear an *okay* as one ever can get from her.

Revolutionary in its implications though Einstein's symbolism was, and at first unproven experimentally, it was nevertheless received with respect, but not with universal respect. In time, as physicists considered the matter, it became documented with a few disconnected pieces of experimental evidence; but these were held together only by Einstein's daring symbolism of deduction and generalization. The symbolism became immense reality at Alamogordo and Hiroshima; the mathematical fiction then became the engineer's El Dorado of power.

At no stage of the development from Berne to Alamogordo was it suggested by any free scientist concerned that these developments were too revolutionary to be continued, but it was both thought and said that the Einstein concept was certainly too wild to get anywhere.

For the story of the development of modern physics is not all sweetness and light. As late as 1923 the writers on relativity theory were accused by competent and respectable mathematicians of "having laid waste a rich cultural domain" —the words of a great mathematician whose name, believe it or not, was *Study*. This rich cultural domain was the algebraic theory of invariants. Professor Study was vexed that the classic notations of that theory were ignored by the relativists who went their new ways, into new countries of the mind where the prospects were more pleasing, despite the fact that the classicists hated the sight of the new vistas.

I often am reminded of these facets of the development of modern physics as I look at the works of modern artists, and hear them discussed. For the things said about modern art by some are not different from what the classical physicists said about relativity. Strictures are heard to the effect that the modernists among the artists also have laid waste a rich cultural domain, and have created a country where no prospect pleases, where the laws of perspective are no more, where all is silly, and "phony"; because the older learning, the older disciplines are ignored.

Art is beauty and beauty is art, they say, and the conclusion is that when there is no beauty there is no art. In the light of the premise, there is no quarreling with the conclusion. But if the premise be changed—and who dares to say, in the light of the principle that the channels of communication of the mind and spirit must be kept open for renewal and development, that it may not validly be changed—the conclusion does not follow. Decidedly, it does not follow at all.

Men of pure science are said to be content—and they usually are—to set down what, for them, is truth, and from that truth to proceed to new truth, or to what, to them, is new truth. In the process they stumble more often than they proceed, they follow more dead-end trails than they find trails which take them to the little hilltops of tentative truth. They discuss, they publish bits of their evidence, and they publish their limited visions, they use each other's shoulders—trying to gain the stature to enable them to get some glimmerings of the direction of the trail of truth to the mountain top of understanding. Such was the progress from Berne to Alamogordo—or rather to Chicago: for it was in the old field house at Stagg Field that what began as an *idea* of atomic energy was realized. There $E = Mc^2$ was proven as objective, experimental truth.

It is the method of free science that truth and error shall be pursued wherever their paths may lead. In science, concepts arise in the minds of free men; and are verified or not verified by experiment and observation, and out of experiment and observation arise new concepts which lead to new experiments and new observation, and so on and on, *ad infinitum*.

Progress in the arts is no different from that in the sciences, pure and applied. The difference lies fundamentally only in the circumstance that progress in the arts cannot be proven:

the chain reaction that was made to occur at Stagg Field has no counterpart in artistic history. In science, as Herbert Ives used to remind the mathematical physicists, the plea that Faraday made to Maxwell that there must be physical meaning for the terms of the equations of physics, will always be a valid point. Indeed, all values are rooted in matter-of-fact events. But you cannot *prove* anything worth proving about a painting.

In the arts, as in science, the process of concept and experiment and observation and then of new concept based on the older experimentation and observation goes on and on, *ad infinitum*. And it is further just as true of the arts as of the sciences that, as George Santayana said, "The only artists who can show great originality are those trained in distinct and established schools: for originality and genius must be largely fed and raised on the shoulders of some tradition." The progression from the alchemists to plutonium is a continuous line—not straight, but continuous; the progression from Raphael to Braque likewise is continuous.

What is generally known as modern art had its origins in the late nineteenth century. So had modern physics. At that time, the leaders of physics were accustomed to think that they had a wonderfully complete, well-verified and apparently all-inclusive set of laws and principles into which all physical phenomena must forever fit; and they were heard to declare —as Michelson wrote in the catalogue of the University of Chicago—that the future of physics lay in the refinement of measurement rather than in new discovery. At the same time established artists were saying approximately the same thing about the future of art.

But in 1896 Becquerel discovered radioactivity and then began a series of discoveries and developments that made physics into a new science. What had been modish and accepted no longer sufficed for adventurous minds in physics; and they found new paths to new truth. So it was in art about the same time: the painters were dissatisfied, as were the physicists, with what was modish and accepted, and they set out to find new paths to new truth and to achieve new means for its expression. As the physicists broke into new domains never dreamed of in the older physicists' philosophy, so modern art was born when artists created something that had never existed before: painting—they hoped and tried—to reveal, "as in a flash intimate, absolute truth regarding the nature of things." Thereafter, the concept of art as the pursuit of beauty was, in their book, inadequate. To them it was just as inadequate as the old Newtonian mechanics were to Lorentz and Minkowski and Poincaré and Einstein—and in just the same sense.

Whether they were right or wrong is not the issue. That question is the wrong question—to which, therefore, there can be no right answer.

The essence of art, as the essence of science, is the *pursuit* of truth and its expression. The difference between them is, as I have said already, fundamentally only that the hypotheses of science may, sometimes but not always, in time be proven or disproven experimentally: the "truths" of art are not susceptible of such demonstration. Yet it must be noted, when using the word *truth*, that the criterion of advance in mathematics is, among mathematicians, not truth but *elegance*. That is to say, a demonstration in mathematics is not judged by concepts of truth or falsity but by its elegance or lack of this quality, and thus its value is a matter of value judgment, not of objective proof—exactly as in the arts.

And this is as it must be. For, from one point of view, science, viewed at any given time, is only a series of hypotheses held for the sake of convenience. When the holding of a hypothesis ceases to be convenient, it is succeeded by another that is more convenient. Thus it was that Planck, having developed his quantum theory out of Maxwell's equations, no doubt took a long stride forward in modern physics; but Poin-

147

caré was able to show that such a development as Planck had made was mathematically not possible out of Maxwell's equations! Yet Poincaré's proof in no way, it seems, affected the convenience of Planck's hypothesis for the advance of physics.

So it is, or ought to have a chance to be, in the domain of art. Those who may be called originators of modern art— in the same sense as the originators of modern physics—felt a terrible need and urgent necessity to paint what to them was the true inwardness of things, their lasting significance; to paint a person as the vessel of an idea, indestructible as a symbol; to put on canvas, as Van Gogh did successfully, a sense of cosmic terror.

These modern artists took as their purpose what John Livingston Lowes says in *The Road to Xanadu* is the only true purpose of all scholarship and all art: "the imagination voyaging through chaos and reducing it to clarity and order is the symbol of all the quests that lend glory to our dust." "*All the quests!*" The painter's imagination and the physicist's, are not differently employed, should not be differently employed: the imagination of both should voyage through chaos and reduce it to clarity and order. It is the only quest that lends glory to our dust.

I continue thus to distinguish between the open and the gullible mind. The question, in the face of the new art, must be to ask what fresh eye and fresh insight is the artist bringing to his work. It is beside the point to ask whether or not he conforms to the laws of perspective of the Renaissance, just as it is beside the point for the atomic physicist to be held to the limitations of the algebraic theory of invariants. Both the artist and the physicist are entitled to attack their problems on much deeper levels than the concepts and tools of the past would allow them to do.

One could pile up any number of examples of the open, but not gullible, mind. Likewise one could pile up any number of examples of the closed and gullible mind.

Clues to the Open Mind

For example, there is Charles Darwin's *On the Origin of Species*. Hardly had it first been issued, a century ago, when the *Spectator* accused Darwin of collecting a mass of facts to substantiate a false principle. The *Quarterly Review* said that Darwin was attempting in his book "to prop up his utterly rotten fabric of guess and speculation" and declared that it was all "utterly dishonourable to science." Darwin's own college at Cambridge would not permit a copy of the *Origin* in its library.

Darwin's old geology professor, Sedgwick, wrote him that the book was "false and mischievous" and added that when he read it he had "laughed till his sides ached." Sir John Herschel, the astronomer, described Darwinism as "the law of higgledy-piggledy."

But I need not multiply my examples. All of you will have those that are better and clearer for yourselves, because they flow from your own fields of interest.

For me, nevertheless, there still remains to relate the poignant example of Edward FitzGerald's translation—which is more than a translation—of *The Rubáiyát* of Omar Khayyám. It appeared in April, 1859, for sale at a shilling a copy. But it found not one buyer at that price; and all 250 copies of the first edition were remaindered at a penny each.

Omar Khayyám of Nishapur on the Iranian plateau, son of a tentmaker, was renowned and respected, in his lifetime, as astronomer and mathematician. He was one of the eight astronomers appointed by the eleventh-century Persian Malik Shah to reform the calendar.

Omar's contemporaries honored him for his mathematical and astronomical computations; but, for his verses, they denounced him as a freethinker. The *Rubáiyát*, in essence, is a plea for tolerance. In it, everything is tolerated except intolerance, and this point of view was offensive to orthodox Moslems. This was said explicitly in *The Book of Learned Men*, an Arabic biographical work of the thirteenth century: "The inner meanings [of Omar's verses] are as stinging serpents to the Mussulman law; hence, the men of his day hated him."

Being disapproved in contemporary eleventh-century Islam, the verses lay in obscurity on through the ages. And the resistances which the eleventh-century Omar's verses met in Islam were no different in kind from the resistances which the FitzGerald translation met in nineteenth-century Christendom. So it was that Edward Cowell, the Persian scholar who had introduced FitzGerald to the *Rubáiyát* manuscripts, wrote that he would not permit a book on the Omar verses to be dedicated to him. "I unwittingly incurred," he said, "a grave responsibility when I introduced his poems to my old friend. ... I admire Omar but I cannot take him as a guide."

In the pre-Darwinian Western World, when things were known or could be known by revelation—especially about human affairs—words such as these by Omar had no takers:

> There was the Door to which I found no Key;
> There was a Veil through which I might not see. . . .

But Omar had seen clearly that the great questions always stand—*all* the great questions of literature and history and philosophy and science—stand outside the limits of finality.

This is my point: all the great questions always stand outside the limits of finality.

Ralph Waldo Emerson declared that the scholar's first duty is not to quit his belief that a popgun is a popgun, although the ancient and honorable of the earth affirm it is to be the crack of doom.

But in this modern world—the world in which the Newtonian mechanics, as I have suggested, have been shown to have less than the divinity which hedged them about for centuries—I conceive that the Emersonian declaration needs a Moeian recension, which is this: Neither shall the scholar quit his belief that the crack of doom is the crack of doom, although the ancient and honorable of the earth affirm it to be a popgun. On the need of that recension, there is the evidence of the reception of Darwin's *On the Origin of Species*.

On the question of the open as contrasted with the gullible mind, I have been telling you that you can decide nothing worth deciding if your point of view is that of a priest of the accepted gods looking askance at the new. There could have been no Alamogordo if the priests of the accepted gods of physics had ruled. There could have been no modern art if Cézanne, for example, had somehow been compelled to paint according to the perspective of Euclidean geometry. Certainly one must recognize changes in value, one must give a chance to men glimpsing new possibilities and new avenues for thought and expression. Likewise, there must be understanding that there are great traditionalists and great innovators both. You must clearly understand that the accepted gods often are good gods, often better than the new. But whether the good gods be old or new, there must be understanding that you get nowhere unless you are a believer in free enterprise in things of the mind and spirit. Only by this way of looking at things will you have a chance to be open-minded, but not gullible.

But having said this much, having said that freedom to think, to feel, to experiment, to innovate, is the *sine qua non*, there remains the question what is the touchstone to determine what is open-mindedness and what is gullibility?

To that question, there is only one answer: Education. Education that brings a command of a wide range of facts, a sense of history; education that develops judgment, connoisseurship, and taste.

And so I now suggest that you get back to your books, for there are very few—and I am not one of them—who can tell you anything that you cannot find, better-stated, in the books and in nature.

A LAWYER'S HISTORY LESSON *

THE AMERICAN PHYSICAL SOCIETY AND

THE AMERICAN ASSOCIATION OF PHYSICS TEACHERS

NEW YORK, JANUARY 26, 1962

WITHIN the month—this month—one of your many eminent members, Dr. Lee DuBridge, published an article which begins like this: "The fact that social and natural scientists seem to have so little to say to each other is one of the tragedies of modern times."

I propose, in a minor way, to try to mitigate what Dr. DuBridge called a tragedy, even while recognizing that an after-dinner speech must be neither too solemn nor too long—above all not too long!

Perhaps, I may as well say at the outset, my credentials as a social scientist may not be deemed very good. For I am a lawyer—only a lawyer it is fashionable to say—and during all my years as a member of the Social Science Research Council I never heard anybody take the floor and declare, or even admit, the law to be one of the social sciences. This always surprised me, in my simple-minded way; for I had thought that the essence of science—in one aspect—is to predict results from known data. And from this point of view, the lawyer's law is more often science than any of the other social so-called sciences.

* Reprinted by permission from *Physics Today* 15, 4 (1962): pp. 30-32, 34.

A Lawyer's History Lesson

The word "law" and the words "social sciences" are, of course, tricky words; and they are used in many senses, which it would be dull to consider now. But, since I am speaking to physicists—and their ladies—perhaps I had better claim that a lawyer's use of the word "law" has a long priority over your use of the word. Your use of the word and my use of it may have no meaning in common, but I do not think that's so, myself.

However that be, when I speak of a lawyer's use of his data predictively, I do not mean merely that the lawyer can predict accurately the result that you surely will have to pay a $15 fine from the known data that you had parked your car by a fire hydrant in New York City and had found a ticket under your windshield wiper.

I mean more than that when I think of the predictive value of a lawyer's data in a lawyer's mind. I have in mind, for a small example, the law that is inherent in the old maxim of the legal learning about criminal libel, that "The greater the truth the greater the libel." Harsh words may well lead to a breach of the peace—fighting in the streets, in other words—and thus the law prosecutes a man who says outrageous things to or about his neighbor, whether the outrageous statements be true or false. Hence, any good lawyer would predict that if a defendant pleaded that his outrageous statements about his neighbor were true, no surer way of getting convicted of criminal libel could be devised. For, as the old woman said in an English court, "I should not mind being called a fool, were I not one indeed."

But I must be wary of going too far in contending that a lawyer can predict legal results from known data. The old sayings come to mind: the lawyer says to his client, "They can't put you in jail for that"; and the client responds, "But I *am* in jail for that."

Persiflage aside, what I really intend to do is to give you some data for thinking about the point made by the philosopher Santayana that "Those who cannot remember the past are condemned to repeat it."

All lawyers know, and you know too, that, if accused of a crime, you are entitled to demand, and get, a trial by jury; but you cannot know *why* unless you know what went on in the minds of Englishmen of the later Middle Ages. "So continuous has been our English legal life during the last six centuries, that the law of the later Middle Ages has never been forgotten among us. It has never passed utterly outside the cognizance of our courts and practicing lawyers."[1]

But even more basic than the question why you are entitled to a trial by jury is, in my mind, the question why you let yourself be tried at all, by any process. You may think this a silly question—to which silly question your obvious answer is that the cops bring you in and you do not have anything to say about it. But it was not always so: in fact, even in our society, it was not so—not very long ago, as time has to be regarded in any view of the history of men.

And clearly, as all of you know, it is not so even today in the relationships of nations to nations. There are no cops to bring a nation in, before a court; and, within very narrow limits, there is, in international affairs, no way to enforce the court's decrees if there were a court to which you could bring the nation in.

It is, indeed, precisely the situation that the shipwrecked sailor explained, with a certain longing: "Captain, if we had some ham we could have ham and eggs for breakfast, if we had some eggs."

I think it fair and evident to say that, at least since the Ten Commandments and the Sermon on the Mount, certainly all western men and practically all men everywhere, have known what's right and what's wrong in the relationship of men to men. And this goes equally as an accurate statement of the relationship of groups to groups, of tribes to tribes, of nations to nations.

---

[1] Pollock and Maitland, *History of English Law*, Introduction, p. xxxiv.

A Lawyer's History Lesson

The question is—and there is no more urgent question of these days—what can be done to make the ideals of the Ten Commandments and of the Sermon on the Mount effective among and between nations? Whence, and how and why can we get the ham and get the eggs to create the longed-for breakfast of peace?

Perhaps, as I think, we may learn something on this subject from the legal history of the Middle Ages, which, as Pollock and Maitland noted, has never been wholly forgotten by Anglo-American courts and lawyers.

We do not know, at rock bottom, how what we think of as government by law got started. But we do know with certainty that when men had once gotten a taste of government by law, they wanted more of the same. A bit of order, a recognition that what is mine is mine—my cow, my ox, my land—always has appealed to the feelings of the generality of men as a good thing. To the generality of men, *yes*; but not to all. The question then was what do you do about those who continue to want to take what is mine and to kill in the process of taking?

This question opens up a large and fascinating chapter in the history of men. The answer seems to be that it had to be made attractive to what we would call malefactors to submit themselves to the judgments of what later became courts. It must have appeared absurd to primitive men—to impute modern thinking to them—to submit their feuds to decisions of courts.

Legal history shows that there were many ways, in primitive law, which were used first to entice and then to compel defendants to submit to the jurisdiction of a court; but I have time to give you only one example—the example of the judgment by battle.

And lest you think I am now using words with some legerdemain of legal meaning unknown to you, I shall say at once that I mean the same thing by battle that you would mean: the plaintiff and the defendant fought it out with swords and javelins before the court—and the man who won the battle, won the law suit. There was no nonsense about proving the facts.

It is easy to imagine how this would appeal to a malefactor —the tough guy who had stolen or killed. He would enjoy an appeal to physical force. And, in time, another factor came in —particularly after the reception of Christianity. This was a belief that Providence will give victory to the right. The God of Battles would take care of that; and the trial by battle became the *judicium dei*, the judgment of God, par excellence.

How far back in history am I now, when I talk this way? Well—it's hard to say exactly, but certainly in the time of Shakespeare, in 1571 to be exact, trial by battle was a going concern. In that year, it is told in the law reports that the judges and the lawyers adjourned to Tothill Fields, near London, where they, with a crowd of four thousand people, assembled to see a trial by battle.[2] And Blackstone in his eighteenth century *Commentaries on the Laws of England*[3] describes trial by battle, at length, as still a part of the law of England.

As Blackstone tells it:

> A piece of ground is . . . set out, sixty feet square, and on one side a court is erected for the judges of the court of common pleas, who attend there in their scarlet robes; and also a bar is prepared for the learned sergeants of the law. When the court sits, which ought to be by sunrising, proclamation is made for the parties and their champions; who are introduced by two knights and are dressed in a coat of armour, with red sandals, barelegged from the knee down, bareheaded, with bare arms to the elbow. . . . The battle is thus begun and the combatants are bound to fight until the stars appear in the evening.

These are Blackstone's words, not mine. And you will agree that it must have been a very colorful day, from sun up to sun down—a day likely to appeal to a certain type of malefactor. Please note again that there was no nonsense about evidence,

[2] Lowe v. Paramour. Dyer 30.
[3] Blackstone, 3: pp. 333-341.

no concern with proof of the facts, no jury, no pleas by counsel: the chap who won the battle won the case.

But you will have observed, from Blackstone's account, that certain rules have appeared: the size of the battleground is stipulated; the judges must be there, to enforce the rules, and so must be the lawyers. You also will have observed in Blackstone's account that the parties *and* their champions must be there.

Well, that was not the end of the whittling down of the defendant's right to insist on trial by battle. Infants, women, and men over sixty were, in time, allowed to decline trial by battle: they might employ champions; and soon the right to employ champions became extended to all able-bodied litigants.[4] And after a while, churches, landowners, and communities commonly retained champions to do battle for them when the alleged malefactor elected to be tried by battle. By this time, swords and javelins were prohibited and the champions fought only with three-foot wooden staves.

Now you see what really happened, and this is the quintessence of my point—that malefactors were obliged to submit to the jurisdiction of a court; and the court made the rules of the trial by battle as they made the rules of all other forms of trial.

After that had been accomplished, it was a foregone conclusion—although vestiges of the right to trial by battle held on until 1819 in England—that, in time, proof by other forms than by battle would come to dominate legal trial procedure.

And so, in time—but remember it took centuries and fairly recent centuries at that—trial by jury, with its rules of evidence and of procedure and its sense of rational justice, became what we all know it to be now.

And do not forget, please—for I shall return to the point later—that, in the long struggle for civil order, the hardest part was the first, to entice and induce, and then to compel, the

---

[4] W. S. Holdsworth, *A History of English Law* 1: pp. 308-309.

alleged malefactor to accept the jurisdiction of a court to decide whether he was a malefactor or not. Thitherto, the malefactor had preferred to decide that for himself!

In the field of what we would call international relations— although the period is an age before there were nation-states —the history runs much along the same lines.

I have written this out for other occasions and I shall not now take your time to go into it—in the interest of that brevity which is said to be the soul of *wit*—wit meaning, in this context, *intelligence* of which I hope I have some, not *witticism* to which I make no claim.

You may take my word for it that the history of the development of law and order as between the feuding barons and marauding groups ran its course in the Middle Ages, along much the same road as the development of law and order as between individuals. The "right"—which *is* the correct word in the context of the Middle Ages—to the spoils of such inter-baronial warfare became the distinctive, recognized privilege of those with enough power to exercise it, for there was no power great enough to restrain. For three long and bloody centuries—the tenth to the thirteenth—in France, this private warfare continued with only the concepts of the Peace of God and the Truce of God to mitigate it, and then only in a limited way.

The difference, the supreme difference between the development of law relating to the individual and the law relating to the feuding barons, was that no way was developed, except by employing greater military force, to get jurisdiction over the predatory barons. The concept of the Peace and Truce of God was a scholar's concept, making the brotherhood of man a logical corollary to the fatherhood of God, and it was good and effective as far as it went. But when the medieval unity of western Christendom disintegrated and when consolidated territorial states appeared as predominant factors, then the concept of the Peace of God went out of the window. And so did the concept of the community of mankind as an effective ideal. In the broadest sense, the history of the era we call Modern is the record of successive attempts to restore that concept as an effective ideal.

And that, in the United Nations, is what we are trying to do today.

I remain an optimist. I remain an optimist because, as Mr. Justice Holmes observed, all the rules of modern law "started from a moral basis, from the thought that someone was to blame."[5] And in the United Nations we have a forum in which the moral basis is constantly stated and in which it is pointed out, for all the world to see, who is to blame.

The history of all law is that law is not law until it has become a habit. When it has become a habit, the question of submitting to the jurisdiction of a tribunal—the supreme question—answers itself. Many events of the past decade indicate that the habit of submission to a tribunal in international affairs is growing.

That the habit will continue to grow, there is no doubt. All observers, anthropological and legal, have noted the sentiment of reverence evoked by the mere existence of law in primitive communities. And we may be sure that the sentiment of reverence for law is not less now among all men than it was in primitive communities.

I have tried, as you have seen, to bring you a lesson of history—of history from a lawyer's point of view, a legal historian's point of view, if you prefer. In doing so, I have been conscious of two dangers of which Mr. Justice Holmes has written a reminder. "One is that of supposing because an idea seems very familiar and natural to us, that it always has been so. Many things which we take for granted have had to be laboriously fought out or thought out in past times. The other mistake is the opposite one of asking too much of history. We start with man full grown. It may be assumed that the earliest

[5] Oliver Wendell Holmes, Jr., *The Common Law*, p. 37.

barbarians . . . had a good many of the same feelings and passions as ourselves."[6] The words are, as said, Mr. Justice Holmes's.

We, who are in the Anglo-American tradition, started on an isolated island site: we were made, from tribes, into one nation by a powerful and skillful and politically wise king, William of Normandy; we were left alone, on our island site, to develop ways to bring malefactors to book and to educate our people in ways of responsible citizenship. Along our thousand year way, we shifted control from king to nobility, from nobility to parliament, and we were able to make this shift because the Renaissance and the Industrial Revolution bred a new force, the educated middle class. Then the settlement of America made a new society, with its ideal that everyone should be as good as the next. And in the United States, very swiftly, freedom under law became a reality; and so did universal education.

Recently there have been added science and technology, tied in with industrial processes, and these have made truly vertiginous the rate of change in some aspects of industrial societies. But they have not made much change in the relationship of men to men, in their degree of competitiveness and cooperativeness—the history of which I have been talking about.

As said, we have had a thousand years to evolve—sometimes smoothly, sometimes not—out of our past. Many of the new nations of our day have no such past. They have taken power without it; indeed, they had no choice but to take power with no long preparation, once enough of their people had been stirred into racial self-consciousness and political awareness. Our long development will not be open to them—not ever.

One may hope, as Ortega y Gasset has written, that

Contrary to general belief, history may advance by jumps, and not always by gradual change. It was the characteristic error

[6] *Ibid.*, p. 2.

of the past century to count upon gradual evolution, and to presume that every whole achievement in history was produced by means of gradual preparation. It was a surprise when facts showed, clearly and undeniably, that in biology and in the spiritual world alike, spontaneous realities could emerge suddenly and in a sense without preparation.

One hopes that Ortega y Gasset is right, and right not only in respect to the biological and spiritual worlds: one hopes so with a hope that is more than hope. But as a lawyer, I see no evidence, in a thousand years of history, for swift change in the relationship of man to man.

And there is another point, which I shall let that greatest of legal historians, F. W. Maitland, state for me.[7] Maitland there discusses the means by which scholars created the concept of the Peace of God.

> The cautious particularity of the canons, resolutions, oaths, their provisoes and exceptions and saving clauses . . . are the very essence of the story. Those who strive for peace are in the end successful, because they are content with small successes, and will proceed from particular to particular, placing now the *villanus* and now the *femina nobilis*, now the sheep and now the olive tree, now the Saturday and now the Thursday outside the sphere of blood-feud and private war. When they are in a hurry they fail, for they are contending with mighty forces.

We, too, shall fail if we are in a hurry, for we, too, are contending with mighty forces.

[7] *The Collected Papers of Frederic William Maitland* 2, "The Peace of God and the Land-Peace," pp. 291-292.

ON QUALITY

SOUTHERN ILLINOIS UNIVERSITY, CARBONDALE,

ILLINOIS, JUNE 13, 1962

YOU have been concerned here—students and faculty—with learning. You have studied history and chemistry, Latin and physics, biological evolution and English, and a full catalogue of other subject-matters besides. You have had to study these subjects in compartments, as it were; because, otherwise, it is thought that the business of learning would be too complicated. However, on my side, for example, I conceive that it would be both feasible and fine to study the writing of English partly by reading the great scientific treatises of Charles Darwin and Thomas Henry Huxley on biological evolution—treatises which are great as science and equally as great as literature.

But I have to recognize that things are not done that way. The professor of English thinks that, to study English, you had better study what he calls English literature—novels, poetry, literary criticism—as the noblest expressions of men and women who wrote English.

That they are noble expressions is certain. But what the professor of English neglects is that there are equally great expressions of the mind and spirit, just as great as literature, expounding the concepts of biology, of law, of theology, and of any other subject you could name.

And the professor of physics overlooks that there are concepts of validity to him and his students expressed nobly in

162

works of what the professor of English truly calls great literature. An example is, of course, H. G. Wells's scientific fantasy *The Time Machine.*

For the biologist there are Shelley's poems with their intimate insights into nature.[1] And for the professor of French there is Laplace's *Exposition du Système du Monde* (Paris, 1796). It is a statement of the first order in celestial mechanics, and likewise is such a beautiful statement in the French language that, for its elegance as French—not for its elegance as astronomy—Laplace was elected to the French Academy. Yet who ever had a chance to read Laplace in a French course?

Along this line of thinking, the examples are legion, and they all lead to the same conclusion: that he who divides up knowledge tears a seamless web which had better not be torn. He tears a seamless web whose beauty is as the rainbow—completely beautiful in its curved sweep from violet to red. The rainbow, of course, also is interesting in its divisions that are useful for scientific analysis; but the divisions are incomplete as a manifestation of the beauty of nature visible to the naked eye.

Similarly incomplete as a manifestation of the brain and spirit of man, are all compartmentations of knowledge, all of which tear the seamless web of man's greatest achievements.

But let me move this discourse out of the realm of generalities into the realm of specific cases.

A couple of years ago on one of his Sunday evening television hours, Edward R. Murrow asked three eminent European and American poets whether or not they could cite any instance of a poem that had directly shaped the course of history. The distinguished poets had no answer, I am sorry to say. They had a chance, literally, to tell the world; but, in the language of baseball, they muffed it.

Yet there is a wonderfully clear instance of a poem directly

[1] John Campbell Merriam, "Shelley and Men of Science," *Christian Register*, December 10, 1936.

163

affecting history—*making* history, indeed—and this is the old English poem *The Vision of Piers the Plowman*, written by William Langland, in the fourteenth century. The poem made history in this way: the actual language of some of its verses became the law of England, and later of the United States, to define what are and what are not valid purposes for that host of organizations set up for charitable, educational, religious, and eleemosynary purposes—colleges, universities, hospitals, humane societies, historical societies, learned societies of all kinds.

The law to which I refer was passed in the forty-third year of the reign of Queen Elizabeth I. One can almost say that the draughtsmen of the law had the *Vision of Piers the Plowman* on his table as he wrote. For certainly he put the language of some verses of the poem into the law, and he used the ideas in those verses to define the legal concepts he wanted defined. In this present world of awful instruments and sluggish consciences, the world should know what William Langland and his poem accomplished. All the world knows that in charity, relief, and education, in the cultivation of learning, the advancement of knowledge, and the progress in culture of society, gifts to what the law calls charitable uses have been under God, of the greatest importance. What the world should know additionally is that, under God, William Langland's poem was the instrument that made gifts to charitable uses effective for these high purposes.[2]

In short, the lawyers and the legislators used the vision of a poet to write their law; and his vision directly affects your lives, and mine, not only on this your graduation day but also on all the days of all our lives.

And now for an instance of the arts affecting science: All of you who have studied chemistry know how much you need glassware—beakers, test tubes, pipettes in all imaginable and

[2] Henry Allen Moe, "The Power of Poetic Vision," *Publ. Modern Lang. Assn.* 74 (1959): pp. 37-41.

164

unimaginable combinations and shapes. And all of you who have used a microscope know that the optical glass in it is the most important part. All these kinds of glass, and all others that have been developed, come from the arts of the glass-blowers—those cunning artists who, in early antiquity on the Syrian seashore, learned how to fashion shapes from the earliest of all plastics, glass. Glass was not made first for windows, not for bottles, but by artists to decorate the noble-man's table and to contain his lady's perfumes. All of its industrial and scientific uses have developed from its artistic beginnings.

And where would the professors of literature, the philosophers, indeed, every scholar, be now were it not for the invention of movable type for printing? And who did that? It was the fifteenth-century Johann Gutenberg, a man whose principal business was the polishing of gemstones and looking-glasses.

And what of the artists? Where would they be without the chemists, primitive and modern, who gave them their painting colors, and their papers, and who smelted and hardened metals so that they could cut stone?

And what would be the course of the architects without the chemists' development of cement for concretes and mortars? And what would architects do without the physicists' and engineers' testings and their calculations of the strengths of materials?

The archaeologists and historians could not have moved into a new phase of their studies without the development by a present-day chemist, Dr. W. F. Libby, of the science of radio-carbon dating. Nor could the anthropologists, studying the movements of ancient populations, make much progress without the biologists' discovery of blood-groups.

All this you may say is so elementary as hardly to be worth saying; and I should agree with that, were it not for the circumstance that, again, what I may perhaps call the battle of the cultures is being fought in the public prints. Sir Charles Snow is all for science as the guiding star by which men and women of the future should set their educational course. Dr. F. R. Leavis—and he is English, too—is all for continuance of *The Great Tradition*, which is the title of one of his books, as the guiding star to the good life. The attainment of wisdom, Dr. Leavis maintains, can best be achieved by studying the greatest works of English imaginative literature—neglecting that the sciences also show their great creative literature and cultural history, forgetting that there have been Darwin and Huxley, Laplace and Benjamin Franklin. And Sir Charles seems not to know that there was a poet, William Langland, who made law with his *Vision of Piers the Plowman*, and certainly he undervalues Shakespeare.

It seems to me that to expound either of the positions in the extreme form that both Sir Charles and Dr. Leavis do is simply to write a recipe for futility, even fatuity. They both are weaving about in partial vacuums of knowledge and thought.

What that partial vacuum is, is clear to me, from where I sit in my work-a-day life, which is, indeed, a very good place from which to see. It is clear to me that each—Sir Charles and Dr. Leavis—is just identifying culture with what he knows best and then calling this the preferred culture for everybody. It looks to me as if each is promoting a cultural patent medicine based on his personal ideology. And, if I may say so, each is promoting a nostrum further based on his lack of knowledge of what goes on and has gone on beyond the fences which bound his own cultural backyard.

Do not, I advise you, pay any attention to this battle of the two cultures, ignited by Sir Charles and fanned to a flame by Dr. Leavis. Do not pay any attention to it because all of it misses the main point.

That main point is quality—quality of intellectual effort, quality of what is accomplished, quality of the intellectual product. That fine American painter Robert Henri stated the true doctrine to a student: "*Anything* will do for a subject: it's what *you* do with it that counts"—provided only that you stay within the officially stated objective of this university: "To exalt beauty, to advance learning, to forward ideas and ideals, to become a center of order and light."

It's what you—students and professors—do with any subject that counts. What the subject is, does not matter: only the quality of the product matters. There is no line of studies that is of itself better, more cultural, more productive of wisdom, leading more directly to the good life, than any other line of studies.

I take it that this is the philosophy of the Southern Illinois University, as it is the philosophy of most state universities; and there is no practical use in arguing for anything else. For, said President Griswold of Yale University a half-dozen years ago: "Our whole national tradition is rooted in the idea that our people shall receive instruction in both learning of intrinsic and learning of extrinsic value and make the most of both, each according to his competence."[3]

To illustrate my point concretely, I say that I have read a book on physical education—kinesiology—which enlarges and ennobles the mind more than some works about literature that I have read.

And I go on to say that the study of science, any science, can be as humanistic and as liberal, as ennobling and enlarging of the mind as the study of, say, Greek sculpture of the age of Pericles. I say with equal assurance that the study of Greek sculpture of the age of Pericles can be as narrowing as the study of the chemical properties of the azo dyes can be, but either study is not necessarily narrowing in either instance. Either can be as ennobling and enlarging of the mind as any other. All history shows that nobody can know or even

[3] A. Whitney Griswold, "The Scholar's Business in American Society," *Saturday Review of Literature*, November 10, 1956.

imagine whether or not a great thing can be done until some-body, somewhere, has gone ahead and done it.

Of this, our country, there is one generalization that may safely be made: that we are great engineers. We will build roads faster and better than anybody ever has done. We will build an Oak Ridge National Laboratory and a Hanford pluto-nium plant, and get them working, faster than anybody else could. We will build more cars than anybody ever has. We will educate more young men and women—and do it well, too—than anybody ever has.

Quantity production we understand; and when one of us has built a better mousetrap than anybody else, the world does not have to beat a pathway to his door to get one, as the old saying goes; we will put it into quantity production and sell it for a dime, everywhere. And let me tell you, too, that the idea and the accomplishment of quantity production are great qualities, themselves.

But, considering our opportunities, we do not invent the world's best mousetraps often enough. We do not manufac-ture a Rolls-Royce. We educate more people than anybody else; but the highest expressions of scholarship, of statesman-ship, of moral goodness, do not appear often enough, consid-ering our broad educational base for their appearance.

Why not? That's the great question; and the question is a question of quality. What should be quality in Carbondale, Illinois? Put in another way, how high should you aim? With what chances of success?

I shall give you my answer, even though you think me an impractical fellow who gazes at the stars, not comprehending their distance.

There was Athens in the fifth century B.C.—you will remem-ber—no bigger than Carbondale, with no demonstrably better genes in its population, in about the same latitude, with about the same climate, and no more adequate food supply, with no institution of higher education as good as Southern Illinois University.

On Quality

Athens was situated on the western edge of what, until then, had been the world's greatest civilizations—in Mesopotamia, in Syria, in Egypt—but those civilizations had gone stale, and as Edith Hamilton says, "the shadow of effortless barbarism" was dark upon the earth.[4]

The words "effortless barbarism" are the clue: the spiritual force of the Athenians' eastern neighbors was no longer white-hot. But the Greeks had that spiritual force and in them was added an amazing clarity and power of thought.

> That union made the Greek temples, statues, writings, all the plain expression of the significant; the statue in its combination of reality and ideality; the poetry in its dependence on ideas; the tragedy in its union of the spirit of inquiry with the spirit of poetry. It made the Athenians lovers of fact and of beauty.[5]

If this was done in Athens, why not in Carbondale? One certain reason is that, after the first-comers, the people in this area lost their pride. And if you doubt that, let me ask you to think of the old capitol of the State of Illinois at Vandalia. Built in 1836, more than a century ago, shortly after the Black Hawk Indian War, it is a noble building, it is a building of quality; it is a monument to the union of extrinsic as well as intrinsic education, of practical as well as artistic expression. It is, as the Greek temples always were, *simple*. The men who planned and built your Vandalia capitol were clear and lucid thinkers and their art, *there*, was like the Greeks', simple. Only people who had lost their pride, who had ceased to be "lovers of fact and of beauty," could have built the junk that surrounds that capitol now. They had lost their pride and with it their faith in the reality of the American dream.

It is a part, a large part, of the function of this University to restore that pride and that faith. That function can only be fulfilled on the basis of quality—the quality of the Univer-

---

[4] Edith Hamilton, *The Greek Way to Western Civilization* (New York, Mentor Book, 1942), p. 7.
[5] *Ibid.*, pp. 185-186.

sity's instruction, the quality of the faculty's scholarship, and also by the quality of the buildings your administration builds.

For buildings are not just bricks and mortar, as the present-day derogatory phrase has it. "The Parthenon was raised in triumph, to express the beauty and the power and the splendor of men."[6] And so should your buildings be raised—and, I shall add, they are.

Quality, quality, quality—this should be your goal, not size, not that *ignis fatuus* of inclusiveness which leads to miring down in the swamps of multitudes of subjects. "Anything will do for a subject: it's what you do with it that counts," I remind you again.

What the architects of ancient Greece did with their subject, when given a temple to design, is what counts. Their size, large or small, does not matter. The Romans built much bigger ones. But the Romans do not live in history because of their temples: they live by reason of the fact that they became the finest law-givers of all time; and they became such because they made their law the instrument of liberation, not, as it had been, for the oppression of peoples. In short, the Romans, too, live in history because of quality—the quality of their freedom-giving law.

And just so this University will live now and hereafter by the quality of what it does.

Similarly, in respect to this University: a pathway will not be beaten hence two thousand years from now, nor now, because of your size, nor because you have built an empire here with satellites elsewhere, nor because you have schools of law, engineering, and medicine. The path will be beaten only because you do what you do, better than anybody else, or at least as well as the best elsewhere.

Hence, let quality be your watchword, let quality be your motto, let quality be emblazoned on your coat of arms.

And when thinking of quality, remember the story of the

[6] *Ibid.*, p. 37.

On Quality

Texan who was having his first look at Niagara Falls. "You haven't got anything like this in Texas," taunted his guide; "you couldn't afford to let all this water go to waste over these falls."

"No," came back the Texan, "but we've got plumbers who could fix the leak."

If you do train plumbers in your vocational institute, that is the quality of plumber I would want to have you train.

And just so, that's the quality of physicist, biologist, playwright, literary critic, historian, I hope that all of you—students, graduates, professors, administrators—will be or have become. Daunted by no work too big, ignoring no work as too small, capable of anything good, brimming over with pride, and full of faith that deserved greatness will ride your banners as did the eagles the standards of the Roman legions—this is the quality I convey for the Southern Illinois University and for all of you.

A GATHERING OF VIRTUOSI

TENTH INTERNATIONAL CONGRESS

OF THE HISTORY OF SCIENCE, PHILADELPHIA

SEPTEMBER 1, 1962

IT is a particular pleasure for the American Philosophical Society to have as our guests the delegates to the 10th International Congress of the History of Science; and it is, if I may say so, particularly fitting that we have this pleasure and this privilege.

For, as you heard during your Symposium on the History of American Science today, our American Philosophical Society Held at Philadelphia for Promoting Useful Knowledge (to state our full title) was the earliest of the American learned societies, as it was the first American group to make scientific inquiry a primary purpose.

And besides that, it is true to say—despite the weighty limitations stated in Dr. Whitfield J. Bell's excellent paper this morning—that there have been few American scientific enterprises, from our establishment in 1743 to the present day, in which the American Philosophical Society, its members, and its resources of money and of prestige, have not had important parts, often decisive parts.

In short, the American Philosophical Society is not only interested in the history of science, all science, everywhere; but also it may truly be said that our history is, in large part, the history of American science.

A Gathering of Virtuosi

But there is even more to the matter than this, which I shall now essay to explain:

This afternoon, you have seen our Independence National Historical Park and you will have observed the architecture of the buildings in Independence Square, particularly the building that we now call Independence Hall. Broadly speaking, it is, of course, in the English style of architecture called Georgian. But you who know the architecture of Georgian England, know that you never saw any building in England that looks like Independence Hall.

Already by the year 1732 when Independence Hall was begun—forty-odd years before our Declaration of Independence from Great Britain—the builders on the American colonies had achieved a distinctive American style of architecture which for want of a better name we call "colonial." That so-called colonial style had a unity although it was different in all the thirteen American colonies—that is, the architecture of the Carolinas differed from that of Pennsylvania and Massachusetts, for examples—and all of it not only differed from any architecture in Great Britain but also achieved greatness in its own right. And it also achieved something else in domestic architecture: it achieved practical universality. Almost everybody in the settled parts of the colonies, rich and poor, had a beautiful house, often small, sometimes tiny, but always beautiful, practical, warm, and livable. This could not be said, I think, of any other eighteenth-century country in the world.

The same distinctiveness and fineness may be said of all the arts of colonial North America. They had their origins, of course, in the arts of Europe—of England and France, of the Renaissance—but all were transmuted by the alchemy of that sense of that limitless space and unlimited opportunity that made the minds and spirits of men different in these North American colonies.

Our eighteenth-century table and decorative silver is readily identifiable as distinctly ours, and so is our furniture. And likewise our easel painting; and no less is our music our own.

Our eighteenth-century arts reflected what we like to think of as the American pioneer virtues: simplicity necessary to stringent times, economy of form and materials, dignity, honesty, good taste, and, in spite of austerity, charm.

What we call our colonial architecture never decayed, never lost its virtues through two centuries. It was one long development; it climbed to a peak as our designers increased in numbers, improved their techniques, and acquired a sureness and grasp of domestic architecture that have never been surpassed in our country and probably nowhere in the world in that period. And then to prove that this had been no accident, we changed to a new style, the architecture of the early republic. This architecture was even more beautiful, even more sure, even more charming and, as fitted the soaring mood of the young republic, less austere than had been the architecture of the Colonial period. We have never been niggardly in acknowledging our debts—intellectual and artistic—to the Old World; and this architecture of the early republic has its debt to Herculaneum and Pompeii *via* the Brothers Adam, the great English designers and cabinetmakers.

He who compartments the facts of history tears a seamless web. Men living make history, and men's minds do not operate in compartments. Thus we may be sure that what happened toward the development of liberty in Independence Hall in 1776 and in 1787 was of a piece with the development of our arts and architecture. Just as they became American with an American style, so it was an American liberty that developed here—the "right to life, liberty and the pursuit of happiness"—and never again, in any part of the world, would men who had ever heard of the Declaration of Independence be content with less than what the Declaration promised. It was a universal Declaration, and, following the writing of the Constitution of the United States, there existed a model for the whole world to make effective the principle of self-government on a federal scale. It, too, was a document of universal application. As Lord Bryce said, it was the greatest document ever struck off by the minds of men at one time—struck off, do not forget to remember, with savages on all the frontiers and very near at hand, always a source of present danger.

I realize, of course, that my canvas is impossibly small considering the scope of my subject matter. But it must fall to the lot of someone to make generalizations from complex data. And he who makes them must hope and believe that he is sufficiently aware of the specialist's detailed studies not to go wrong in his generalizations.

I have spoken of the ideal of the universality of our beautiful American architecture; that architecture and its universality both were American inventions. And all men know the universality of our ideal of liberty, which, too, in its universality, was an American invention. It was so for all men, everywhere, from then until now. Liberty was not news, as the saying is, but universal liberty was; and this was an American invention.

And this ideal of the attainable universality of liberty, and of all other good things too, was the ideal of the American Philosophical Society. It was so stated often by our Founder Benjamin Franklin. He and his colleagues addressed themselves to the improvement of the *Genus humanum*, mankind in general.

Talk about *Societas generis humani* was, of course, prior to the eighteenth century, found in many writings, and in particular in Cicero's *De Officiis*. But until Francis Bacon in the seventeenth century, the concept had no particular effect toward bettering the lives of the *Genus humanum*. What Bacon's ideas proposed, in essence, was to reverse the whole course of human history, as previously understood. Remember that he spoke to men who for centuries had been oppressed by the dogma of the helplessness of fallen humanity. "Such teachings," said Bacon, "if they be justly appraised,

175

will be found to tend to nothing less than a wicked effort to curtail human power over nature and to produce a deliberate and artificial despair. This despair, in its turn, confounds the promptings of hope, cuts the springs and sinews of industry, and makes men unwilling to put anything to the hazard of trial." These words, as said, are Francis Bacon's.

Benjamin Franklin and his colleagues were the inheritors of this point of view, of these purposes. And surely no men inherited such purposes more gladly; no men ever were more delighted to put anything and everything to the hazard of trial.

However, they were not only inheritors of points of view and of purposes: they added elements of their own. And as I have read among the books and papers relating to the early history of our Society, I have come from my reading with the deep conviction that its particular character, at least during its eighteenth-century formative period, could be summed up in one word "Communicate." This word, in the context of the early history of our Society, meant to make everything available to everybody: one has a duty to put in common, to make readily available *to all* whatever is learned or may be made useful to mankind, whatever may dignify, ennoble, and help men everywhere.

This emphasis on communication was deliberate and all-pervading; and, if I may say so, it was very American. This American Philosophical Society's emphasis was not, as I read history, strongly characteristic of the European learned and scientific societies of the time.

Thus, I shall hazard the observation that, again, the American contribution was to universalize, to have as purpose, to make all good things—whether architecture, liberty, or knowledge—available to all mankind. And this, I shall go on to say, is still the best and most distinguishing feature of what the world calls "Americanism."

The American Philosophical Society was designed to be a

A Gathering of Virtuosi

society of "virtuosi or ingenious Men." Our charter, of 1780, proclaims that "the experience of ages shows that improvements of a public nature, are best carried on by societies of liberal and ingenious men, uniting their labours, without regard to nation, sect or party, in one grand pursuit, alike interesting to all, whereby mutual prejudices are worn off. . . ."

The international character of our Society is further declared in the final section of our charter which, as Dr. E. G. Conklin—one of our great presidents—used to remind us, was written in the midst of a seven-years war when national antagonisms were intense: ". . . nations truly civilized (however unhappily at variance on other accounts) will never wage war with the Arts and Sciences, and the common Interests of humanity. . . ."

You may know by these quotations from our charter how much Dr. Franklin would have approved your meeting with us here. But even Dr. Franklin, in his most ambitious dreams, could not have foretold that this day—this first of September, 1962—would come when, in *his* Philadelphia, scholars representing the scientific societies of the world would gather under the auspices of his American Philosophical Society. There is no doubt that he would have regarded such a gathering of "Virtuosi," his word for you, as a happy fulfillment of his universal, humane philosophy.

And this is important for us who now constitute the Society; because, as we think of him, Dr. Franklin lives among us still.

177

ON THE NEED FOR
AN ARISTOCRACY OF BRAINS
AND CHARACTER*

COSMOS CLUB, WASHINGTON, D.C.

APRIL 5, 1965

IN his *History of English Law*, F. W. Maitland, the most lucid and farsighted of English legal historians, quotes a text from St. Paul: "It is better to marry than to burn." And then Maitland dares to comment, on a text of Scripture, mind you: "Few texts have done more harm than this." Similarly, from the scriptures of the United States, I shall quote Thomas Jefferson's "All men are created equal" and shall dare to comment that few texts have required more explanation than this.

You will note that I have given what the young would call a Patrick Henry twist to my daring. For you will remember his famous speech in the Virginia House of Burgesses:

> Caesar had his Brutus, Charles I his Cromwell and George III [here he was interrupted by cries of "Treason"] may profit by their example. If this be treason, make the most of it.

There is no doubt that, at the time it was said, the saying that "All men are created equal" needed to be said, and especially that it needed to be said in the context of the Declara-

---

* Address at conferral of the Second Cosmos Club Award, 1965. Copyright 1965 by the Cosmos Club. Reprinted by permission.

tion of Independence. Nevertheless, I shall dare to say flatly now that few unqualified statements have done more harm than this. If this be treason, you may make the most of it.[1]

Equality in abstract mathematics is a reasonable concept. But men are not abstractions, and no two of them are equal in comparable ways. On the contrary, they are, in fact, differentiated endlessly throughout all the details of their physical and mental attributes and their social history. To say that all men are created equal is—as everybody knows and nobody doubts nowadays, but nobody says—the apotheosis of error. But that it, nevertheless, has had the widest possible effect on thinking is no doubt true.

As a wise nineteenth-century Scotsman said in a time and place of no racial tensions:[2]

> There is, in truth, no fallacy more dangerous because there is none more inviting than that which brings what is complex and obscure under what is familiar and simple. And into this fallacy our grandfathers certainly fell, when, in vehement reaction against inequalities which had come to seem intolerable, they could not rest satisfied with anything short of the affirmation of the "Equality of Men." It was more than fallacy. It was bad policy. . . . It is a maxim in controversy that the best weapons are not the most sweeping denials, which do indeed but offer a needlessly large target for rejoinder. But the revolutionary writers of a hundred years ago did not observe this. Grant that, in revolt against political and social economic inequalities, they were right; it was not therefore necessary to invoke anything so large as equality of men. It would have been enough to make out a case for equality before the Law; or for equality in vote and in eligibility to office; and for effectual abatement of inequalities of social status, and of fortunes. But they did not think so. . . . They took up a position which they

---

[1] As every schoolboy knows, the date of our Declaration of Independence was 1776. By 1789, enlightened thought on the subject of equality had progressed to the point that Article I of the French Declaration of the Rights of Man and of the Citizen says, in Thomas Carlyle's translation: "Men are born equal and remain free and equal in rights."

[2] John MacCunn, *Ethics of Citizenship* (Glasgow, 1894), pp. 2-3.

thought to be strong because it was extensive, and even by public declaration proclaimed the "equality of men."

They paid the inevitable penalty. It quickly appeared that in their zeal to be besiegers, they had opened lines so wide that they had themselves in their turn become the besieged.

I submit that this is the situation now developing in the United States.

One of the difficulties of saying anything in words is that it cannot be said all at once, as a painting or a photograph often can be fully understood at a glance. So I must ask you to bear with me until all the words now needed to be used have been said.

In particular, I ask you to believe that I know I am living in the contemporary world. I am not speaking of being besieged by people of any race, but of the crowd from whatever race. All my life's work shows that I have acted on this belief; selections of persons made without regard to race, creed, or ancestry, on the merits of the individual.

I also know, historically, that there have been great civilizations among all races; and that all those civilizations had their roots of greatness in an aristocracy. The Greek and Roman aristocracies come first to our Western minds, and so do the Florentines of the Renaissance and the English of Elizabeth and Shakespeare. But we must not forget the Incas of Peru and their predecessors, the Mayas of Middle America, the Pharaohs—including the Ethiopian Pharaohs—of Egypt, the Chinese of many dynasties, the Balinese, the Icelanders. And so it goes, including the Virginia, Pennsylvania, New York, Massachusetts, and other aristocracies of brains and character from whence came our Founding Fathers.

That some of these aristocracies were hereditary is clear; that none of them survived long without new genes from outside the hereditary aristocracy is equally clear. Indeed, the greatest names of the greatest civilizations are mostly non-hereditary: Shakespeare, Ghiberti, Galileo, Cervantes, Copernicus, Bruno, Thucydides, Pericles, Einstein, hosts of others, including Christ himself—all came from the people. Winston Churchill did not, nor Elizabeth I, nor the composer Bach; and they show that aristocracy is possible in and out of any social class and that it does not consist of any social class. For history is replete with kings and emperors and dukes and counts, who were, in modern parlance, no-accounts or worse. But the Pannonian peasant's son, a private soldier named Aurelian who became emperor of Rome—as wise as he was brave—was an aristocrat of another color, of the only color that counts.

And so likewise were the water-boys who became kings in the ancient Middle East. They became kings of their realms; and kings of the realms of the minds of men were all those who, through the ages, found new truths and new means for their expression.

They were able to affect the lives of all subsequent civilized men, because they were not equal: they had that effect because they were superior.

A society becomes great only by path-breaking greatness within it. It is, I think, likely that greatness will appear more often by a leveling up of the crowd along the streets. But assuredly, it will not come by any process of leveling down; and most assuredly it will not come unless the leveling up is of such a kind as to provide freedom to think, to experiment, to speculate in thought and action, to state new truths or what to the staters is truth, and to make good on freedom-loving action. I would add that freedom-loving action has no long-term chance unless its purpose is stated with force, courtesy, taste, and a sense of historically minded resolve. For "the just prejudices," as John Burke called them, of an organized people must be taken into account. The species remains wise even if individuals be foolish.

If I have made my position clear to this point, there remains to ask: Where would I go from here? Whence comes an aristocracy of brains and character, an aristocracy with a conscience and taste and a sense of history?

It is worth nothing to say that such an aristocracy cannot possibly come in this mid-twentieth century and by way of proof to point to the crime in our city streets, the tasteless demonstrations and the sit-ins on our university campuses, the unpunished perjuries in our courts, the fast-buck crowd that holds nothing sacred. For these have been phenomena of all societies, even in all the great ones, even in the greatest of all, Athens of the fifth and sixth centuries B.C.

I instance ancient Athens because, there and then, men had learned, in the words of Pericles' Funeral Oration, that "the secret of Happiness is Freedom, and the secret of Freedom is Courage."

Pericles said more, on that occasion, also worth adverting to, and Gilbert Murray[3] has summed it up: "The Athenians love beauty, but have not luxurious tastes; they cultivate the mind without any loss of manliness."

> As to wealth, of course, it is useful for many purposes; but it is not with us a thing to boast about or to display. No one in Athens need be ashamed of being poor, unless indeed his poverty is due to lack of industry and good work—then he may well be. Unlike other cities, Athens expects every citizen to take an interest in public affairs; and, as a matter of fact, most Athenians have some sense of public affairs. We believe in the value of knowledge as a guide to action; we have a power of thinking before we act and of acting too, whereas many people can be full of energy if they do not think, but when they reflect, begin to hesitate. We make friends abroad by doing good and giving help to our neighbors; and we do this not from some calculation of self-interest but in the confidence of freedom and in a frank and fearless spirit.

That, as Thucydides painted the picture in Pericles' words, was what Athens was in her greatest days. And how much like the United States of today it was!

[3] *Hellenism and the Modern World* (Boston, 1954), pp. 38-39.

Aristocracy of Brains

But there is another side of the picture of Athens in her greatest centuries which also is like the United States of to-day. Let us now look at that. Plato[4] says that his fellow citizens had an insatiable love of money and that, in their law suits, half the people were perjured.[5] "Patently, few nations have a history so full of unblushing lies; and in later days *Graeca levitas* supplanted *Punica fides* as a byword with the honest Roman."[6]

> The essential qualities of a race should be found in its most eminent representatives. But a passion for morality is very subordinate (to say the least) in the genius of some of the greatest Greeks. To judge by their remaining fragments, there was none in Sappho and her peers. It is not conspicuous in Homer or Herodotus: we shall not learn mercy or righteousness from Achilles or Odysseus. Aristophanes, a Greek of Greeks, paid even less countenance to the view which sees in Hellenism a superior type of Christianity, purged of dogma and adorned with the graces and gifts of culture; and it is at times chastening to remember, as it is in general better to forget, that many of the most graceful Greek vases are offerings dedicated to unnatural vice.[7]

And so it goes, or rather *was* in ancient Greece in her greatest period. And how applicable to the United States if we substitute the names of some modern writers for those of the ancients!

But to estimate the greatness of a civilization, our own or others, we must fix our eyes not on weaknesses but on strengths. Just as in estimating the power and worth of Christianity we should look to the lives of the Saints, not to the atrocities of Churches, so in estimating the value of Greek civilization we should look to "Pindar and Pericles and Thucydides before whose minds had passed the visions of art or

[4] *Laws*, 831.
[5] *Ibid.*, 948.
[6] Sir Richard Winn Livingstone, *The Greek Genius and Its Meaning to Us* (Oxford, 1915), p. 42.
[7] *Ibid.*, pp. 25-26.

the conception of science, or the dreams of a race of beings living a beautiful, complete and human life."[8]

So also should we think in estimating the worth of our American civilization and the possibilities of our having a Great Society.

It is said of Socrates that the power of his thought—the continuing power—lay in his adding moral genius to intellect, the wedding of thought to morality.[9]

Or as Plato put it,[10] the main thing to be learned is the conduct of life—"how to manage your home in the best possible way, and to be able to speak and act for the best in public life."

"That was the university education of an Athenian."[11] One could wish it were a larger part than it is of the university and college education of mid-twentieth-century Americans. There are now about 500,000 of them, college and university graduates, each year. Multiply them by the forty years of their post-university lives, add the millions we already have, and the total will number 30 million or so. And that would be enough of an aristocracy—if they were aristocrats of brains and character—and would be the largest aristocracy there ever has been.

But, alas! Not all are aristocrats of brains and character, though I believe a larger percentage of them are, and more have it in them to become so—and to be aristocrats, too, with a conscience and a sense of history, representing the wisdom of the species.

They are not going to increase by teaching from hot-shot professors who know only their specialties, or who concentrate too much on their specialties. But let me say, in the same breath, that the professors by and large do teach much more than specialized information. They also make the classic virtues live, train tastes to shun the trash of the mass media,

[8] *Ibid.*, p. 20.   [9] *Ibid.*, pp. 218, 224.
[10] *Protagoras*, 318.   [11] Livingstone, p. 213.

illustrate the virtues of restraint, and make—literally *make*—cultured appreciators of the best.

The Lord will bear witness that I am not one to decry specialization. I have devoted a large part of my life to fostering it. But, also, all through my working life I have tried to foster something more, and that is the concept of good citizenship in the specialists. For example, I told a congressional investigating committee in the fateful year 1952 that the fruits of American freedom are what make our country strong, and I convinced them that the Guggenheim Foundation, in seeking to help scholars and artists to achieve leadership, knew that "no man or woman could have a part in making our country strong unless he is a good citizen, devoted to the principles which are basic to our strength." I made the statement stick, because I could prove the facts and because, in this kind of situation, deeds and attitudes count, whereas words of exhortation have practically no meaning.

In times past, the cements that bound bodies politic together have been many, depending on time and place—family solidarity, religion, monarchical loyalties, commonly held political ideas. Now the cry is that these cements hardly exist, that peoples now have lost their bearings, and that there is a great rebellion a-growing against the failures of society (whatever that may mean), the predilections of the economists, the vacillations of legislatures—and much that is similar, besides.

I wonder about all this: I wonder to the point of disbelief. I do not believe that there are here and now, proportionately, more crookedness, more crimes, more discontent than there were in the best centuries of ancient Greece, or among the greatest lawgivers of all time, the Romans, or among the Elizabethans who brought Englishmen out of the Middle Ages into the modern world.

These ages all had their conflicts and discontents, just as deep and widespread as ours. But—and not too slowly either—the chief conflicts and discontents of the ages were worked out. To make my point, I shall cite only one example out of many, from Rome in her great days. The patricians, the aristocracy to use another word, made what we would call the "image" of the Roman state. And while there was always a degree of resistance to the image—by which I mean the *mores*, the ways of doing things—there also was a high degree of acceptance by the mass of Roman society. Indeed, the plebeians accepted and fought for the patrician image of Rome, as they, gradually, demanded and got a larger participation in the fruits of its successes. "It is conceivable that Roman civilization deteriorated and was superseded when the whole of Roman society had been culturally plebeianized and the Roman image was blurred and incoherent."[12]

But the situation is very different in the United States of the twentieth century. We have a vast pool of potential patricians. They are not being plebeianized; they are being exalted by education. Five hundred thousand of them a year are getting bachelors' degrees from our colleges and universities. As previously said, they and their fathers and mothers will amount to thirty million. They now arrive at college about one hundred per cent better prepared to grapple with college curricula than we were: any college admissions officer will tell you so. And the colleges that know their students will tell you something more and something very important: that going with their trained brains is, in the great majority, a strong will to contribute to the society which has made all this possible. They have a feeling for quality of expression, a greed for knowledge, a sense of history, even a sense of personal religion, in greater numbers and in greater percentage, than ever before in the history of the world.

Such an aristocracy does not visualize the restoration of inherited privileges, it does not depend on having money, it has no resemblance to oligarchy or plutocracy, it is of all

[12] A. L. Kroeber, *An Anthropologist Looks at History* (Berkeley and Los Angeles, 1963).

races, it is largely self-made. Rather, the effectiveness of such an aristocracy calls for a social consciousness to ensure, on the one hand, recognition, by the community at large of this community's "best" and, on the other hand, the recognition that, by virtue of something more solid than unreflecting prejudice, and by common consent, they represent what is noble and of good repute.

There are no easy answers to great problems and we shall get only disappointment if we expect soon to find answers to ours. We cannot get answers by longing, or by fiat, or, perhaps least of all, by legislation. On great questions, we—as in all past ages—will fail to get answers if we are in a hurry.

But my thesis is that we have a better chance than any people ever had to maintain an aristocracy of brains and character. And the reason we have that chance comes principally from the wide-spreading of our education, its high quality in the development of intellection. There is needed only one ingredient more than we have; and what this ingredient is has never been stated better than by Edwin Bidwell Wilson, from whom I learned more, and learned to understand more, than from any other man. Professor Wilson wrote:

> It was my privilege as a young man to become acquainted with a considerable number of distinguished scholars of the generation of Willard Gibbs who seemed to me to be much alike in their simplicity, dignity and friendliness—gentlemen of the old school we youngsters called them. They did not wish to be hero-worshipped, they were not patronizing; they did not proselytise, they were living examples of what the best in university life has been, is now, and will be so long as there are youth who are inspired by such examples to try to become in all simplicity worthy successors to them.

It remains to be added that such inspirers are not only professors and teachers so employed. They are, equally powerfully, the physicians, the lawyers, the businessmen, the farmers, the carpenters, the garagemen, the Pullman porters, the

187

public servants of every community—the men and women that the youngsters, in old-fashioned language, look up to, living examples of what the young may be inspired to become. Of all such is an aristocracy of brains and character made up. Such men and women never are satisfied with a "modest competence" in matters of character and intellect; they "go for broke" toward a higher level of humanity. As John Burke said, they have both "a disposition to preserve and an ability to improve, taken together."

However, Rome, in its greatness, and the same had been true of ancient Greece, had not the facilities, had not the machinery in being, for developing a new aristocracy. But England before and in the age of Elizabeth, and afterward, had training grounds for an aristocracy of brains and character, in the universities of Oxford and Cambridge, in the law schools of the Inns of Court, in the Royal Society of London, and above all in the developing parliamentary procedures of the House of Commons with their emphasis on the history of English institutions and on the conscience of a rising Puritanism.

We inherited all that, we emphasized much of what was best in all of it, and we developed further much of its best: manhood suffrage, widespread education, easy flow upward, based on some kind of merit, between classes. And we developed, besides, easy flow downward—based on non-merit—in classes, to the point that the saying "from shirtsleeves to shirtsleeves in three generations" became true and current. Ours was and remains no hereditary aristocracy, based on money or on anything but personal merit.

But now it seems to some people to be "much easier than before to believe that America is visibly sick with a malady that may do all of us in," as Richard Hofstadter wrote in *Encounter*, October, 1964. Democrat Hofstadter then was writing about what he feared to be the prospects of Senator Goldwater's election. Happily, he was wrong about that, by a landslide matter of fifteen million votes! And this Republican non-Goldwater Moe does not have to take seriously his diagnosis that we have *any* sickness that may do us ail in. That we have sicknesses is certain; that they are incurable and may do us in, is, on the face of the record, so improbable as to be pessimistic moonshine.

For we are not in the condition of ancient Athens in her greatest centuries, where, Plato testified, half the people were perjurers, where the audiences of Demosthenes were described as "a barbarous people, an assembly of brutes." We are not that, by far: we are, indeed, a sound people in a country where at least half the houses do not have to be locked at night. What we have of crime and poverty is bad, but not serious enough to do us all in, nor widespread enough either.

Mr. Justice Holmes once remarked that he wished to be remembered as "the upholder of the respectable and the commonplace." It was an incomplete statement; his whole life showed that what he wanted most was scope for the unusual in thought and action. And so do I, while not losing sight of the merit of the respectable and the commonplace. The simple and enduring truths, are, indeed, the wisdom of the species; and we shall forget them at our peril. Among those truths, which are perhaps a little less self-evident than they used to be, are those that may be indicated by the verbs "to respect," "to revere," "to look up to," "to emulate." But evident or not, these truths are effective in the great commonalty of our American life. Indeed, it is utterly safe to say that we are more morally conscious than ever before in our history, or probably in any people's history.

And so it is my thesis, based on that general morality and on the great numbers of trained intellects among us, that we shall achieve the needed aristocracy of brains and character, an aristocracy with a moral conscience and a sense of history. We shall achieve it surely; and, if pressed, I should say that we have it already, although there are, indeed, too many aberrant factors to suit me, just as there were too many such factors to suit Plato in the greatest days of ancient Greece.

Without an aristocracy, we should be lost; having it, we surely shall be saved. That is, indeed, what our manifest destiny is, our cultural, nonterritorial manifest destiny: to have the greatest aristocracy of brains and character the world has ever known. Having that aristocracy is the only way to the Great Society. There is no other way.

The way to it, you see, is the way of the respectable and the commonplace, the unheadlined and the uncomplicated— the commonplace, in Abraham Lincoln's words, "that is something more than common," the commonplace of American life that holds out the American promise to all people of the world, for all time to come.

This is what I believe, what I cannot help believing. I thank the Cosmos Club for giving me a forum in which to say it.

THE CURSE OF PEDANTRY

AMERICAN COUNCIL OF

LEARNED SOCIETIES, WASHINGTON, D.C.

JANUARY 20, 1966

MR. Justice Holmes used to admonish, even before he was a judge, that the laws that govern us, at any given time, are dependent on "the felt necessities of the time, the prevalent moral and political theories, intuitions of public policy, avowed or unconscious, and with the prejudices which judges (and Congressmen, if I may add a word to Mr. Justice Holmes's saying) share with their fellow-men." Mr. Holmes, of course, used the word prejudice in its primary, not its invidious, sense.

In the line of Mr. Holmes's thought, you should have no doubt that the law which sets up and governs the National Foundation for the Arts and Humanities and which controls us was enacted to meet the felt necessities of the present time. In the seeing to it that the necessities became felt, the American Council of Learned Societies surely had a major part. For the ACLS took the lead in the formation of the Commission on the Humanities, and it was the Report of this Commission that focused the attention of Congress on the legislation we celebrate.

That this felt necessity, brought to a head by the ACLS, was a long time developing, is true. But let us not forget what

The Curse of Pedantry

John Adams wrote in the eighteenth century—that he had to study politics and war, so that his sons might study the useful arts and philosophy, so that his grandsons might study the arts. The second President of the United States had historical and political sense.

So did Thomas Jefferson, the third President of the American Philosophical Society, as he was of the United States. And it is to be noted, too, that Mr. Jefferson was President of the Philosophical Society twice as long as he was President of the United States; and, I dare say—because Julian Boyd told me so—enjoyed it twice as much! For the American Philosophical Society did then, as it does now, consider all knowledge to be within its province. The Society and its presidents have made no exclusions, then or now, among the sciences and the humanities as is commonly done nowadays. And so it was that Mr. Jefferson, as President of the United States, in his second inaugural message of 1806, delivered when he was President of the American Philosophical Society, declared that all areas of learning in the United States should be "placed among the articles of public care," "all parts of which contribute to the improvement of the country." So said Mr. Jefferson; in short, he urged the development of all learning as a federal responsibility.

One could follow the development of John Adams's and Thomas Jefferson's "felt necessities" through a century and a half, and see them develop, in an up and down kind of way, taking account of "prevalent moral and political theories" until the felt necessities became "intuitions of public policy."

And this brings us up to the Bush report, *Science: The Endless Frontier*, published in 1944. Then, as Professor Don K. Price, Dean of the Graduate School of Public Administration at Harvard, wrote in his recent (1965) book *The Scientific Estate*, "the traditional policy of the United States" was reversed in two ways: "it [the Bush report] persuaded universities and private research institutions that they had to ask the government for support and persuaded the government that basic science, as well as applied research, deserved support." "But . . . hardly anyone," continues Dr. Price, "stopped to ask the fundamental question: how is science, with all its new power, to be related to our political purposes and values, and to our economic and constitutional system?"

But there was one questioning voice, and in the self-congratulatory spirit that prevails here today, I shall remark that the questioning voice, asking the fundamental question, was mine.

For as chairman of one of Dr. Bush's advisory committees, I wrote the report's chapter on the discovery and development of scientific talent. You may read on pages 142 and 143 what I said, in 1944, about the fundamental question, stated by Dr. Price. Here, I shall quote only a few sentences, as follows:

> The statesmanship of science . . . requires that science be concerned with more than science. Science can only be an effective element in the national welfare as a member of a team. . . . We could not suggest to you a program which would syphon into science and technology a disproportionately large share of the nation's highest abilities without doing harm to the Nation, nor, indeed, without crippling science. The fruits of science become available only through enterprise, industry, and wisdom on the part of others as well as scientists. . . . There is never enough ability at high levels to satisfy all the needs of the Nation: we would not seek to draw into science any more of it than science's proportionate share.

You may think, in the year 1966, that these are reasonable and quite innocuous statements. Yet in 1945 and into 1946 I was told, with a good deal of violence, that I certainly had gummed the works. Nevertheless, I persisted, and in 1946 I told the American Association for the Advancement of Science, meeting in Boston, that unless science desisted from its then purpose to hog it all, free science might well be something that their successor scientists would read about but did not have.

193

The Curse of Pedantry

The denouement is pleasant to record: the voice of science now pleads eloquently for humanistic learning.

So much for history, with just the remark that we shall forget it at our peril. The peril would come from forgetting Mr. Justice Holmes's guides, "the felt necessities of the time, the prevalent moral and political theories, intuitions of public policy, avowed or unconscious."

In government one should be out in front, but must not be too far out in front. I do not regard this as counsel of timidity; I do regard it as counsel of wisdom. The wisdom of it lies in this: Considering the 6,000 three-year fellowships, chiefly for humanistic studies, that the Office of Education plans to award in 1966 for graduate studies, rising to 7,500 in 1967-1968, and considering the funds now available to the National Endowment for the Humanities, the prospect for humanistic studies is bright, financially brighter than it ever has been. For 1966-1967, the Office of Education's commitment for its graduate fellowships is $55,000,000.

To continue to merit such support by the taxpayers' money, we must put ourselves into position to demonstrate some impact of our efforts on our total American culture. To put it more bluntly, what the Humanities Endowment does with the taxpayers' money must, to merit continuing support, make some impact—visible, recognizable impact—upon the lives of people outside the academic community. In Mr. Justice Holmes's language, what the National Endowment for the Humanities does, must become one of the felt necessities of our time.

Saying what I have just said decidedly does not mean that works of scholarship should not receive support. There's no question that they should; for they are basic to advance in thought, in morality, in political theory, in taste, and even in manners. The formal education of the Founding Fathers and their lifelong studies show this to be true beyond a doubt. We should not expect too much of history, but neither should we

194

The Curse of Pedantry

think that what is commonplace to us has always been so. As the Founding Fathers were, those responsible for the operations of the National Humanities Endowment should be, or at least must try to be, men of the past, present, and future.

This is a tall order; and my saying, so far, has been much too generalized. So let me go on to say something more, and thus, no doubt, get myself labeled, by I hope only a few, as somebody who should not be allowed to be loose in the land. What I shall add now is simply this:

The curse of humanistic scholarship in my time has been pedantry. You all know what I mean and I need not define it. Sometimes when viewing what passes for fine scholarship and what I regard as its excesses of picayune malaise, I have seen in it a new scholasticism, with a more than alexandrine twist. But we must strive to make the so-called humanistic learning humane—that is, human. Otherwise, it is just a sterile business, without any impact that is worth a tinker's dam on American culture, on the good life, on the pursuit of happiness, on the rights of men, on political liberty, on freedom of the mind. The study of literature, to adduce only one example, should cultivate human judgment, developing both taste and moral feeling.

The National Endowment for the Humanities will not in my time, nor in Barnaby Keeney's, encourage, support, stake, or grubstake what we and our Council deem to be pedantry.

The classics, *yes*; medieval and Renaissance studies, *certainly*; philosophy, *of course*, but not logomachy; history, my best love, but not desiccated antiquarianism; law, which in some aspects is fertile humanistic territory, but not pettifoggery; linguistics—but I have enumerated enough to give you the general idea of the way my mind runs.

And lest there remain any doubt about the way it runs, I shall say that I agree with what George Steiner of Churchill College, Cambridge, wrote recently:[1] "A man would have to

[1] *The Listener*, 21 October, 1965.

195

be an outright optimist or gifted with self-deception to argue that all is well in the study and teaching of English literature. There is a distinct malaise in the field, a sense of things gone wrong by default."

Well and good, you may say; you might even say, *okay*. But in either case, you will ask, "What is to be the determiner?"

To that I can only respond by making a personal statement: I am a lawyer and I am, in what I regard as the best of legal systems, a case lawyer, in the Anglo-American legal tradition. I believe that justice and equity are best done by deciding the particular case; that no man has good enough brains, or a large enough vision, or enough wisdom, to pronounce a generalized proposition applicable to all cases. I distrust builders of complicated systems of thought about human affairs supposed to be universally applicable; I detest the glorifiers of abstractions who write their abstractions in a lingo mostly private to themselves; and the same goes for artists who say nothing to my favorite human characters, Tom, Dick, and Harry, or, as Lord Bowen, a great English judge, used to put it, to "the man on the Clapham omnibus."

They are great persons, are citizens Tom, Dick, and Harry, and so are citizens Anne, Jane, and Sue: and no matter what bus they ride, they are anxious to learn and are capable of much more learning than they are usually credited with. The Act under which the National Endowment for the Humanities operates declares that "democracy demands wisdom and vision in its citizens and must therefore foster and support a form of education designed to make men masters of their technology and not its unthinking servant."

That is what the law says we must do. We shall do it by fostering such scholarship as has a concern—and here again I quote from the Act—for "a high civilization," with "dedication and devotion" to the end that the vision and imagination in our fellow citizens may make them masters of their technology and their fates.

This is at once a high ideal and a stern command.

THE ROLE AND OBLIGATIONS
OF MUSEUMS
AS A SCHOLARLY RESOURCE*

MUSEUMS CONFERENCE, BURLINGTON, VERMONT

AUGUST 23, 1966

A special delight of getting old, wrote Justice Holmes in one of his eightieth years, is that "there are fewer and fewer to whom I feel the need to show a youthful deference." Another delight of getting old is to remember what happened, which, though it may be in the books in the libraries, still is not adverted to. I am sorry that I am not as old as Justice Holmes was when he said these wonderfully helpful things. But there was one development, remembered by me and germane to my assigned topic, which will afford us some historical perspective on the question of the role and obligations of museums as a scholarly resource.

I refer to the development of scientific scholarship in the United States following the First World War. The National Academy of Sciences had been created by Act of Congress in 1863, during President Lincoln's administration, to be the scientific adviser to the government of the United States. When World War I was in sight for us, there clearly appeared

* Reprinted by permission from *Museums and Education*, ed. Eric Larrabee, Smithsonian Publication 4721. Papers of the Smithsonian Institution Conference on Museums and Education, University of Vermont, August 21-26, 1966 (Washington, D.C., Smithsonian Institution Press, 1968), pp. 24-34. Copyright 1963 by Smithsonian Institution Press.

to be the need, for purposes of national defense, of more scientific research on broader fronts than the universities then were able to cope with. Hence, in 1916, there was spun off—as the lawyers say—from the National Academy of Sciences, the National Research Council, the Academy's operating arm, which was to get urgent research done. By present-day standards, what the National Research Council was able to get done then was not great in terms of specific accomplishments of applied science; but its truly great accomplishment was to show that in the upcoming modern world scientific research was something we, as a nation, could not do without.

In this year you may think this so elementary as to be hardly worth saying, but this was not so in 1919. Then, the nation had to be convinced of what everybody today knows to be true—that scientific research is an indispensable ingredient for progress, even for survival, in the world as it is. I say the nation had to be convinced of this; and from that statement I except nobody; persons in government, university administrations, industrialists, even many scientists themselves had to be convinced. They were content with what we had. They pointed with pride, and justifiable pride, to our prior industrial progress, our railroads that spanned the country, our development of rust-resistant wheats, our inventions of ingenious tools, and to much besides—practically all matters of applied science.

The principal vehicle for convincing the nation was the *Bulletin* of the National Research Council started in 1919. In it, the giants of those days—Elihu Root, statesman and lawyer; George Ellery Hale, astronomer; John J. Carty, president of the Bell Telephone Laboratories—wrote both the words and the music for their gospel theme that you cannot have applied science unless you have pure science to apply. George Ellery Hale named four corporations, one of which he said then spent as much as three million dollars annually for research—which would be peanuts now—"and in all cases the resulting profits are so great that their laboratories and staffs are constantly expanding," and they continued to expand until today, when corporate research expenditures annually are reckoned in the billions of dollars. Dr. Hale even thought it necessary to quote an 1873 statement by John Tyndall, distinguished English physicist, "It would be a great thing for this land of incalculable destinies to supplement its achievements in the industrial arts by those higher investigations from which our mastery over Nature and over industrial art itself has been derived."

Today it seems incredible that such things needed to be said in 1919; but those who said them in 1919 were not fools, nor were they misinformed about the necessity to say them or about the first and primordial need for the scientific progress they pleaded for. That need was for scientists trained for deeds of original discovery, in sufficient numbers to make the difference between a rushing current of scientific discovery and a trickle that would not wash the test tubes of my present-day grandson's chemistry set. So they established the National Research Council Fellowships with funds granted by the far-seeing Rockefeller Foundation. The results of the ensuing studies have been incalculable for scientific development in the United States. Most of the early National Research Council Fellows studied in Europe, for there was the Pierian spring of scientific discovery from which they could drink deeply. But this is another story into which I cannot go in detail here.

What I shall submit now is that the situation of the humanistic museums of this country, insofar as they are scholarly resources, is pretty closely parallel to that of this country's universities and colleges in 1919. The term "humanistic museum" is one I had to coin during my tenure as chairman of the National Endowment for the Humanities, to make it clear that the museums, which the Humanities Endowment proposed to assist, fell within the provisions of the Act of Congress creating the Endowment—museums of history, archaeology, anthropology, etc. (If you should ask me what I meant to include under etc., I should have to say that I do not know exactly; and I should like to be instructed.)

I said just now that the present situation of the humanistic museum is about what the situation was in respect to the scientific laboratory of 1919. It is about the same because, by and large, we do not have personnel qualified to use what is in our laboratories—our collections. We surely do not have enough trained persons. We do not pay well enough to attract and keep the best. Our humanistic museums—probably all museums—are, indeed, the neglected stepchildren of the American educational enterprise, as, indeed, are all the humanities. Moreover, the humanistic museums are, if I may put it so, the unintegrated stepchildren of our educational enterprise.

There are deep and ancient historic reasons for this state of affairs. And here I shall pause to remark that, in our line of work, as in the line of inquiry assigned to me, we must be historians, or else, assuredly, we will be nothing. Historically, the development of societies has been, in the Western World, from a "noble warrior" culture to a "scribe" culture. "Education is a collective technique which a society employs to instruct its youth in the values and accomplishments of the civilization in which it exists." Thus in Arabia at the time of the Prophet, when society was dominated by an aristocracy of warriors, education was of a predominantly military kind: as such, it aimed at training character and building physical vigor rather than developing the intelligence. But in more refined (as we would call them) civilizations, the legacy of the past, embodied in written form, pressed heavily; and in such civilizations, education was dominated by the technique of writing. These were the "people of the Book," as the Koran calls the Jews and Christians, with a respect not unmixed with astonishment.

This kind of account could go on for a long time; so per-

200

Museums as Scholarly Resource

haps I had better compress a couple of millennia into a couple of paragraphs. The education of classical antiquity was by the book, and when Christianity took over, it organized education around the Book of Books, the Bible, as the source of all necessary knowledge about life. In all post-classical education, through the so-called Dark Ages, through the Renaissance, into modern times, the people of the Western World remained "people of the Book."[1] We still are. Except in the sciences, scholarship still is largely out of the book and out of manuscripts in the library. And, no matter how much a man knows about, say, the weather, the seasons, the ways of life on the frontier or in the wilds, the proper cycle of fallow fields, he is not accounted an educated man unless he has learned it from books. We still are "people of the Book."

There is still another historical sequence that must be mentioned. Derived from a Greek word meaning "temple of the Muses," the ideal museum in Mediterranean antiquity was thought of as covering the whole of human knowledge, covering the fields of all the Muses. But I know of only one that attempted to do so in those days—the Museum of Alexandria, Egypt. Yet even it had not appeared out of nowhere. It was, in effect, a vaster and more inclusive form of the philosophical community—philosophy in those days referring to all knowledge, as it did even in our Benjamin Franklin's day—created by the early Pythagoreans and copied by the Academy of Plato and the Lyceum of Aristotle. The Museum at Alexandria was founded by the first of the Ptolemies of Egypt at the beginning of the third century B.C. It lasted—or at any rate its library did—until its pillage by decree of the Christian bishop, Theophilus. That was in 389 A.D. "The term 'museum,' after the burning of the great institution at Alexandria, appears to have fallen into disuse from the fourth to the seven-

[1] In respect to the summary in this and the preceding paragraph, see R. I. Marrou, *A History of Education in Antiquity* (New York, Sheed and Ward, 1956).

201

teenth century, and the idea which the word represented slipped from the minds of man."[2]

But despite this fact, it is worth trying to find out what the Museum at Alexandria amounted to and what was done there. It was under royal patronage.

> It attracted not only poets and men of letters into the city but the most eminent scholars of the day—geometers, astronomers, physicians, historians, critics and grammarians. These "museum pensioners" . . . lived in community, close to the palace. They had no taxes to pay and no duties to perform. . . . Functionaries appointed by the king looked after the scholars' material needs so that . . . they could devote all their attention to their studies. They had wonderful facilities for their work—Botanical and Zoological Gardens and their world-famous Library. . . . The Museum was essentially a centre for scientific research, not advanced education: the scientists and scholars . . . were not obliged to give any lectures. Nevertheless, they did teach. Good is self-diffusive, and knowledge has a natural tendency to spread: this is generally recognized to be one of human nature's fundamental characteristics.[3]

This passage says several things important for us now: that the museum, a center of collections of objects and specimens, was a research center, and only peripherally a center for teaching. "We know that the scholars in the Museum did in fact attract disciples, and accepted and educated them."[4] But it was not until much later, in say the third century A.D., that it had professorial chairs in the main branches of knowledge. It was under the Roman Empire that the Museum at Alexandria became a center of higher education at a time when there were still no universities. To a lawyer like myself, historic precedent has important meaning. It enlarges our perspective and forces us to think and "to test the validity and cogency of the reasons for our choices: it makes our decisions conscious ones."[5]

[2] *Encyclopedia Britannica*, 11th ed., *19*: p. 65, *s.v.* "Museums of Science."
[3] Marrou, pp. 260-261.   [4] *Ibid.*, p. 261.
[5] *Ibid.*, p. xiii.

Museums as Scholarly Resource

Conscious of the origins of museums, I am more than delighted to be aware that, given its collection of objects, the primordial museum was a place for research. So it should and must continue to be. Knowledge should emanate from the museum's collections and, in accordance with its natural tendency, will spread. E. McClung Fleming has truly remarked that:

> The library and the museum constitute the two halves of our memory of the past . . . but it is the rare historian who can read the museum's artifact as freely and as accurately as he can read the library's printed book or written manuscript. The artifact is a social document, but the historian has tended to ignore this primary source in his preoccupation with printed and manuscript material. He has consulted only one-half of our memory of the past.[6]

This is familiar stuff to all involved professionally with museums today. Saying it to them is like preaching to church-goers who do not need the preaching, whereas the preaching is needed by the unconverted who do not go to church. In the present case, the unconverted are generally in the universities where, by and large, they still are "people of the Book." Many of my readers will know all this, better than I do. You also know, and you should believe, what Wilcomb E. Washburn has said: "In a great museum, as in a great university, research into the unknown must be the passion that dominates all and on which the functions of conservation and education depend."[7]

Louis C. Jones has pointed out that the historian from the ivory tower of a university finds in a good museum the same regard for scholarship, standards of research, and devotion to history as a discipline as prevail in his tower. This is as it should and must be.[8] But the sad part of the tale is that there are too few "good museums" in Louis Jones's sense, with

[6] "Early American Decorative Arts as Social Documents," *Miss. Valley Hist. Rev.* 45 (1958): p. 276.
[7] *Museum News* 40 (1961): p. 19.   [8] *Ibid.*, p. 16.

staffs trained to such standards of knowledge and excellence of scholarship that their future in the total American educational enterprise will demand. Hence, the first need in the effort to make our humanistic museums live up to their potential as a scholarly resource is to train staffs for research —that is, to produce new knowledge.

From good research flows good teaching in the college and university; from good research flow accurate, understandable, telling museum exhibits. The museum staffer must understand the role of the artifact in its own contemporary society. It must be understood before it can be interpreted. The staff must be scholars, not just keepers of things. For, as G. Carroll Lindsay has written,

> To arrive at even a general impression of a historical era, one must study not only what was written, but also what was sat upon, eaten and eaten from, ridden on, and lived in and with. This sort of thing is found most easily and in greatest quantity and variety in museums.[9]

The Reverend Ebenezer Brewer, in his *Dictionary of Phrase and Fable*, tells of a little old seventeenth-century lady who used to say to her pastor that she "had found great support in that blessed word 'Mesopotamia.'" Well, in our times the blessed word is "research" and many have found great support in *that* word. It is not as mellifluous, indeed. It has produced, for some of those who account it blessed, pots and pots of money. It has accounted, in some, for slackness in teaching. It has led many to think that they are entitled to carry on research and do nothing else to pull their freight in the educational boat. Of course, I now refer to research in the universities: "research" has not had, in the museums, anything like the support the old lady derived from the blessed word "Mesopotamia."

I plead for research as the only way for the humanistic museum to achieve its proper role as a scholarly resource. But,

[9] *Curator* 30 (1963): pp. 236-244.

in so pleading, I do not forget to remember that, in these United States, the scholar—particularly the humanistic scholar—historically has had an obligation to teach and to teach well. So far as the scholar in the museum is concerned, I would not diminish that obligation. The scholar in the museum has an educational obligation—in his exhibitions, in his labeling of objects, in his advice to the little old lady who wants to know how grandmother made hominy that tasted so good, and in many other ways besides.

The museum is the only educational institution that teaches the old and the young and those in between, from the cradle to the grave. As S. Dillon Ripley has said, the museums' "exhibits must be brought into everyone's life as meaningfully as the supermarket. In our system of education, we assume that one can be educated only by learning to read. But objects are as much documents to be read as the printed page." A live cow (I once had a secretary in New York City who never had seen one), George Washington's campaign boots, a treadmill, a double-bitted ax are objects to be read. A museum requires the services of scholars and teachers as well as exhibits designers.

Dr. Ripley makes another most sensible and practical observation.

> If then we must do more in the open education we present to the millions who throng museum halls each year, let us do so with all speed, conscious that in this way we may gain support for the inner programs of research and higher education in our laboratories. The two must go hand in hand, each program dependent on the other, deriving new meaning and understanding the one from the other.[10]

It usually is my dour fate to be obliged to address audiences a good many of whose numbers know more about my assigned subject than I do; and this subject is no exception. But, if I have been discouraged—as I have been—by what must be the

10 *Museum News* 43 (1964): p. 18.

Museums as Scholarly Resource

relative nonoriginality of what I have written, perhaps I am entitled to remember what John Adams said about the Declaration of Independence—that there "is not an idea in it but what had been hackneyed in Congress two years before." And perhaps I may take comfort in Thomas Jefferson's reply that it was not his purpose "to find new principles . . . to say things that had never been said before, but to place before mankind the common sense of the subject," and to harmonize "the sentiments of the day whether expressed in conversation, in letters, in printed essays or the elementary books of public right." Not that I delude myself that I have said anything as important as Mr. Jefferson said in the Declaration of Independence, but only that I think it may be valuable enough to engage my time and yours with my setting down in one place what seems to me the enlightened common sense of the subject.

Perhaps a new day is dawning for the museum; for in 1965 the Congress of the United States, in passing the legislation that established the National Foundation for the Arts and the Humanities, declared "that democracy demands wisdom and vision in its citizens and that it must, therefore, foster and support a form of education designed to make men masters of their technology and not its unthinking servant," and "that a high civilization must not limit its efforts to science and technology alone but must give full value and support to the other great branches of man's scholarly and cultural activity." The museum must play a great part toward achieving such a purpose. Furthermore, in 1966, the Legislature of the State of New York appropriated $600,000 for all kinds of museums to be administered by the New York State Council on the Arts.

The National Endowment for the Humanities has decided to start a training program for museum personnel, and most of the monies appropriated to the New York State Council on the Arts will be used for the same purpose. I have been, and shall continue to be, associated with both of these training programs. For I believe, as did those who promoted the development of science after the First World War, that the first necessity for the development of museums in the total American educational enterprise, is to create a better trained and larger staff for research, for education, for exhibits design. That is what museums need most. Money is needed for this purpose, of course, but I confess to harboring the hope that not too much money will be earmarked for research; for it would be bad news, indeed, if "research" became the only blessed word in the museums' lexicon.

I began this paper by remarking, with Justice Holmes, that at my age it is a pleasure to think that there are fewer and fewer to whom I feel the need to show a youthful deference. Even so, there are not many whom I am minded to commit to the nether regions; but among them are those who think that research scholarship is the answer to everything. In our many-faceted line of work, it decidedly is not; whereas, in my opinion, a knowledgeable concern for the humanistic scholars is that the first requirement of the humanities be that they be humane—that is, human and not pedantic. This is truth to me; for it is something I just cannot help believing. And what I cannot help believing *is* truth to me.

One final word: I would reserve a block of rooms in the nether regions—the most uncomfortable rooms there are in hell—for those who use the word "museology." For the use of that word would kill any hope that we are human; indeed, its use would prove that we are ignorant pedants, than whom there are none more ignorant. And I hereby offer a reward of one hundred dollars of my own cash, in United States currency, to anyone who will invent a better word, satisfactory to one who no longer feels the need to show a youthful deference.

ENGLISH

AND AMERICAN LIBERTIES

SIX hundred years ago, Geoffrey Chaucer observed in *The Canterbury Tales* that, come April, "than longen folk to goon on pilgrimages." And so, consonant with the dictum of the finest poet in the English language, in April my wife and I made a pilgrimage to England, whence we have just returned. But we did not take to the road from the Tabard Inn at Southwark to Canterbury, as Chaucer's pilgrims did. Instead, like the Clerk of Oxenford—which I once, myself, had been—we hied ourselves to Oxford and the tiny thatched village of Forest Hill, nearby.

The Clerk of Oxenford said to the landlord of the Tabard Inn when he was told to tell his tale: "Hoste," quod he, "I am under your yerde; ye han of us now the governaunce, and therefor wol I do you obeisaunce."

I said the same thing to our host, Dr. Detlev Bronk, when he ordered me as did the landlord of the Tabard Inn to "Telle us some merry tale, by our fey."

Merry I shall not be—nor was the Clerk of Oxenford merry in his tale. Here is mine.

As said, we went to the tiny village of Forest Hill where my son, on his first sabbatical, had rented a seventeenth-century house for his family. We stayed there. In the churchyard of the thirteenth-century village church I often went to read the names on the headstones and to think about these people, people whose names are not inscribed on history's page—the people who never had said anything that could be remembered nor done anything that could be recalled—as Disraeli once put it, I hope, sardonically.

But they were the people who had won at Crecy and Poitiers, at Waterloo and Bosworth Field, even at Forest Hill in Cromwell's army; who had died at far away Balaklava and Khartoum and Yorktown; and who—not inscribed on history's page—stubbornly and patiently, had stood firm for the English liberties that became ours.

The Bicentennial of American Independence is coming up in the year 1976. The members of the American Philosophical Society had great parts in the forging of American Independence—Franklin and Jefferson, John Adams, and Tom Paine, Washington, David Rittenhouse, Cadwallader Colden, the Biddles, the Hopkinsons, the Wistars.

Their lives have been told in the *Dictionary of American Biography*, and their praises have been sung in legions of books. And when the American Philosophical Society celebrates the two-hundredth anniversary of American Independence, their great parts will not be forgotten. But let us not forget that they became great because they had some extremely stiff competition. Back of them was the people—a politically sophisticated, mature people—who produced the leaders, elevated them to power, and sustained them. The quality and distinctive character of that generation is lost in the *Dictionary of American Biography*.

Like the people in the churchyard at Forest Hill who had said nothing that is now remembered, who had done nothing that is now recalled, they nevertheless were the people upon whom the great men of 1776 were utterly dependent for action. They were "the representatives of the Free Men of the

209

Commonwealth of Pennsylvania," the men of the county seats, of the shires, of the villages and towns who, quite literally, pledged their lives, their fortunes, and their sacred honor that the American Colonies might become free and independent.

But what do we know about them? Alas, we know little or nothing. I should like to know whether or not enough may be learned about them to make it possible to produce what I here tentatively call a "Biographical Dictionary of the American Revolution." The theme of such a work would be no less than the transformation of state and society in America in the late eighteenth century: how, "acting for all mankind," in Mr. Jefferson's words, America became the world's ideal for freedom and liberty, and also became the world's example in practice. Of no other part of the world may this be said with equal truth.

In the eighteenth-century colonies of America, a cause was carried—or was lost—at the ballot box. The same is true today; but it was even more true when governmental units contained fewer people. Then, the farmers and the villagers, the tradesmen and the mechanics, knew, by their words and deeds, their leaders' worth; and they both elected and sustained those leaders.

They constituted, indeed, an American aristocracy—an aristocracy of brains and character—an aristocracy not of birth or wealth, not of race or social class, an aristocracy largely self-made. In short, they were recognized by their communities to represent the communities' "best," and by common consent they represented what was noble and of good repute.

These are the men and women I hope some day will be made understandable in a "Biographical Dictionary of the American Revolution"—people without whom there would have been no American Revolution.

At the American Philosophical Society, we think of Benjamin Franklin as omnipresent; and, as his unworthy successor in the presidency, I try to be guided by concepts he would approve. I have no doubt that he would approve of this project.

The host of the Tabard Inn decreed, as he instructed the pilgrims before they started for Canterbury:

> Who-so be rebel to my judgment
> Shal paye for all that by the weye is spent.

I trust that our host of tonight, Detlev Bronk, will not think that I have rebelled at his justment that I should tell my tale; and I hope that he will not decree that I shall pay for all that on tonight's way is spent upon this magnificent dinner. For he is as the Franklyn in the Canterbury Tales, of whom Chaucer wrote:

> With-oute bake mete was never his hous,
> Of fish and flesh, and that so plentevous,
> It snewed in his hous of mete and drinke,
> Of alle deyntees that men coude thinke . . .
> His table dormant in his halle alway
> Stood redy covered all the longe day.
> At sessiouns ther was he lord and sire;
> Ful ofte tyme he was knight of the shire.

And so, Sir Detlev, knight of the shire, on behalf of all this goodly company, I thank you.

APPENDICES

APPENDIX I

VINTAGES REMEMBERED

EXCERPT FROM THE REPORT
OF THE PRESIDENT
JOHN SIMON GUGGENHEIM MEMORIAL
FOUNDATION 1962

AS I sit down at my table to write the last Report I shall write for the John Simon Guggenheim Memorial Foundation, a short novel by J. M. Scott, *The Man Who Made Wine*, comes hauntingly to mind. Mr. Scott's book is the story of Michel Rachelet, *maître de chai* of the Château La Tour-St.-Vincent, for many years vintner of that estate in the Medoc, on the eve of his retirement. I am Rachelet.

In the story, Rachelet reviews in his taste-memory, sensitively and evocatively, all the vintages for which he had been responsible—some good, some fine, some superb; and he is pleased to think that all have been workmanlike. There had been difficulties in many years, caused by wars, shortage of help, shortage of money. But Rachelet is satisfied that the vintage of each year had been as good as the grapes of that year, despite extraneous difficulties, had permitted him to make the wine. Again—perhaps too full of pride—I am Rachelet: I, too, am satisfied.

At the end of the story, a boy comes into the vineyard and Rachelet remembers how it was with him when he was young:

> A strange emotion flooded through Rachelet. . . . But it was not sadness. It was something else.
> He refilled his glass and raised it to the fascinated child:
> "We who are on the way out salute you who are on the way in," he said softly. "There will always be good young wine coming on

215

in the *chai* and good young fellows who love the vines. . . . May the good God show you what He has made me see."

Again, I think like Rachelet. And, like Rachelet, I am contented. . . . Rachelet had reviewed his vintages in his memory and on his palate. Similarly, I review my vintages in my memory and with my eyes and ears. . . .

—HENRY ALLEN MOE

APPENDIX II

RETROSPECTIVES

REVEREND JUSTIN J. HARTMAN, Minister of the Acton Congregational Church, Acton, Massachusetts, at the Sherman Congregational Church, Sherman, Connecticut, on October 8, 1975:

WE MEET here this afternoon as friends and family to give thanks for the life of Henry Allen Moe. It can truly be said of him that he changed the course of history. But, unlike so many history-changers, he changed it for the better. He did not bring wars or revolutions, nor did he build an industrial empire. Rather, he liberated others to give the world dances, paintings, music, novels, sculpture, and new kinds of photography. He enabled scientists to work in their laboratories that they might come to new understandings of our marvelous universe. He, himself, although not a scientist, was made a member of the National Academy of Sciences, a most remarkable honor. It was done in appreciation of his advancement of science.

After coming back from England where he had earned a law degree in the 1920's, he intended to embark on a career in law in this country—an intention never carried out. Instead, Mr. and Mrs. Simon Guggenheim sought him out and asked him to help them devise a memorial to their young son who had died. After Henry Allen Moe had toured the country and had talked with many people, he came up with the plan for the John Simon Guggenheim Foundation. He became its first secretary, later its secretary general and, in 1961, its president.

The Foundation's purpose was to assist men and women to carry on original research in all fields of knowledge and creative activity in the arts. During Dr. Moe's thirty-nine years with this foundation, he supervised the granting of millions of dollars to

217

encourage these endeavors. To read the names of the recipients of these awards is to read a Who's Who in the American arts and sciences in the twentieth century. Recipients included persons from Latin America, the Philippines, and the Caribbean, as well as United States citizens.

How many books in the libraries of America have in their preface a tribute to "Henry Allen Moe without whose help this book could not have been written"? Nor did Dr. Moe's help stop with the granting of money. He was a friend and mentor of those he helped. He kept in touch with them through a voluminous correspondence, and he seemed to be able to remember what all of them were doing. He saw them when they were in New York, and he encouraged them to feel that the Foundation was their intellectual home. Nor was his friendship limited to those who had been granted awards. He befriended the "rejects" as well, and many came back to him through the years for more encouragement.

Henry Allen Moe does not easily fit into any of those pigeon holes we like to use for classifying people. Conservative, surely in many ways, yet a pioneer in recognizing and appreciating new art forms. He saw that photography could be an art form as well as a commercial venture, and he helped it become just that. One associate said that no one before him had ever thought about giving awards to poets, composers, choreographers, and photographers. He was tough, determined, hard-working, yet gentle, benign, and compassionate. His professional life was rich, full, and rewarding but, nearly always, there was that counterpoint melody in a minor key—physical pain.

Injured in a serious accident while serving in our Navy in World War I, he applied for a Rhodes Scholarship from his hospital bed in an application so impressive that a member of the committee of selections for Rhodes Scholarships visited him in the hospital. Since all the regional scholarships had been awarded, the visitor helped arrange a special one—an unusual honor!

Dr. Moe was one of those all-too-rare members of the human species who think more about tasks to be done, causes to be served, others to be helped, than they think about themselves. In all the years I knew him, I never once heard him refer to his wartime injury or complain of pain or suffering.

He moved in the world of the great, the near great, and the would-be great. Yet he was always true to himself, guided by his own deep principles, never sacrificing his own integrity. Perhaps a man who has been so close to death is not easily frightened by lesser dangers. He once said, "I have never got anywhere by being scared." This fearlessness stood him in good stead in the 1950's when he was called to testify before congressional committees. It was in the days of McCarthyism, when reactionary forces lashed out at the great philanthropic foundations and seemed to take special delight in harassing the creative artists and writers who challenged conventional thought.

In what I believe was his finest hour, Dr. Moe explained to the committee, in defense of such foundations as his own:

> We are not God and we cannot foresee the future. . . . Foundations operating on the frontiers of knowledge must take chances to achieve results. If the foundation should attempt to prescribe what shall be orthodox in politics, science or in any other manifestation of the mind or spirit, it had better not be in existence.

The New York Times, in an editorial commending Dr. Moe's testimony and his work at the Guggenheim Foundation, concluded that editorial with this comment on judging foundations:

> Foundations must be judged by the quality of the work performed by the recipients of their aid. We think that they have met the test and are continuing to meet it with credit to themselves, with honor to their country, and with benefit to all humanity.

In a letter written to me that same winter, he enclosed a speech with the comment, "I have only one speech. . . . It is on the importance and the power of freedom."

Yet this man who advised governors and presidents, gave counsel to Nobel prize winners and avant-garde artists, had a real appreciation for us ordinary people in Sherman. He enjoyed a life-long friendship with Theodore Rogers and I felt that a part of Dr. Moe's life came to an end when we buried Theodore Rogers in this churchyard on a lovely May day a year ago last spring. In 1947, when we started a community newspaper in Sherman that chronicled local happenings and featured articles by many strictly amateur writers as well as some by professional writers, Henry Allen Moe became one of our most ardent fans. He said that no matter what other periodicals were demanding his attention, *The Sentinel* always came first. He particularly enjoyed the articles by Nellie Worden, who wrote about everyday Sherman life with complete truthfulness. Indeed, she wrote with a candor that very few professional writers—who are bound to think about their prose style—can ever achieve. I almost believe that, if Nellie had asked him for a grant, he would have given her one!

At least in his earlier years, Sherman was a deep well from which he drew refreshment and strength that enabled him to go back to his job renewed and simplified. The Moes bought an old house and, for many years, adamantly refused to add city conveniences to it. They had those in New York, they wanted something different in Sherman. Physical labor was an antidote to his mental exertions on the job. He found a kindred spirit in Victor Butterfield, one-time president of Wesleyan University, part-time Sherman resident, and all-time hard worker both physically and mentally. Henry Allen Moe had a deep love and respect for New England. New England stood for the things he believed in: freedom and a kind of fierce independence. As Robert Frost said, "We love the things we love for what they are." With this love of New England, he wanted to feel like a New Englander. And what better way is there to feel like a New Englander than to become a builder of stone walls, which he did become.

I believe it was the dam he built across Quaker Brook that pleased him most of all. For a man who works with intangibles— ideas, structures of society, committees, people's minds—there comes a very special reward in creating something that you can see and feel, and know that it will be there long after you are gone. And what could be more tangible than a huge cement dam? "This dam," he once said to me, "will last longer than anything else I have done."

To do justice to the work of Henry Allen Moe, the doer of justice would have to write a book. A tribute such as this can only hint at his many achievements.

So wide were his interests and so varied his achievements that he seemed like a Renaissance man set down in our twentieth century.

Retrospectives

MRS. JOHN D. ROCKEFELLER 3rd, President of the Museum of Modern Art:

HENRY ALLEN MOE and his wife Edith hold a very special place in the affections of all of the trustees and members of the staff of the Museum of Modern Art and we are proud to join with the New York State Council on the Arts in asking Dr. Moe's many friends to join together in paying tribute to him.

For thirty-two years Dr. Moe served with the highest distinction as a trustee of the Museum. For two years he was our chairman, and for twenty-eight years a vice chairman. Throughout these many years he contributed, consistently and generously, of his time and his wisdom through active and committed service.

On this occasion on behalf of William Paley, chairman of the Board and myself, I would like to reiterate the Board's resolution expressing our lasting appreciation of Dr. Moe's devotion to the Museum and the wise counsel which, for more than two-thirds of our history, he brought to the conduct of our affairs. The resolution concluded with gratitude for the singular example that he set by his high sense of duty, judiciousness of temperament, kindliness of spirit, and strength of character, as a trustee, as an officer, and as a friend.

Appendices

PAUL HORGAN, Author:

IN honor of his felicitous union of thought, word, and enduring meaning, let Henry Allen Moe have the first word:

"About me, physically," he wrote in a letter during one of his recurring and agonizing trials with a First World War injury received while a naval officer, "about me physically, I get a little better each day and have no complaints. Of course, I, being as I am, will not be wholly content until I can lay up a stone wall. But I have a little sense, and shall not press Nature's processes too far or too fast."

A year later, much restored, and back at his semicircular desk where his work literally surrounded him, he wrote:

"I guess I agree with Sartre in his saying that the ultimate evil is to make abstract that which is concrete."

From these brief extracts—brief but not small, for nothing I ever knew him to say or do was small, in his sense of proportion and towering honesty—it is possible to base important elements of his likeness. Having wisdom, he knew the positive value of patience. At the most sophisticated of jobs, he was in tune with nature's rhythms.

Being a man of the most naturally fastidious taste, he disdained the vulgarity of personal complaint. If given cause for offense, he made little or nothing of it, for he had the gift of seeing deeply what lay before, and he could project keenly what must come after, and so the irritation of any present moment was met with his customary indifference to inconvenience, or somebody's luckless unawareness of the proper thing.

Being as he was, the idea of *making*, the beautiful union between concept and execution, was as native to him in scale either great or small as any other element of his nature. To build a wall with his own hands was a fine, clear problem to solve with skills of his own. Either was a concrete undertaking. Both had his full respect for what they were in all their basic simplicity.

With this kind of respectful regard for the commonplace concreteness of which so much of our life is made, he was able also with his particular genius to envisage a great abstract design for our culture which, as he would carry it out, came sensibly and handsomely into concrete form. He spent forty years of his eighty-one in creating out of an abstraction—an original idea of

222

contributing to the world's aggregate of cultural achievement—an entirely concrete institution whose purpose fed roots in thousands of the most fecund lives of this century, and continues to do so. Out of these roots grew works of the arts and sciences, of public life, and of education, which enriched the society and gave a pattern for a whole new concept of how to put wealth to work through chosen individuals for the direct benefit of the general enlightenment.

It is a marvel to contemplate the range and depth of his mind and his versatile interests through the years during which he gave substance to his vision.

In any field of intellectual or technical work there was hardly a value he could not weigh, hardly a name he did not know, hardly a veteran or newcomer with whose achievement he was unfamiliar, and indeed, in many cases, of which he was not the actual sponsor as president of the great Foundation he first headed. It is a guess confidently to be made, further, that no patron of talent was ever more generous than he in the liberty which he bestowed, along with largesse. Once he gave his belief in the recipient of a grant, he made no move to dictate how the grant must be used. On the basis of a specific project, he gave support not only to that, but to a career, a life; and it is to be doubted that he ever forgot a name of the thousands of men and women whom he materially encouraged, or the particular work they did under his encouragement, or the results of it, both personal, and historical, throughout the intellectual record of two generations. If you were to subtract him and his influence from the cultural landscape of this country in the last half-century, a crater would be left too vast to be measured, as we can scarcely measure his greatness today. We can merely allude to what we know of him. The future will know more: but safely we can say that he was one of the very great Americans of this century.

His public life was a model of selfless duty. In it, his commitments ranged through an extraordinary variety of interests. His board memberships—often in the post of chairman—for museums and other educational institutions, were too numerous to list here, though it is good to recall now, in the Museum of Modern Art, that he served it as chairman and vice-chairman. As a trustee of Wesleyan University, he was, along with President Butterfield and Professor Sigmund Neumann, a prime mover in the establishment of Wesleyan's Center for Advanced Studies which for

223

ten years was a national model upon which many similar centers have been created. As the first chairman of the National Endowment for the Humanities, though other commitments obliged him to serve but briefly, he set continuing goals for that increasingly significant social instrument. His appointment to that chairmanship was only one of the dozens and dozens of honors with which he was invested here and abroad, and it may be taken as symbolic of his stature in contemporary society.

Of the great plenty of academic honors which were bestowed upon him, his honorary Doctorate of Laws from Oxford University gave him, I think, the greatest pleasure—not so much for the special prestige which it represented, but because of his years in Brasenose College as a Rhodes Scholar. As he wrote on a post card from there in recent years, "This is my college, and I love it. . . ." For the American Philosophical Society, of which he was president for eleven years, he had very grave respect, and he sustained in the most natural way the dignity, elegance, and wit of its first president, Dr. Benjamin Franklin.

If he saw instruments of culture reaching beyond national boundaries, it was his native land, this America, whose historic, intellectual, and spiritual vitality lay closest to his heart. These he served with vigor, astuteness, and breadth of understanding and, further, with that indefinable beauty of character which made him uniquely the man we remember.

We do not grieve for him, for that he would not want. But we exult in him, though that, too, in his utter selflessness, he would never have imagined as his due. But it is, in the end, the personal man whom we keep alive intimately in our love and regard. In his undemonstrative way, he gave these in plenty to countless people.

To risk an intimacy, I quote again from one of his hospital letters, in which with the minimum of words he expressed the fullest love with the lightest touch. "Edith," he wrote, "is in the pink, having weathered my ups and downs here for the past 8 weeks. When I'm able to move about she's the one who will be entitled to a bit of gaiety." For let the comradely gaiety and the wit, the conviviality and the unaccented charm, the lovely, gentle, and direct penetration of his intelligence, be remembered along with the less informal but splendid and far-reaching acts of his work.

Finally, in the decades of my privileged friendship with and knowledge of this triumphant man, there was one familiar human attribute which I never found in him. This was pride of self. Proud he was, to be sure, of what was achieved by those writers and artists, scientists, teachers, and public servants, to whose careers, and through them to our lives, he gave the energy of his ruling faith.

For all his significant thought and feeling went not for himself, but for others, to foster the enhancement of human life, that it continue to grow toward that goal which quite unselfconsciously he arrived at for himself—the goal of being civilized in the greatest possible degree.

Appendices

CHARLES FRANKEL, Professor of Philosophy, Columbia University:

IN 1954 I was a Guggenheim Fellow, working on a book in Paris. In describing my plans at the time when I applied for the Fellowship, I had said that I intended to move to England in May. But now it was the end of March, and somehow it seemed inappropriate to leave France. I wrote Mr. Moe to tell him of my change of plans, and detailed good scholarly reasons why it was desirable that I stay where I was. He replied quickly and briefly: "But of course! Paris in the spring. Where else should one be?"

A year or so later I ran into another side of the man. He had written me a letter asking my judgment about something or someone, and, in the course of answering, I mentioned that I had just accepted appointment to a Columbia University committee which, for the next eighteen months, would examine the University's activities and recommend a design for its educational future. The assignment seemed to me an exciting one, and I said so to Mr. Moe. His reply, once again, was instantaneous, and, once again, he did not waste words. He thought I ought to be doing philosophy, not working on a committee. And while he did not say so in so many words, he strongly implied that anybody worthy of a Guggenheim Fellowship ought to have had enough judgment to see that for himself.

This was the wonder of Henry Allen Moe. He was himself an extraordinary committeeman—organized, imaginative, spirited, generous, with dangerous powers of persuasion. He sacrificed himself unsparingly in collective endeavors. Yet he thought that committees did not do the ultimately important work of the world, but only the necessary work—and not always that. The important work was always and inescapably the work of an individual, of a mind and a sensibility following its own independent path. The bet had to be made on individuals. And once that bet on an individual was made, there could be no fixed rules. If a man wanted to stay in Paris, then he ought to stay in Paris, and forget about giving reasons. The reasons would not be as good as the instinct that led him to want to stay. Especially if he were in Paris.

With the greatest of respect to the people who make the decisions in the great foundations today, there is too often something that is missing from their planning and thinking. It is something very simple, and it is what Henry Moe possessed and exemplified. It was joy—joy in doing, and joy, particularly, in the life of intellect and discrimination. He loved wine and this was continuous with his love of good writing, and both of these were continuous with the excitement that he felt in scientific inquiry or writing a book or composing a sonata. He was a patron of the arts and sciences not out of abstract conviction but out of pleasure in them. He helped scholars, writers, and artists (he had superb judgment about them) because he knew what made them tick, and he ticked to the same beat.

The Guggenheim Fellowships were awards of unmatched distinction for this reason more than any other. They represented not a plan but a continuing act of informed judgment. They had no elaborate rationale behind them. They spoke for themselves, as any achievement in the arts or sciences speaks for itself.

Yet there is something else, of course, that they also represented. They spoke for Henry Moe's special conception of democracy and his special kind of faith in it. Only individual ability, only individual promise, counted in those awards. He wanted to give good people a chance to do their best. He did not think that democracy meant distrust of excellence; he did not suppose that a belief in equality necessitated a relaxation of standards. He thought that a democratic society could be—had to be—firm yet generous, shrewd but imaginative, joyous, tough, discriminating. And in himself he combined just these qualities. He proved, better than any abstract argument, the possibility and the nobility of the social ideal for which he lived.

Appendices

HAROLD W. KEELE, Attorney:

I SUPPOSE I could very properly say that I never met Henry Allen Moe. In matter of fact, he burst upon me with the suddenness and pent-up fury of a tropical hurricane. I had come to Washington in the summer of 1952 as general counsel of a Congressional committee to investigate foundations. Quickly I learned that the foundations had decided to boycott the entire investigation. Imagine then my surprise when an utter stranger stamped angrily into my office one morning and after identifying himself as Henry Allen Moe announced that he was there to do battle in defense of foundations and particularly the Guggenheim. "And," he added for good measure, "let me tell you, Mr. Keele, I am a hell of an operator." On that day I was given the opportunity of seeing Henry Allen Moe at his magnificent best—bold, fearless, determined—ready to engage the enemy on any terms in defense of his beliefs and his beloved foundation. There were some tense moments that morning, but out of that encounter there grew a firm and cordial friendship between us that lasted as long as Henry Allen Moe lived.

More importantly, Henry Allen Moe came away from that meeting determined to assist the Cox Committee in its work. From that moment he waged a spirited and successful campaign to persuade the foundations to cooperate fully with the Cox Committee. This proved to be to their great and lasting benefit and assisted them in successfully withstanding the scurrilous attack launched against them two years later by the Reece Committee. It was one of Dr. Moe's most important contributions to philanthropic giving and much of the credit for the almost universal acclaim accorded the work of the Cox Committee rightly belongs to Dr. Moe.

Of the many eminent persons connected with the foundations with whom I dealt during the Cox Investigation, the one who, in my estimation, towered above all others was Henry Allen Moe. I think the characteristics that impressed me most were his indomitable courage and his uncompromising honesty. Where others were timid Dr. Moe was bold. Where others sought to shy away from admissions of error Dr. Moe freely admitted mistakes. Nor did he shrink from criticizing those who used their eminence in the artistic or scientific field as a platform for their political views. For example, I cite the following from his testimony before the Cox Committee:

Retrospectives

I disapprove of these chaps, Mr. Counsel, who use their scientific and other eminence for the purpose of giving expression to views which, if they did not possess their scientific eminence, would not be listened to at all. . . . I object to all professionals, including professors and movie stars and every other category of professionals, who step out of their professional roles while using their professional eminence to get a hearing for something that they couldn't get a hearing for if it were not for their professional reputations. . . . I disapprove of it, but I can't do anything about it, and I wouldn't do anything about it if I could. After all, it's a free country and from my point of view everybody has the right to make a damn fool out of himself in his own way if he wants to.

To my way of thinking that is pure quintessential Henry Allen Moe. His contribution to society was unique and it was monumental. The record is there for all to examine but it is only we fortunate ones who knew him well who can know the measure of his greatness as a man. He was a giant among men of large stature.

Appendices

ERIC LARRABEE, Writer and Editor:

HENRY was set apart from the rest of us by his extraordinary ability to be realistic without in any way losing hope. Wise in the ways of the world, and holding few illusions about mankind's capacity for knavery and folly, he nonetheless had no room for cynicism in himself and little but disdain or pity for it in others. He simply assumed that an objective worth achieving would be as energetically pursued by those he trusted as he himself would pursue it. He had small patience with web-spinners or with those whose motive was self-interest. He preferred substance to shadow; his attention was directed to the matter at hand. With Henry in the chair, one could be assured that the business of the meeting would be handled with dispatch. Having served from its inception as vice-chairman of the New York State Council on the Arts, he was in a very real sense its guiding light. Believing as he did that no board is better than its staff, he gave to those whose work he directed unstinting confidence and support. He knew how to guide without meddling, and he never overstepped the often narrow line which separates the two. From this same perception of the role came his unique gifts as a good counselor. Like so many who rejoiced in his friendship, I turned to him again and again when important decisions were to be made, secure in the knowledge that everything said to him would be carefully weighed and considered, and responded to by clear, unequivocal, and—as often as not—uncannily prophetic advice. In this, as in so much else, he had no equal.

230

Retrospectives

JOHN HIGHTOWER, New York State Council on the Arts:

HENRY ALLEN MOE was the New York State Council on the Arts' charter vice chairman. He brought to the Council a steadfast conviction "that without the artist there is no art," and watched with unyielding patience his early insistence of this principle gradually evolve into the Creative Artist for Public Service program which established the Council as one of the nation's foremost sources of direct support for the work of creative individuals. For those who came to respect "Moe's rules of order" whenever he conducted a meeting, we also observed with admiration a man who combined a poet's insights with a lawyer's appreciation of structure. In 1971, the New York State Arts Council honored Dr. Moe with a special citation at the New York State Award ceremony for bringing to the deliberations of the Council "a philosophy of art which provided the foundation walls on which its policies have been built."

In 1972 he was asked by Governor Nelson Rockefeller to continue serving the Council as honorary vice chairman for life.

His conviction that art was an elemental thread in the fabric of all societies has left an indelible mark on a number of institutions that will miss his sagacity and cannot replace his unswerving dedication to the humanizing qualities he knew the arts engendered. In his eyes there was a profound twinkle of unerring wisdom that seemed born of a puckish belief that life was concurrently marvelous and mad—and an understanding that each of these qualities possessed considerable truth.

He was one of our country's true statesmen for the arts. He will always be remembered as a giant in our midst for the openness of his mind, the integrity of his vision, and the humanity of his spirit.

231

Appendices

WALKER O. CAIN, Architect, Centurion:

HENRY ALLEN MOE was a member of the Century Association for forty-six years and of the American Academy in Rome for thirty-three. That he gave generously of himself to both will be no surprise to those present and in both his ideas were felt to the end. Only last Thursday we saw his name as sponsor of a newly elected Centurion and it seems only last week that I telephoned to request and receive his emeritus wisdom on current Academy problems. Wisdom may be the word most often encountered in describing Henry Moe, probably because it suggests the judicial nature of many of his contributions. Yet there was a time, undoubtedly a brief moment, when his wisdom was not permanently established, although clearly anticipated. If this sounds heretical, I give you the result of Russell Lynes's recent research, an excerpt from a letter to the Admissions Committee, dated 1928. It has been properly declassified.

Written in Chicago, October 27, 1928

Committee on Admissions,
The Century Association,

Gentlemen:

It may be an unusually broad reason I have for commending Henry Allen Moe to your Committee. I have heard he is an intelligent man and I know he is in charge of the interesting and potentially valuable Guggenheim fellowships. Those fellowships will be more useful the wiser he is, and where more wisdom to be picked up casually than at the Century Club? So let's elect him for the good of the Universe.

Vilhjalmur Stefansson

Well, they did elect him, and he did acquire or increase his wisdom, and if the Century can be pardoned for thinking it gave Henry something, it is certain that he returned it many times over. Henry served on almost every committee at one time or another. This being an occasion of happy reminiscences it is appropriate to report that two of the most important (in their fashion) were committees he invented, both of them related to wine. One was the Wine Committee and the other the Vintage Festival—the first to select wine, the second to celebrate it. Once a year, Henry would assemble a group of artist members, assign them areas of the wall, and establish a theme. Overnight there

232

would appear cheerful cartoons in glorious color, depicting factual or allegorical celebrations of the grape.

During the long afternoon and evening Henry was always to be found counselling, advising, selecting that perfect Latin quotation, refereeing debates, and in general urging the team forward. And it was always Henry who defended his artists when their murals occasionally exceeded the bounds of conventional taste.

The American Academy in Rome, in some ways on a parallel course with Henry's Guggenheim Foundation, borrowed from Henry's experience in the search for young artists, a search that absorbed much of his life. How does one identify the genuine article in the chrysalis stage? How to ensure the highest development of the best talent? These questions contain the essence of the problem that the Academy and Henry wrestled with together.

In his various roles, Henry had to listen to a lot of praise, even flattery, and it never seemed to damage or corrode him. Perhaps he felt, as Adlai Stevenson once put it, "Flattery won't hurt you, as long as you remember not to inhale."

Henry remembered.

Appendices

NELL EURICH, Educator and Author:

To a very few individuals is given the ability to choose wisely and well others with creative talent. To single them out from the multitude, before they have given real evidence of their talent, is even more rare. And to have one's predictions fulfilled is truly rare.

Henry, albeit his sparkling eyes and gracious charm, could not be bamboozled. Deception fled from his presence and honesty held constant. Yet, how did he see or feel the potential in some, not in others, and with notable confidence back his choice? You may not realize it, but speaking objectively, I am not a recipient, never an applicant, always in the wrong place at the wrong time.

One day a young man, new to his position at the Guggenheim Foundation, walked into the office of a young woman teaching at the University. of Minnesota. She was startled when learning his name and purpose. She was an applicant—Marjorie Nicolson. In a beginner's surroundings, they talked, and then she became a Guggenheim Fellow and later dean at Smith College and the first woman head of a graduate department at Columbia University. She became a first-rate scholar of the seventeenth century and —my teacher.

Others were even more widely notable. The names are legion: Conrad Aiken, Edmund Wilson, Samuel Barber, Vladimir Nabokov, Saul Bellow, Martha Graham, Jacques Barzun, Stephen Vincent Benét, Brand Blanshard, Peter Blume, Louise Bogan, John Cage, Sally Carrighar (the naturalist), Aaron Copland, Hart Crane, Rachel Carson, Henry Steele Commager, e e Cummings, John Dos Passos, Douglas Moore, Lionel Trilling. From the long list I seem to have chosen especially from arts and letters; those in the natural sciences and social science were equally great in achievement. Above all Henry Allen Moe gambled on creativity, on the possibility for original research and expression, on performance.

Later, Henry was on the selection committee for the Aspen Award in the Humanities. His unerring eye now operated on the already great, and his judgment strongly influenced the selection of Benjamin Britten, whom he called the "Orpheus of western music"; and of Constantinos Doxiadis, the "Callicrates of world architecture and planning."

Henry might easily have chosen the participants for the Olym-

234

pic Games, as we remember that the Games included poets, at least in the fifth century. He could have managed the games as well.

One last word about the "rejects" in his process of selection. Many of them became his life-long friends, guided by his advice and the new opportunities he helped them to find and recognize. The family of talent sponsored by Edith and Henry Allen Moe is indeed world-wide, and one of them may be our first settler on those beguiling planets in outer space.

Appendices

THOMAS M. MESSER, Director of the Solomon R. Guggenheim Museum:

HENRY ALLEN MOE, sometimes Dr. Moe, and often just Henry, was so ubiquitous and pervasive a personality within our institutional world of culture and within the sphere of the humanities that his removal from it compares to the fall of a great warrior who thereby leaves the field of battle in at least temporary disarray. Yet nothing about Henry was warlike, and the large movements he engendered were created through the most restrained and almost unnoticeable means. His efforts, therefore, toward desired and desirable ends always stood in inverse ratio to the results themselves. For while characteristically the effects were telling, the originator's motion was gentle and muted.

By knowing about everything, by having passed through every situation, not just once but dozens of times, by grasping always the structural foundations and by recognizing surface phenomena for what they were, Henry could activate things by a nod, a smile, or a rhetorical question. As a trustee of the Solomon R. Guggenheim Foundation (what was he not a trustee of?) he never argued a point, never seemed to decide. Instead he would listen attentively to my lengthy analyses, to ask eventually with the barest twinkle in his eyes, some such question as, "Does this worry you, Tom?" Since of course it did, and since everyone felt in his question the hitherto suppressed and masked issue, decisions followed by way of foregone conclusions. Henry always seemed to say, "Tibi dixit, tibi dixit," as we would resolve the riddles brought to the surface through his questioning.

Yet this posture of passivity could be discarded as Henry would suddenly appear fully visible with a supportive "All right, let's go ahead with it." Or even more importantly, effectively timed public praise when one needed it most.

Remoteness and involvement, intellect and passion, vision and common sense, and many other such polarities seemed to coalesce in Henry Allen Moe's rich human texture where, in the end, all was balanced and perfectly formed. No wonder, therefore, that he occupied in the minds of those around him the highest mountain top unto which messages, problems, and issues of some gravity were referred for ultimate arbitration. Even now it seems as if to reach Henry one would need to mount just a little higher.

236

Retrospectives

HENRI PEYRE, Long Sterling Professor of French at Yale University; since 1970 Distinguished Professor at the Graduate Center of the City University, New York:

AMONG the many tasks which Henry Allen Moe accomplished with indomitable energy and talent, his direction of the John Simon Guggenheim Foundation was primary. A young lawyer barely over thirty, fresh from his years as a Rhodes Scholar in Oxford, he was chosen by Senator Guggenheim to organize and lead that most original of Foundations. The country had emerged from World War I with the sudden realization of its immense power: it had the good will, the economic resources, the skilled manpower required to fulfill its new destiny, which was nothing less than to assume the leadership of the Western World. But it still lagged behind in advanced research and in pure science. The stress had long been laid on empiricism and on pragmatic know-how. The time had come for America to encourage also its most promising speculative thinkers, its artists, its humanists, its educators.

At a time when the collective pursuit of knowledge and team work tended to be emphasized, Henry Allen Moe chose to stress the inventiveness and the intellectual independence of the individual researcher. Incessantly, he was on the look-out for non-conformists, for scientists formulating a bold hypothesis and eager to push back the frontiers of knowledge, for scholars ready to rise above pedestrian tasks and to reinterpret a portion of history, of literature, of social studies. He traveled across the country, searching for promising talents, consulting with former fellows of the Foundation about the new trends in their discipline. His warmth and his admirable selflessness soon won him devoted friends among college administrators, heads of laboratories and scientific institutes, publishers, eminent artists, writers, thinkers. The Guggenheim Foundation, thanks to his guiding spirit, became one of the most respected fraternities of talents; it did much to make friends for this country among Canadians and Latin Americans. It assumed in the United States the role which, in other lands, is often fulfilled by Academies and by Ministries of Education.

With the assistance of his choice of an able staff and a discerning committee of selection, it was not too difficult to choose physicists, biologists, humanistic scholars. Henry's patience and clear-sightedness were exemplary. His lawyer's gift to read critically through texts and to go straight to the heart of any matter stood him in good stead. So did his admirable impartiality. But the lawyer and the administrator in him were wedded to a talented writer of prose and to a lover of the arts. From the outset, he made it a rule to reserve a considerable number of fellowships for American novelists, poets, dramatists, artists, composers. It took flair and insight to read into an early novel or a young man's poem, into a painting or a sculpture by an artist yet unknown, the promise of genuine talent. Henry and his staff never claimed impartiality. Yet they seldom made an error or passed over a person who later reached greatness. He well knew that no one is truly competent to run a business, a big organization, even a country, who does not have something of the artist in him. Indeed, the roster of writers, painters, sculptors, and musicians selected as Fellows by the Guggenheim Foundation is an impressive list. The flowering of American art and literature in the middle of the twentieth century, the impact of American creativeness upon the world at large, have been due in no small part to the discerning taste and to the thoughtfulness of Henry Allen Moe. Seldom has so much, in the realm of the spirit, been achieved by the steadfast and generous devotion of one outstanding individual.

Retrospectives

CURT RICHTER, Psychologist, Johns Hopkins Hospital, Baltimore, Maryland:

HENRY ALLEN MOE was a member of the American Philosophical Society for thirty-three years and its president for eleven years.

In our lecture room in Philosophical Hall, Washington, Franklin, and Jefferson look down on us from portraits on the front wall over the speaker's table. There Henry Moe stood on the first day of each fall and spring meeting. His whole manner left no doubt in our minds about the wonderful things that were in store for us for the next few days. He promised to put before us what he called a "feast of reason"—and with his garnishments of comments, wit, and humor it was always indeed a feast.

He had the ability to establish a happy responsive relationship between the speaker and the audience. And with his wide range of interests in all fields of learning—science, art, and literature—he was able to put the new useful knowledge in its proper place.

The highest compliment that we can pay him is that in character, statesmanship, and high regard for learning and freedom he was as much like Benjamin Franklin and Thomas Jefferson, his predecessors as president of the Society, as he could possibly be. Franklin was president of the Society for twenty-one years, Jefferson for seventeen. Henry Moe was the twentieth-century embodiment of these two great men.

The Society as it is today—with its high standards of learning and scholarship and its interest in the lasting things of life—owes very much indeed to Henry Moe. Our thinking about Henry must always include his wife Edith, who shared his great affection for the Society. Finally, it can be said that we not only respected him but loved him and shall always miss him.

239

Appendices

FREDERICK SEITZ, President of Rockefeller University:

AMONG the short stories of O. Henry that were popular a half-century ago, there is one about a devoted New Yorker who not only loved our city, with its countless institutions and activities, but explored it continually from top to bottom. One day he came across the expression "man about town" and, intrigued with it, set about searching for someone with the range of interests and activities to match the expression. But after several months he had to admit failure.

About that time, a group with which he was involved was written up in the press. In commenting about him and his role, the newspaper said that "among his many friends he is universally regarded as the ideal example of a man about town."

Henry Allen Moe was far more than a man about town—though he surely was that. As our collective comments indicate, he was more precisely a "man about the world"—and, in fact, a very large world. Hardly a corner of the universe of worthwhile things escaped his boundless energy and zeal, which we all admired and loved.

Henry's initial professional interest was in mathematics, although he ultimately decided upon jurisprudence. Indeed, he always displayed the qualities of a great attorney when matters merited his attention. However, his deep involvement with scholarship at the most elite level insured that he would meet, as a peer, with leaders in other academic fields. In this way he became friend and adviser to the scientific community, with which he developed close bonds. In turn, the scientific community gladly provided guidance in his never-ending quest for the most brilliant and creative young scholars whom he wished to help on their way.

Recognizing his unique role in behalf of the well-being of mankind through science, the National Academy of Sciences gave him the most distinguished award it can bestow—the Hartley Medal, established in 1913 by Mrs. Helen Hartley Jenkins in honor of her father, Marcellus Hartley. This award, also known as the Public Welfare Medal, is unique in that it is awarded for outstanding application of science to public service, rather than for achievements within a particular scientific discipline. Through the award the Academy indicates its high regard for the medalists—many of them not research scientists—by conferring upon

240

the recipient special privileges of membership in the Academy, including the right to present papers at Academy meetings.

I would like to read the letter which Detlev Bronk, who was then president of the National Academy of Sciences, sent to Henry Moe in April, 1958, informing him of the award:

Dear Henry:

It is my pleasant privilege to inform you that the Council of the National Academy of Sciences, on the nomination of the Committee of the Marcellus Hartley Fund, has unanimously voted to confer on you the Public Welfare Medal at the time of the Annual Meetings of the Academy in Washington this April. We hope that you will be willing to accept this award at our Annual Dinner on the evening of Tuesday, 29 April, at the Shoreham Hotel.

The Public Welfare Medal is awarded for eminence in the application of science to the public welfare. It is also awarded in order to associate with the Academy those active in affairs closely related to the concerns of the Academy and for whom we have especially high regard. Our charter does not provide for honorary members; a holder of the Public Welfare Medal is, however, virtually that.

Among those whom we have thus sought to honor in previous years were General Goethals, S. W. Stratton, Wickliffe Rose, John D. Rockefeller, Jr., Karl Compton, David Lilienthal, James R. Killian, Jr., and Warren Weaver.

I am sure I need not tell you how great would be my personal satisfaction to make this award to one whom I hold in such high and affectionate esteem.

Yours sincerely,
Detlev W. Bronk

In response, Dr. Moe stated:

Dear Det:

There are some good things of the world in which you and I move which one notes, with a glow of pleasure, that his friends have received and which, it never crosses one's mind, he might himself receive. One of these is the Public Welfare Medal of the National Academy of Sciences: I remember my joy when Warren Weaver got it, and Jim Killian and Karl Compton and David Lilienthal.

And now it is for me! Although I can hardly believe it, I accept with the utmost in pleasure and shall be present on 29 April to

receive it from you. That you will confer it upon me will add immeasurably to my pleasure and my satisfaction—and Edith's.
 You are all too good to me!

Sincerely yours,
Henry Allen Moe

You will recall that Cyrus the Great requested that his tomb at Pasargadae bear the simple inscription, "I was Cyrus, King of the Persians," whereas our own more democratic, if not more modest, Benjamin Franklin requested the inscription "Benjamin Franklin—printer." The scientific community would have been deeply pleased had Henry requested the inscription, "I was Henry Allen Moe—scientist."

Retrospectives

ROBERT SHACKLETON, Librarian of Bodley and Fellow of
Brasenose College:

WHEN Henry Allen Moe sought a Rhodes scholarship in 1919 one
of his referees claimed: 'It is almost impossible to over-state this
young man's case,' and another wrote: 'Wherever Henry Moe
goes, he will lead.' His mid-western university did not have extensive contacts with Oxford and Henry, in order to make up his
mind about the choice of a college, is said to have spent an hour
over works of reference in the New York Public Library. But
Frank Aydelotte, who was at Brasenose, probably advised him
and the Warden of Rhodes House, commending the young scholar to Brasenose, wrote, 'Aydelotte thinks very well of Moe.'

At the outbreak of World War I he had enlisted in the United
States Navy and rose to the rank of Lieutenant (j.g.) in the Naval
Reserve. During his service he was in command of a submarine
chaser and for a time taught mathematics and navigation at the
Naval Academy. After the Armistice on duty on a battleship, he
was in an accident in which he suffered serious injuries. He spent
a year and half in a Naval Hospital. When he was discharged
his surgeon said to him, 'I am sorry my boy, but you will never
be able to walk again.'

He went up to Brasenose in January 1921. On the same day,
Carl Newton, likewise a Rhodes Scholar and a Dartmouth graduate, arrived at Brasenose and became a life-long friend. He has
kindly supplied information for this notice. Moe arrived at Brasenose on crutches. On his vacations he had to be lifted on and off
railway carriages by his Brasenose companions, but he was
grimly determined to walk again and worked unremittingly to
restore the torn muscles of his shattered legs. When, several
years later, he returned to the Naval Hospital walking with a
scarcely noticeable limp, his old surgeon said to him delightedly:
'Get out of here, Moe, you walk better than I do.'

He read law, achieved a first in the Final Honour School, and
went on to take the B.C.L. Though prevented by his war injuries
from playing an active part in sport, he participated fully in College life. He belonged to the literary society named after Walter
Pater and to a notorious luncheon club, the Vampires, which
often incurred the wrath of the disciplinary officer. His contemporary Noel Hall, later Sir Noel and Principal of the College, says
that he was much loved and incapable of belonging to a clique,

243

and those of his contemporaries who survive retain the most affectionate recollection of him. After the B.C.L., he was appointed to teach at Brasenose, being named Hulme Lecturer in Law. A story from this period is still told in the College. He pinned up on the College board a notice to his pupils, signed simply 'Moe.' The Vice-Principal, W.T.S. Stallybrass (Sonners), facetiously congratulated him on having become a member the House of Lords, whereupon the young lecturer hurried to the lodge, took out his pen, and inserted the word 'Hank' before 'Moe.' He taught only for a year in Oxford and returned to America to begin his career at the bar and as a foundation officer.

Both Oxford in general and Brasenose remained close to his affection. When his foundation work brought him to Europe, he revisited Oxford and took a close and practical interest in its affairs. In 1928 he became treasurer of the Association of American Rhodes Scholars (an office he held for 37 years) and was instrumental in setting up that enlightened body, the American Trust Fund for Oxford University. In the 1950s he helped J.N.L. Myres, then Bodley's Librarian, to create the organisation of Bodley's American Friends. The Bodleian was dear to him, and the building of its new Law Library owed immensely to his foresight and enthusiasm, and to his capacity for communicating enthusiasm to others. When W. E. van Heyningen sought to raise funds for the new college, St. Cross, of which he was Master, Moe spontaneously invited to dinner at the Century Club a group of those potentially interested, and ever after the well-being of St. Cross College was close to his heart. Still later he assisted his own College to set up the Brasenose Foundation for American old members of the College.

He was always interested in the Eastman Professorship in Oxford and when it was proposed to build a house for the holders, Moe made it his personal concern. A British architect produced a design for a house in the most modern style. Moe said that this would not do. He supplied a photograph of an English Cotswold cottage and an American architect was instructed to build a house to that pattern. The result is the charming house which stands at the end of Jowett Walk.

He was greatly cherished at Oxford. Brasenose elected him to an honorary Fellowship and the University gave him an honorary D.C.L., two distinctions of which he was very proud. In the splendid portrait by Franklin Watkins, painted for the American Philosophical Society, he is wearing an Oxford D.C.L. robe (borrowed, as it happened, for the occasion from Dean Rusk) and a Brasenose tie.

His last visit to Oxford was particularly memorable. It was in 1973. His left leg, still ailing from his naval accident in the First War, had been amputated, and, as if to demonstrate that he was still young in spirit, he had set off on a European tour. He was housed in a ground floor room in College and as a special concession, Brasenose not yet having gone coeducational, his wife Edith was allowed to sleep in College to look after him. He dined at the High Table in his own right and Edith dined as the Principal's guest. One night, the President was to broadcast and was expected to announce his resignation. The speech was due at 4 a.m. British time. They borrowed a transistor radio and an alarm clock in order to hear the speech. The next day, Hank was angry and disappointed. When asked if he had met the President he replied that, a life-long Republican, he had been personally acquainted with every President of the United States from Theodore Roosevelt except the last. Shortly after, they left for Paris, the Villa Serbelloni, and Rome, in the best of spirits and full of zest for life.

He had the record and the capacity to be a distinguished academic but preferred to stand outside the purely university world. But his work for the Guggenheim and Rockefeller Foundations, his presidency of the American Philosophical Society, and his brief service as the first director of National Endowment for the Humanities made him a dominant figure in the intellectual life on two continents. He had a remarkable ability to assess the quality of specialists in fields remote from his own. He was devoid of pomp and could show the same interest in the problems of a graduate student as in those of a university president. He believed that personal contact promotes the circulation of ideas, and he had the imagination to translate this belief into action. He was a warm-hearted and generous man, a great man and a lovable man, and western civilisation owes much to him.

Appendices

FRANCES GILLMOR, Writer and Folklorist:

I AM HAPPY when I think about Henry Allen Moe. The first time I met him was at his office just before I started on the Guggenheim Fellowship year which has illuminated all my work since. He was warmly interested in my plans, and made me comfortable when I was just undertaking them. Truly he had a genius for making people comfortable.

When I came back I called again at his office. He mentioned that he had always remembered the goat bells in the early morning at Delphi—and by a miracle the only things I had brought back from Delphi were two goat bells. I hurried to my hotel and brought one to him. He wrote afterward that his grandson had taken it outside the house and rung it for him to make him feel that he was in Delphi.

Once he wrote me a postcard from Portugal to say that he and Mrs. Moe had been watching a fiesta procession in the street below their balcony. Out of the hundreds of Fellows whom he had known, how could he remember that I was working on folk drama and fiestas, and so send me that kind and personal card?

I will always remember with gratitude, as all Fellows must, that I was privileged to have known him. He was a great man, gentle in his concern for people.

Retrospectives

DUMAS MALONE, Biographer of Thomas Jefferson:

I KNEW Henry Allen Moe first as a fellow Centurion, while I was a professor of history at Columbia University. During that period I was twice a Guggenheim Fellow, working on my comprehensive biography of Thomas Jefferson. After my return to the University of Virginia, where I am now a professor emeritus and bear the honorific title of biographer-in-residence, I saw a good deal of him in connection with the National Endowment for the Humanities which he was setting up.

Henry Allen Moe always impressed me as a man of rare balance. In administering the Guggenheim Foundation, he manifested great flexibility, while maintaining the highest standards. He invested in men—very diverse men—rather than in topics and granted them the utmost freedom, rightly believing that they could be trusted to make good use of their time. In setting up the National Endowment for the Humanities he showed the same catholicity of spirit and insistence on excellence without a trace of pedantry. I mourn him as a friend and salute him as a creative statesman in the realm of learning.

Appendices

LEWIS MUMFORD, Author:

ONE personal experience long ago gave me the measure of Henry Allen Moe as a sensitive judge alike of ideas and men. In 1932 I had received, at my own request, a limited Guggenheim award, enough to maintain four months of travel and study in Europe. That stipend served me well in the preparation of both *Technics and Civilization* and *The Culture of Cities*. But the two remaining books in my "Renewal of Life" series had still to be written; and the nature of these books had not yet had time to crystallize in my mind. Having already some insight into Dr. Moe's methods, I decided not to submit a definite project: instead I asked for a whole year solely for untrammelled study and meditation on the historic life of man. This must have been an unusual request, and the favorable final decision could have been made only by an unusual man, who knew that orderly institutional and scholarly criteria must sometimes be set aside in order to keep the spirit alive. From then on, I went to Henry Moe whenever I needed advice about seeking—or avoiding!—professional commitments to other institutions as well as his, confident his response would be that of a wise and liberated mind.

Retrospectives

GORDON N. RAY, Present President of the John Simon Guggenheim Memorial Foundation:

FEW of the procedures Henry Allen Moe followed to uncover and encourage talent were reduced to writing. Rather, he preferred to carry them in his head, where they could be constantly adjusted to meet changing situations. Though he relied on "finger-tip feel" to a great extent, he invariably drew on his remarkable acquaintance with authorities in every field to verify his instinctive reactions.

His mild manner concealed a strong and positive personality. One soon discovered that he held firm views on most subjects. He was not a man to delegate authority, preferring instead to keep in personal touch with every application and all aspects of the Foundation's correspondence. This characteristic may be regarded as further testimony to his strong sense of obligation to the trust placed in him.

His control of detail was meticulous. He seldom dictated his correspondence. He usually drafted his letters in longhand in his firm distinctive script. Only after he was thoroughly content would they be turned over to Miss Sherman to be transcribed. In consequence, his letters were not only models of clarity and force, but also invariably stamped with his personality.

He was kindly but firm in dealing with the Fellows, always sympathetic to their problems, yet anxious to spur them on to do their best work without interference. Indeed, his strong belief in the power of freedom underlay all his relationships with them.

Appendices

JOAQUIN LUCO, Scientist, Santiago, Chile:

OUT of his grief at the death of his son, Senator Simon Guggenheim took a Maecenas's view of the living. The John Simon Guggenheim Memorial Foundation was created in 1925 in order to "promote the advancement and diffusion of knowledge and understanding, and the appreciation of beauty, by aiding without distinction on account of race, color or creed, scholars, scientists and artists of either sex in the prosecution of their labors."

The Senator's intent took form under the guidance of Henry Allen Moe, a young lawyer who, having graduated from Oxford University, returned to North America in 1924.

Chile was one of the first South American countries included in the Foundation's program. Since 1930 the Foundation has granted annually and without interruption, many fellowships to scientists and artists in our country. Today these Fellows—all who are alive—have paused to meditate on the significance in their lives of having been Guggenheim Fellows, and they have tried hard to recall even the tiniest detail of the meetings that they had with Dr. Moe.

Dr. Moe was not only the president of the Foundation, he was much more: he was the human factor in it, the man who welcomed Fellows as a friend and as a teacher. From the first moment, each one of us, upon entering his office in New York, perceived the personal warmth that emanated from him. Later, around the strange horseshoe-shaped mahogany desk, the newcomer learned to appreciate his wisdom and concern.

The Foundation never was an impersonal organization; it was Henry Moe who understood the present and guided the future of each Fellow. It was that way at the beginning and in that way it has continued. It could not be any other way, since the Foundation has willingly attempted to provide the necessary liberty so that the creative powers of those selected could make beauty and knowledge their objectives. Henry Allen Moe was the guiding spirit.

In 1957 he visited Chile. He came to learn about the life of each of the Chilean Fellows. He left with an award from our Government.

250

Retrospectives

LOUIS C. JONES, Folklorist and Writer:

DURING the last two decades of his life, Henry Moe was closely identified with the village of Cooperstown and its major institutions. That relationship had its origins at the Museum of Modern Art during the years when Stephen C. Clark, Sr., was president and chairman of the Board and Henry was his very close adviser. After World War II, Mr. Clark turned more and more of his attention and energies to the remaking of his beloved village into a medical and historical center whose significance would rest not on size but on quality. Henry was not only privy to these plans, he was an active and constructive contributor to them.

One of the areas where Mr. Clark sought Henry's advice in 1946 was the search for a director of the privately endowed State Historical Association and its Farmers' Museum. Now I remind you that Henry was a compulsive gambler—he bet millions of Senator Guggenheim's dollars on untried youngsters in whom he had caught the promise of winners. This time he stretched the odds about as far as they would go: he recommended to Clark for director of a historical society and two museums a man who had never had more than one semester of American history—and that in high school, a man who knew nothing whatsoever about museums, who had never administered anything, and who wanted to continue his life as a college teacher. Against all common sense, Mr. Clark took Henry's advice and offered me the job. Against my better judgment I accepted and stayed, until I retired twenty-five years later.

I tell you this to make a point: Henry had a most remarkable instinct for understanding the chemical interaction of men, of estimating the chances of an individual's success in a given situation. He was a pinpointer of potentialities.

During the '50's, Mr. Clark drew Henry more and more into the dramatic growth of the Cooperstown institutions: the Bassett Hospital became a model rural medical center; the Baseball Hall of Fame became a religious shrine for the fans; the Farmers' Museum and the Historical Association innovated programs and practices that set them apart as forerunners to be followed. By the early 1950's Henry was on all these boards and those of the Clark family foundations. Then suddenly in the fall of 1960, Stephen Clark died and Henry Moe became president and chair-

251

man of the Board of the Hospital, the Historical Association, and the Farmers' Museum.

Mr. Clark's will greatly enriched the Clark and Scriven Foundations with the understanding that they should benefit Cooperstown and the surrounding rural community. It was Henry who suggested and then guided the Clark Scholarship program, giving an opportunity for a college education to hundreds of youngsters who otherwise would have had no such chance. Henry invested the same concern for the individual, the same thought and care on those high school seniors as he had on the Guggenheim Fellows.

I want to speak of Henry Moe as Chairman of the Board, a role not always understood among the leaders of our cultural agencies. He expected the director and his staff to generate ideas and early on to share them with him. Then there was give and take, always measured, always realistic, concerned with the art of the possible. If, finally, the idea seemed sound, step by step he would work out the plans for its eventuation. Chairman and director each knew exactly what responsibilities were his. I went through this process hundreds of times with him, but I never really understood it until the morning after his funeral, when I sat and studied the stone dam he built on Quaker Brook with his own hands. Each stone had been evaluated, carried to the place where it would hold the maximum weight, do the most good. This was the way he engineered the foundation on which we built at the Historical Association, the Cooperstown Graduate Programs which have revolutionized the education of history museum personnel and art conservators and created a new field in American folk culture. This was the way he brought to pass a new library and new buildings at the Farmers' Museum. The lines of communication were always open between us, and when there were problems he saw them as mutual problems for the chairman and the director to solve together. In all this he invariably valued the human equation; no one was ever a statistic to Henry Moe.

I served under his presidency for twenty years, under his chairmanship for twelve. Never once in all that time did he overstep that thin line which separates the prerogatives of the officer of the board from those of the director. In my view, he was the ideal chairman of the board, but that fact pales before another: he was one of the best friends I shall ever have.

Retrospectives

THE CLARK FOUNDATION
AND COOPERSTOWN INSTITUTIONS:

HENRY ALLEN MOE gave to us the full measure of his rare experience as one of the masters of the intellectual world. He also gave unstintingly of those qualities which marked his life: a genuine concern for the individual and his or her potential, a freedom of spirit that rose to the new idea and untried experiment, courage and a shrewd wisdom coupled with a firm decisiveness. And these virtues were mellowed by his humor and a never failing sense of proportion. His dynamic influence will mark our institutions as long as they survive.

> THE CLARK FOUNDATION
> *Stephen C. Clark, Jr., President*
>
> THE FARMERS' MUSEUM, INC.
> *Stephen C. Clark, Jr., President*
>
> THE MARY IMOGENE BASSETT HOSPITAL
> *Robert E. Brosnan, President*
>
> NEW YORK STATE HISTORICAL ASSOCIATION
> *Henry R. Labouisse, Vice President*

Appendices

DR. CHARLES ALLEN ASHLEY, Director, Mary Imogene Bassett Hospital, Cooperstown, New York:

HENRY ALLEN MOE served the Mary Imogene Bassett Hospital as a member of its Board of Trustees from 1946 to 1975 and as president and chairman from 1962 to 1975. The successful teaching hospital depends on an integrated and balanced combination of the talents and aspirations of a diversity of individual professionals. Henry Allen Moe brought to his role at the Hospital his years of experience in evaluating and encouraging the drive and performance of individuals. In his personal contacts he exhibited a persistent and optimistic enthusiasm for the potentials of youth. It was a treat to observe him in his warm contacts with young people. He made clear his intolerance of mediocrity and his insistence on precision. When a work met his high standards we all basked in his delight in a job well done.

His enjoyment of good company, good talk, and good food added a dimension of pleasure to the intellectual stimulus of our contacts with him. He had the patience to listen to long complicated medical and scientific presentations and helped to focus attention on the essential problems. While helping us pursue the Hospital's missions in medical education and research, he insisted that we keep the care of the individual patient as the center of our attention and drive.

The courage and cheerfulness with which Henry Allen Moe endured years of great physical pain will remain a source of strength and determination for all of us.

Retrospectives

J. KELLUM SMITH, JR., Trustee of the American Academy in
   Rome:

HENRY ALLEN MOE was a trustee of the American Academy in
Rome from 1942 until his death on October 2, 1975—a span of
thirty-three years. He was awarded the Academy Medal in December 1970.

He brought to the affairs of the Academy not only a fine legal
and practical mind but a wealth of experience in and intelligent
sympathy with the world of the arts and of humanistic scholarship. His acquaintance among artists and the professoriate was
wider than that of any other trustee—indeed, wider than that of
any imaginable trustee. This result was produced by a happy
confluence of his natural enjoyment of fine minds and spirits
and his long and remarkable career as President of the John
Simon Guggenheim Memorial Foundation, which it is not too
much to say he invented; invented and cast in his own mold, for
it was his instinct for quality in people that made the Guggenheim
Fellowships the prized awards that they soon became and continued to be. That same instinct for quality he brought to the
deliberations of the Academy, combining with it a sharp and
critical common sense that some traced to his Minnesota origins.

A man of international eminence, who dined with the great,
honored innumerable boards and committees by his presence,
and wielded much influence in artistic and scholarly affairs, he
was conspicuous throughout his life for a special integrity and
forthrightness, and for a *humanity* that is not always, but always
should be, acknowledged as the central element in humanism.

255

Appendices

EMANUEL WINTERNITZ, Art Historian, Musicologist, Curator
  Emeritus of Musical Instruments, Metropolitan Museum of
  Art:

THE magnificent tributes paid by countless people to that magnificent man, Henry Allen Moe, listed his positions, titles, honors, and professional relations; but little has been said about his inimitable way of doing business as a foundation man. Even his long and witty goodbye letter to the Guggenheim Fellows in 1963 retains an official idiom and does not quite reveal the inner man and his unique personal way of conducting foundation business. I quote two paragraphs from it:

> On this day of my retirement, I go on to assure you that the usual connotations of retirement have no application to me, and that you will not need to think of me as being either idle or indigent or—as a retired friend added the other day—dead.
>
> There is no sadness in my retiring but contentment in having done a job as well as I possibly could do it. And that's the way I shall attend to my next jobs.

The following letter, reacting somewhat critically to Mr. Moe's goodbye letter, may reveal a bit of the impact the unofficial Mr. Moe made on a man who, as a young immigrant of 1938, had learned to take Mr. Moe as the wise and encouraging exponent of a new hospitable country:

August 2, 1963

Dear Mr. Moe,

On returning from Europe I found your letter of June 30 and I am certainly glad to have this description of all your variegated projects, plans and, last but not least, your kind little autographed supplement.

However, being a habitual back-talker, I should like to register some criticism. The trouble with your letter is that *you* have written it, and not another, unbiased person who could have talked more freely about Mr. Moe. Then, there might have been a little paragraph about "Mr. Moe and the visitor," describing what must have been the daily routine of Mr. Moe but a unique experience for any visitor coming for help or advice or even the harsh truth. This paragraph would describe Mr. Moe listening quietly to the visitor and concentrating on his words without any visible effort, and giving him the feeling that nothing, nothing in the world, existed for Mr. Moe in this half-hour but the visitor and his worries or plans or thoughts, however queer they might be. Such half-hours are not easily forgotten by a visitor. They may give him back, under certain conditions, a trust in humanity, and lift him out of the world of Madison Avenue, and encourage him more than any money grant could do to follow his scholarly ideals. And all this without sentimentality, in the most matter-of-fact way in the world. I am sure, now that Mr. Moe "retires" to more work than before, he will not change his habits with visitors.

Of course, a museum organ-grinder hesitates to write such a critical letter to the president of the American Philosophical Society, but once in a while, in our world of conventions, one should give vent to one's feelings.

With compliments to your mother, to Mrs. Moe, and to Mr. Moe himself,

As ever yours,
Emanuel Winternitz

The unofficial, unpedantic Mr. Moe was revealed to me, however, much earlier in a single unforgettable sentence. This is the story. In 1945 I applied for a Guggenheim Fellowship for writing a book on musical instruments in relation to the development of musical style. I received the fellowship. When my script for the book was well under way, an unexpected thing happened. A well-known private publisher of art books asked me whether I would be interested in writing a book on musical autographs, analyzing a selection of them with emphasis on the graphological aspects. I was passionately interested, though less in graphology than in the musical script as embodiment and evidence of the act of musical creation and as a gold mine for the study of working habits of composers.

The sudden appearance of a publisher known for good graphic work and interested in a topic dear to my heart since childhood, when I looked at venerable scripts of Haydn, Mozart, and Brahms in Vienna libraries, was little short of a miracle. There was, however, some difficulty. My commitment to the Guggenheim Foundation was for another topic. I certainly needed the consent of the Foundation. But would it be tactful to ask for a radical change after having been treated so kindly the first time?

I visited Mr. Moe and hesitantly explained my problem. "Are not both projects concerned with music?" he asked. I protested. My first book idea, musical instruments, I insisted, was quite different from the study of musical script. "But does not musical

257

Appendices

style play a role in both projects?" Mr. Moe said. I still insisted. There was a pause, and I am sure in retrospect that Mr. Moe was more aware than I of the absurd and comical fact that I was actually trying to dissuade the Foundation from granting my request. Then Mr. Moe said very seriously, with only the faintest indication of amusement in the corners of his mouth and eyes: "Dr. Winternitz, we don't buy books, we buy men." That settled it. It was an unforgettable sentence, reflecting the inner Mr. Moe, his unpedantic directness and matter-of-factness, and above all, his generosity, warmth, and honor.

(From The American Council of Learned Societies Newsletter, Fall-Winter, 1975-1976)

APPENDIX III

RECORD OF SERVICE AND RECOGNITION

UNITED STATES HEARING
ON THE NOMINATION OF HENRY ALLEN MOE
TO BE THE FIRST CHAIRMAN
OF THE NATIONAL ENDOWMENT FOR THE
HUMANITIES, FEBRUARY 25, 1966

NOMINATION

HEARING

BEFORE THE

COMMITTEE ON
LABOR AND PUBLIC WELFARE
UNITED STATES SENATE

EIGHTY-NINTH CONGRESS

SECOND SESSION

ON

HENRY ALLEN MOE, OF NEW YORK, TO BE CHAIRMAN OF
NATIONAL ENDOWMENT FOR THE HUMANITIES

FEBRUARY 25, 1966

Printed for the use of the
Committee on Labor and Public Welfare

U.S. GOVERNMENT PRINTING OFFICE
WASHINGTON : 1966

59-940

II

NOMINATION

FRIDAY, FEBRUARY 25, 1966

U.S. Senate,
Committee on Labor and Public Welfare,
Washington, D.C.

The committee met at 10:40 a.m., pursuant to call, in room 4232, New Senate Office Building, Senator Lister Hill, chairman of the committee, presiding.

Present: Senators Hill (presiding), Morse, Yarborough, Randolph, Pell, Kennedy of Massachusetts, Nelson, Javits, and Prouty.

Committee staff members present: Stewart E. McClure, chief clerk; John S. Forsythe, general counsel; Robert Barclay, professional staff member; and Stephen Kurzman, minority counsel.

The CHAIRMAN. The committee will kindly come to order.

We have before us the nomination of Henry Allen Moe, of New York, to be Chairman of the National Endowment for the Humanities, for a term of 4 years, to which office he was appointed during the last recess of the Senate.

I may say that the doctor has a wonderful record. I do not think I have ever seen a finer, more— -

Senator JAVITS. Would the chairman yield?

The CHAIRMAN. Yes.

Senator JAVITS. May it be understood that Senator Prouty must leave, and other members will not be here——

The CHAIRMAN. Yes.

Senator PROUTY. I regret having to leave because I would like very much to stay and hear the remarks of Dr. Moe. I think he has an outstanding record, and certainly is worthy of the appointment to the position for which he has been nominated.

The CHAIRMAN. Please leave a proxy.

Senator PROUTY. Yes, I will.

The CHAIRMAN. Dr. Moe, as I have said, you have a wonderful record, and many great accomplishments, and we will be very happy to have you at this time make any statement you might see fit as to your qualifications for this position of Chairman of the National Endowment for the Humanities.

Senator JAVITS. Mr. Chairman——

The CHAIRMAN. Senator Javits.

Senator JAVITS. May I have the pleasure of introducing our distinguished——

The CHAIRMAN. Your distinguished constituent?

Senator JAVITS. Yes, my constituent.

The CHAIRMAN. Of whom you are proud.

Senator JAVITS. Yes. I have known Henry Allen Moe for many years, and of course, as the chairman said earlier to me personally—

and I hope the chairman will put the marvelous quotation he used in the record—his record is very unusual and very outstanding. We are very proud of him in New York.

It may perhaps characterize Henry Allen Moe to my colleagues in the Senate if I tell them this: I have only one question about Dr. Moe, and that is, notwithstanding the fact that he will now be an official of the U.S. Government, I very much hope he will nevertheless be able to continue on a personal and informal basis to advise with the wide range of people who need advice as to where to go and how to go for foundations. He is the one person in all of New York, perhaps in the United States, who knows the whole range of foundations, and just how to go about applying to them, and who to go to for each particular subject. There are many projects that might be marvelous in themselves, but still can't get anywhere because they are applying to the wrong foundation.

I just say that to characterize what we think about Dr. Moe in New York.

Senator YARBOROUGH. I have been one, as you know, to work on each of these arts and humanities bills, and naturally I am greatly pleased to see the high qualifications of the nominee to this position who comes here in the person of Dr. Moe. I know that I have been working on them ever since I have been with this committee. Senator Case, of South Dakota, was the sponsor of a bill to create a National Academy of Culture and I was the chairman at the hearing held on that bill.

Senator JAVITS. I introduced the bill in 1949, as you know, so I want to see it well handled.

Senator YARBOROUGH. You were in the House at the time, I believe.

It has been a great pleasure to see all this growth of support for such a measure.

The CHAIRMAN. Well, we will be happy to hear from you now, Doctor.

Senator MORSE. Mr. Chairman, may I interrupt you a moment?

The CHAIRMAN. Surely.

Senator MORSE. I must return to finish a speech that is now in the typewriter. As you have a quorum now, may I leave my proxy with Mr. Randolph?

The CHAIRMAN. Yes. And thank you, Senator Morse; we appreciate your presence.

Senator MORSE. Thank you.

Dr. Moe, please accept my apologies that I have to leave. I wish I could be here.

However, since neither the committee, nor you, sir, need me at the moment, I must leave.

The CHAIRMAN. All right. Now, Doctor, you may proceed, sir.

Record of Service

Dr. MOE. I don't know what to say, Senator.

I discussed the matter of my appointment, when the word had come through from the White House that I was wanted, with some of my colleagues, as to whether or not I should accept this, and they said, "Well, of course you must, you have a public duty to accept it, because all your life, all of your life's work has led up to this kind of thing."

I think I have nothing further to say, Senator.

The CHAIRMAN. I think that anyone who will look at your record will certainly be absolutely persuaded that what you have said is true, your life's work has certainly eminently prepared you for this position to which you have been nominated. And unless there is some objection, I shall put in the record at this point the doctor's record.

(The biographical sketch of Dr. Henry Allen Moe follows:)

HENRY ALLEN MOE

Born in Wright County, near Monticello, Minn., July 2, 1894.

Primary and secondary education in public schools of St. Paul, Minn. College education at Hamline University, St. Paul, Minn.; B.S. degree 1916. Reporter, St. Paul Pioneer-Press and St. Paul Dispatch, 1915-17.

In 1917—enlisted in U.S. Naval Reserve as Seaman second class; retired 1920 as lieutenant (jg)—retired for injuries sustained in line of duty. Rhodes Scholar at the University of Oxford, Oxford, England, 1920-23; studied law. B.A. degree in jurisprudence 1922; bachelor of civil law, 1923.

Lecturer in law for Brasenose and Oriel Colleges, University of Oxford, 1923-24.

Simultaneously with Oxford legal studies, studied law at the Inns of Court, London, and was admitted to the bar of England—1924—of the Inner Temple, barrister at law.

The attached record shows what I have done since returning to the United States from the University of Oxford; it was compiled at the request of the Honorable John W. Macy, Jr., Chairman of the U.S. Civil Service Commission, when my appointment to be Chairman of the National Endowment for the Humanities was under consideration. At that time I wrote Mr. Macy that I had never merely lent my name to any of the organizations I had served, but always had pulled

Appendices

my weight in the boat—as he knew personally from my service as a trustee of Wesleyan University in Middletown, Conn.

The names of organizations preceded by asterisks (*) are those from which I have received compensation: to all others my services were gratis.

PRESENT SERVICES TO EDUCATIONAL, CHARITABLE, CULTURAL, AND GOVERNMENTAL ORGANIZATIONS

American Philosophical Society (the oldest learned society in the United States, founded at Philadelphia by Benjamin Franklin in 1743). Member since 1943; president 1959 to date.

New York State Historical Association, Cooperstown, N.Y. Member of the board of trustees since 1947; president 1951 to date; chairman of the board of trustees since 1961.

Farmers' Museum, Cooperstown, N.Y. Member of the board of trustees since 1947. President 1961 to date.

Mary Imogene Bassett Hospital, Cooperstown, N.Y. Member of the board of trustees since 1946; president since 1962; chairman of the board of trustees since 1962.

*The Clark Foundation, New York, N.Y. Member of the board of trustees since 1955. Consultant from 1963 to date.

*The Scriven Foundation, New York, N.Y. Member of the board of directors since 1955. Consultant 1963 to date.

(The Clark and Scriven Foundations, in addition to other kinds of grants for charitable and educational purposes, award scholarships for higher education to graduates of high schools in the area of Cooperstown, N.Y. After 2 years of such grantings of scholarships, about 175 students, who—by and large—would otherwise have no chance for higher education, are now on our scholarship rolls.)

Leatherstocking Corp., Cooperstown, N.Y. Director since 1965.

Wesleyan University, Middletown, Conn. Now trustee emeritus, presently member of the management committee of Wesleyan's Center for Advanced Studies.

New York State Council on the Arts, vice chairman from its establishment (1960) by the Legislature and Governor of New York, to date.

*John Simon Guggenheim Memorial Foundation, New York, N.Y. Principal administrative officer 1925 to 1963 with titles of secretary, secretary general and president. Member of the board of trustees 1945 to date (provides fellowships to scholars and artists of all kinds to assist their studies; citizens of the United States, of all the American Republics, of Canada and of the Philippines are eligible for the fellowships.)

*Harry Frank Guggenheim Foundation. Trustee, 1965 to date.

Maud E. Warwick Fund for Orphans of World War II, New York, N.Y. Member of the board of trustees 1945 to date; executive vice president 1945 to date. (Provides scholarships to assist American orphans of World War II to obtain higher education.)

Member of Committee of Award of the Vetlesen Foundation, New York, N.Y., to select recipients of $25,000 prizes for eminent scholar-

266

ship in the earth sciences, 1960 to date. (These prizes are awarded biennially on a worldwide basis.)

Member of Committee of Award of the Aspen Institute for Humanistic Studies, Aspen, Colo., to select recipients of the $30,000 Aspen Awards for eminence in the humanities and the arts, 1963 to date. (These awards are made annually on a worldwide basis.)

Member, board of trustees, Museum of Modern Art, New York, N.Y., 1943 to date. Vice chairman, 1945-59, 1961 to date. Chairman, 1959-61.

Member, board of trustees, Institute of Modern Art, New York, N.Y., 1960 to date. Chairman of the board during the same period.

Member, board of trustees, the Allen Tucker Memorial, New York, N.Y., 1946 to date. Chairman of the board, 1961 to date. (Provides scholarships for American artists.)

Member, board of trustees, Louis Comfort Tiffany Foundation, New York, N.Y., for a dozen years or so. (Provides fellowships for American artists.)

Member of the board of trustees of the American Academy in Rome, 1941 to date. Member of the executive committee during the same period except for the years 1955 and 1956. (Provides fellowships for American artists. scholars, architects, composers of music to enable them to study at the academy's headquarters in Rome, Italy.)

Member of the Advisory Committee of the Ditson Fund for Music, Columbia University, New York, N.Y., for 20 years or so to the present date.

Escuela Agricola Pan-Americana, Tegucigalpa, Honduras, member of the board of trustees for a half dozen years; chairman of the executive committee since 1963. (This is an American school, supported largely by American funds to educate middle-American youth in practical agriculture and agricultural management.)

Year 1963 to date: Member of a committee, named by the American Association of Museums (Washington, D.C.) to solve the problem presented in 1963 when the trustees of the Cooper Union, New York, N.Y., announced that they would close the Cooper Union Museum of Decorative Arts and dispose of the collections. (As of this date, I think we have the problem solved; but it may not be announced yet.)

*University of California, Berkeley. Regents' lecturer, spring 1965 —my services being those of adviser to the dean of the graduate division.

Association of American Rhodes Scholars. Member of the board of direction, 1928 to date; treasurer, 1928 to 1965.

Association of American University Presses. Chairman of the advisory council, 1964 to date.

New York University. Member of the President's Advisory Council, 1965-   .

NOTE.—The Leatherstocking Corp. is the only business organization with which I have been or am connected: all others, nonprofit.

Trustee, Science Service, Washington, D.C. (an institution for the popularization of science) for the past 6 years or so.

Appendices

Member of the board of trustees of the Rockefeller Foundation, New York, N.Y., 1944-60; and member of the executive committee during the same period.

Chairman of the Committee for Inter-American Artistic and Intellectual Cooperation, under the coordinator of inter-American affairs (who was Hon. Nelson A. Rockefeller) during World War II. This organization arranged for the sending of American scholars and artists to Latin America and for the bringing to the United States of Latin American scholars and artists—the selected persons chosen on the bases of high levels of accomplishment and personal merit.

Year 1945: Chairman of a committee under Dr. Vannevar Bush, Director of the Office of Research and Development, to make a study of the "discovery and development of scientific talent in American youth." See Dr. Bush's report to President Franklin D. Roosevelt: "Science: The Endless Frontier."

As chairman of the committee, I wrote in our report to Dr. Bush, pages 142-143:

"President Roosevelt's letter to you looks toward a science that will be a decisive element in the national welfare in peace as it has been in war. He said, 'New frontiers of the mind are before us, and if they are pioneered with the same vision, boldness, and drive with which we have waged this war we can create a fuller and more fruitful employment and a fuller and a more fruitful life.' It is clear that the letter refers to science as the word is commonly understood, or, more technically described, to science now within the purview of the National Academy of Sciences, that is, to mathematics, the physical and biological sciences including psychology, geology, geography and anthropology and their engineering, industrial, agricultural and medical applications. To science in this sense, therefore, the recommendations in this report will be limited.

"The statesmanship of science, however, requires that science be concerned with more than science. Science can only be an effective element in the national welfare as a member of a team, whether the condition be peace or war.

"As citizens, as good citizens, we therefore think that we must have in mind while examining the question before us—the discovery and development of scientific talent—the needs of the whole national welfare. We could not suggest to you a program which would syphon into science and technology a disproportionately large share of the Nation's highest abilities, without doing harm to the Nation, nor, indeed, without crippling science. The very fruits of science become available only through enterprise, industry and wisdom on the part of others as well as scientists. Science cannot live by and unto itself alone.

"This is not an idle fancy. Germany and Japan show us that it is now. They had fine science; but because they did not have govern-

268

ments 'of the people, by the people, and for the people' the world is now at war. This is not to say that science is responsible: it is to say, however, that, except as a member of a larger team, science is of limited value to the national welfare.

"The uses to which high ability in youth can be put are various and, to a large extent, are determined by social pressures and rewards. When aided by selective devices for picking out scientifically talented youth, it is clear that large sums of money for scholarships and fellowships and monetary and other rewards in disproportionate amounts might draw into science too large a percentage of the Nation's high ability, with a result highly detrimental to the Nation and to science. Plans for the discovery and development of scientific talent must be related to the other needs of society for high ability: science, in the words of the man in the street, must not, and must not try to, hog it all. This is our deep conviction, and therefore the plans that we shall propose herein will endeavor to relate the need of the Nation for science to the needs of the Nation for high-grade trained minds in other fields. There is never enough ability at high levels to satisfy all the needs of the Nation; we would not seek to draw into science any more of it than science's proportionate share."

Member, Advisory Committee on Tax Exempt Foundations, U.S. Treasury Department, 1963-64.

Director at large, Social Science Research Council, New York, N.Y., 1940-43; member of the council's committee on problems and policy, 1941-46.

Member of committees to select Rhodes scholars for 17 years, 1933-51. Member of the board of direction and treasurer of the Association of American Rhodes Scholars, 1928 to 1965.

Trustee of the Institute for Current World Affairs, New York, N.Y., 1933-53. Chairman of the investment committee, 1936-46. (Provides training grants for young newspaper men, chiefly American citizens, to enable them to live in and become authorities on selected areas of the world.)

Member of the board of trustees of the Wooster School, Danbury, Conn., 1943-48. Secretary of the corporation during the same years.

Trustee, Marine Biological Laboratory, Woods Hole, Mass., 1951-56.

Year 1963: Member of the committee (formed by the W. B. Saunders Co., Philadelphia, publishers of medical books) to select two medical scholars for writing fellowships of $15,000 each.

Member of the board of trustees of the American Institute for Persian Art and Archaeology, 1930-33. Secretary of the corporation and member of the executive committee during the same years.

*Columbia University, New York City. Lecturer in law, 1927-29.

Member of the editorial board, the American Scholar, publication of the Phi Beta Kappa Society, for several years.

Adviser for several years to the Hearn Fund, Milford, Del., on scholarships to assist the higher education of boys and girls living in the vicinity of Milford.

The Oberlaender Trust, Philadelphia, Pa.: Trustee from about

269

1931 to about 1953 when it wound up its activities. (This foundation was established to foster good relations with Germany; when Hitler came to power this became a futile enterprise and from then on the moneys of the trust were devoted to the assistance of German-Austrian refugee scholars—who had escaped or were booted out by Hitler —in the United States. For an account of the trust's assistance to such persons, see "The Refugee Intellectuals: The Americanization of the Immigrants of 1933-41," by Donald Peterson Kent, Columbia University Press, 1953.)

HONORARY DEGREES, AS OF NOVEMBER 1965
(In approximate order of receipt, in each category)

Doctor of humane letters
Hamline University, St. Paul, Minn.
Kenyon College, Gambier, Ohio.

Doctor of laws
Johns Hopkins University, Baltimore, Md.
Columbia University, New York, N.Y.
Wesleyan University, Middletown, Conn.
Yale University, New Haven, Conn.
Swarthmore College, Swarthmore, Pa.
University of California, Berkeley, Calif.
Northwestern University, Evanston, Ill.
Brown University, Providence, R.I.
Rockefeller Institute (now Rockefeller University), New York, N.Y.

Doctor of letters
New School for Social Research, New York, N.Y.
Princeton University, Princeton, N.J.
Emory University, Atlanta, Ga.
Southern Illinois University, Carbondale, Ill.

Doctor of medicine
Catholic University of Chile, Santiago, Chile.

Doctor of civil law
University of Oxford, Oxford, England.

AWARDS AND HONORS, APART FROM HONORARY DEGREES

Honorary fellow of Brasenose College, Oxford.
Public Welfare Medal, National Academy of Sciences, Washington, D.C., "for eminence in the application of science to the public welfare."
Award of Merit, National Institute of Arts and Letters, New York, N.Y., for "guiding, through three decades, the encouragement of art and artists in an enlightened manner" (1955).
Award of Merit, Philadelphia Museum College of Art, Philadelphia, Pa., for "wise custodianship of the Guggenheim Foundation which brought new knowledge and fresh images into the world" (1963).

Record of Service

Honorary member of Phi Beta Kappa, Johns Hopkins University chapter.

Cosmos Club Award (see attached citation) 1965.

Fellow of the American Academy of Arts and Sciences, Boston.

Corresponding member, Massachusetts Historical Society.

Fellow of the Royal Society of Arts and Manufactures, London.

Of the Inner Temple (London), barrister at law.

Member of the New York bar.

CITATION—HENRY ALLEN MOE
DISTINGUISHED EXPONENT OF SCIENCE AND THE HUMANITIES

Foundation executive, lawyer, humanist, Henry Allen Moe is recognized throughout the scholarly world for his dedicated services and inspired participation in the promotion of the sciences, humane letters, and the arts.

Through his association with foundations and learned societies over a period of forty years he has played the role of a superb catalyst and in a remarkably creative manner has made possible the fulfillment of talent and promise. He has guided the selection of thousands of young men and women for advanced research or artistic creation, and has given them encouragement, advice, and recognition. With an open mind toward the progression and even the vagaries of an advancing culture, he has shown an uncanny genius in recognizing potential. He has detected some of the best of the avant-garde while encouraging the solid performance of veterans still capable of further accomplishment, standing as ready to support an action painter or a twelve-tone composer as a nuclear physicist or an existentialist philosopher. In this he has exhibited courage, breadth of understanding, and faith in the future, and his influence has been pervasive, salutary, and universally respected.

As President of the American Philosophical Society he is a worthy successor to Benjamin Franklin, whose breadth of learning and deep wisdom he emulates.

For his eminent contributions to the advancement of science, literature, and the arts in America and for his distinguished leadership in the field of foundation administration, the Cosmos Club of Washington is proud to designate Henry Allen Moe as the second recipient of the Cosmos Club Award.

Si monumentum requiris, circumspice.

The CHAIRMAN. Senator Pell, you have been very much interested in this legislation.

Senator PELL. I would also just like to support Senator Javits and say how delighted we are with the nomination of Dr. Moe, and I am happy, and I think the foundation is very lucky indeed that he is willing to take this responsibility on at this time.

The CHAIRMAN. Are there any questions on the part of any memmer of the committee? If not, Doctor, we want to thank you very much, and your record will go into our complete record.

Senator YARBOROUGH. Mr. Chairman, I have one other comment.

The CHAIRMAN. All right.

Senator YARBOROUGH. For the record, I am glad to see, as a matter of personal satisfaction, somebody older than I appointed.

Dr. MOE. I am the oldest man here.

Senator YARBOROUGH. Congratulations.

The CHAIRMAN. Dr. Moe, I said to you and to Senator Javits, and I will repeat it for the record, a quotation from the pen of the eminent Ralph Waldo Emerson, "Do not say things. What you are stands over you the while, and thunders so that I cannot hear what you say."

Now, with this record you have here, there is no need for you to even speak; it speaks so beautifully, so eloquently, so magnificently for your qualifications for this position. We want to thank you very much for being here with us. We are glad you came.

Dr. MOE. Thank you all.

Senator JAVITS. Mr. Chairman.

The CHAIRMAN. Senator Javits.

Senator JAVITS. Is a motion in order?

The CHAIRMAN. We will go into executive session, Senator.

(Whereupon, at 11 a.m., the committee went into executive session.)

O

INDEX

273

Index

Amersfoort, Holl., 52
Amherst College, 30
Amsterdam, Holl., 51
Andrew, Saint, 126
Angell, James Rowland, quoted, 35-36
Anglo-American law, 10, 12, 19, 132, 155, 196
Anglo-American tradition, 160
Annals of Internal Medicine, 48n
Annals of the Missouri Botanical Garden, 61n
Ann Arbor, Mich., 8
Antarctic, 30
An Anthropologist Looks at History (Kroeber), 186n
Antofagasta, Chile, 31
An Apologie for Poetry (Sidney), quoted, 125
Aquinas, Saint Thomas, 119, 129
Arabia, 15, 107, 120, 200
Ariovistus, King, 49
Aristophanes, 183
Aristotle, 20, 201
Armageddon, 135
Army, U.S., 37, 38
The Art Museum in America (Pach), 67n
Ashley, Charles Allen, 254
Asia, 109
Aspen, Colo., 267
Aspen Award in the Humanities, 234, 267
Association of American Rhodes Scholars, 244, 267, 269. *See also* Rhodes Scholar(s); Rhodes Scholarship
Association of American Geologists and Naturalists, 30; secretary's report quoted, 30
Association of American University Presses, 267
Assyrians, 104
Athens (anc.), 168, 169, 182, 183, 184, 189. *See also* Greek civilization
Atlanta, Ga., 270
Attorney General *vs.* Downing, 128n
Augustine, Saint, 126
Aurelian, Emperor, 181
Aydelotte, Frank, 243
Aztec civilization, 83

Babel, Tower of, 106
Babylon, 105, 106, 120, 122.
    See also Mesopotamia

Bach, Johann Sebastian, 19, 55, 181
Bacon, Francis (1561-1626), 17, 175, 176; quoted, 175-76
Balaklava (Crimean War), 209
Balinese, 180
Baltimore, Md., 68, 77, 239, 270
Barber, Samuel, 234
Barnett, Lincoln, 64, 64n
Barton, Henry A., 33
Barzun, Jacques, 234
Baseball Hall of Fame, 251
Becquerel, Antoine Henri, 70, 93, 98, 146
Beirut, Lebanon, 121
Bell, Whitfield J., xiii, 172
Bellow, Saul, 234
Bell Telephone Laboratories, 198
Benét, Stephen Vincent, 234
Bengal Asiatic Society, Library of, 140
Benjamin Franklin Lectures, 79
Bentham, Jeremy, 8
Berkeley, Calif., 267, 270
Berne, Switz., 143, 144, 145
Berytus, Lebanon, 121; Law School, 121
Bible, 66, 108, 201
Bicentennial of American Independence, 209
Biddles (family), 209
Bill of Rights (U.S.), 85, 86, 110
Binney, Horace, 136; quoted, 136
"Biographical Dictionary of the American Revolution," 210
Black Hawk War, 169
Black Sea, 109
Blackstone, Sir William, 9, 156, 156-57, 156n; quoted, 156
Blanshard, Brand, 234
Blume, Peter, 234
Bodleian Library (Oxford), 140, 243
Bodley's American Friends, 244
Bogan, Louise, 234
Bologna, It., 129
The Book of Learned Men (Arab.), quoted, 140, 149-50
Boston, Mass., 21, 30, 33, 193, 271
Bosworth Field, battle of, 209
Bougainville (isl.), 23
Bowen, Charles Synge Christopher, quoted, 196
Bowman, Isaiah, 30
Boyd, Julian, 192
Bracton, Henry de, 9
Brahms, Johannes, 257

274

Index

Index

276

Index

Einstein, Albert, 27, 53, 63-64, 64n, 69, 70, 90-91, 91, 94, 98, 115, 143, 144, 147, 181; quoted, 64, 69
Elamites, 104, 105, 106
Elicker, Paul E., 33
Elizabeth I, 131, 132, 134, 164, 180, 181, 188
Emerson, Ralph Waldo, 17, 19, 30, 137, 138, 150; quoted, 15, 16-17, 17, 29
Emory University, 270
"Empirical Research and the Development of Economic Science" (Mitchell), 84n
Encounter, 188
Encyclopaedia Britannica, 131n, 139n, 202n
England, 5, 208, 217, 226; arts and architecture, 173, 174; Bar of, 5, 265; Catholic, 131; fourteenth-century, 128, 129; institutions, 188; law, 8, 9, 10, 64-66, 126, 128, 129, 131, 153, 154, 156, 157, 164; liberties, 11, 209; nineteenth-century, 66; Protestant, 132; seventeenth-century, 18, 109, 120; universities, 188
English (lang. and lit.), 14, 28, 130, 162, 162-63, 164, 166, 196, 208
English, the, 5, 66, 154, 180, 185
"English Justinian," 9
"Equality of Men," 179-80
Erewhon (Butler), 29
Escuela Agricola Pan-Americana, 267
Ethics of Citizenship (MacCunn), 179n; quoted, 179-80
Ethiopian Pharoahs, 180
Euclidean geometry, 151
Euphrates River, 97, 102, 104
Eurich, Nell, 234
Europe, 3, 38, 51, 52, 54, 67, 109, 110, 117, 120, 129, 173, 176, 199, 244, 248
European, 53, 84, 110, 163
Evanston, Ill., 270
Exposition du Système du Monde (Laplace), 163

Faraday, Michael, 27, 146
Farmers' Museum, 251, 252, 253, 266
Farnsley, Charles and Nancy, xiii
Fenimore House, Cooperstown, N.Y., 83

Finian, John F., 61n
First Minnesota (regiment), at Gettysburg, 59
FitzGerald, Edward, 122, 139, 140-41, 141n, 149, 150; quoted 140, 141, 142, 150
Fleming, E. McClung, quoted, 203
Flexner, Abraham, 69
Florentines, 180
Florida, University of, 97
Fond du Lac, Wis., 59
Forest Hill, Oxford, Eng., 208, 209
Fosdick, Raymond, quoted, 45
Founding Fathers, 85, 86, 100, 110, 180, 194, 195
France, 49, 50, 67, 158, 173, 226
Frankel, Charles, xiii, 226
Franklyn (*Canterbury Tales*), 211
Franklin, Benjamin, 59, 119, 166, 175, 176, 177, 201, 209, 210-11, 224, 239, 242, 266, 271
Freeman, Douglas Southall, 83, 84
French (lang. and lit.), 163
French, the, 37-38
French, Academy, 163
Frost, Robert, quoted, 220

Gainesville, Florida, 97
Galantière, Lewis, quoted, 81-82, 82
Galileo Galilei, 27, 180; quoted, 116
Gambier, Ohio, 270
Gaul, 49
George III, 178
George IV, 65
German-Austrian refugee scholars, 270
Germanic barbarians, 82
Germans, 49
Germany, 268, 270
Gettysburg, battle of, 59
Ghiberti, Lorenzo, 180
Gibbs, Willard, 187
Gildersleeve, Basil Lanneau, 74
Gillmor, Frances, 246
Gilman, Daniel Coit, 74; quoted, 74
Girard (Stephen) Will cases, 136
"Glacio-Aqueous Action in North America" (Hitchcock), 30
Glanvill, Ranulf de, 9
Glass, W. Bentley, xiii
God, 12, 50, 51, 84, 89, 100, 126, 127, 128, 130, 135, 136, 139, 156, 158, 161, 161n, 164
Goethals, George Washington, 241

277

Index

Index

Holdsworth, W. S., 157n
Holmes, Oliver Wendell (Justice), 10, 36, 39, 46, 69, 123, 159n, 160n, 189, 191, 194, 197, 207; quoted, 10, 44, 159, 159-60, 189, 191, 194, 197
Homer, 183
Honduras, 267
Hopkinsons (family), 209
Horgan, Paul, 222
Hudson Valley Rent Wars (col. Am.), 52
Hunter, Walter S., 33
Hurrians, 104, 106
Huxley, Thomas Henry, 138, 162, 166

Icelanders, 180
Illinois, 169
Incas, the, 83, 180
Independence Hall, Philadelphia, Pa., 59, 173, 174
Indians, American, 51, 60-61, 111
Indies, 61
Industrial Revolution, 160
Inner Temple (London), 5, 265, 271
Inns of Court (London), 188, 265
Institute of Current World Affairs, 33, 269
Institute of Modern Art, 267
International Congress of the History of Science, 172
Iran, 140, 149
Irnerius (jur.), 129
Islam, 107, 110, 120, 140, 142, 150
Israelites, 110
Italy, 15, 129, 139
Ives, Herbert, 146
Ivins, William M., Jr., 61, 61n; quoted, 61-62, 62-63
Iwo Jima (isl.), 23

Japan, 38, 268
Jefferson, Thomas, 54, 55, 106, 108, 119, 192, 206, 239, 247; quoted, 56, 100, 178, 192, 206, 210
Jenkins, Helen Hartley, 240
Jews, 200
Joffre, Joseph Jacques Césaire, 67
Johns Hopkins Hospital, 239
Johns Hopkins University, 68, 74, 98, 270, 271

John Simon Guggenheim Memorial Foundation, 5, 6, 15, 25, 29, 31, 34, 45, 69, 77, 185, 215, 217, 218, 219, 223, 228, 233, 234, 237, 247, 249, 250, 255, 257, 258, 266, 270; Advisory Board, 68; Charter quoted, 250; Committee of Selection, 68. See also Guggenheim Fellow(s); Guggenheim Fellowship(s)
Jones, Howard Mumford (President, American Academy of Arts and Sciences), quoted, 21
Jones, Louis C., 203, 251
Jusserand, J.A.A. Jules, quoted, 130
Justinian I, Emperor, Code of, 121, 129
Justus, Saint (bishop), 126

Keele, Harold W., 228
Keeney, Barnaby C., 195
Kent, Donald Peterson, 270
Kenyon College, 270
Keynesian economics, 27
Khartoum (campaigns), 209
Killian, James R., Jr., 241
Kimball, Fiske, 58
Koran, 200
Kroeber, Alfred Louis, 186n; quoted, 168

Labouisse, Henry R., 253
Langland, William, 66, 125, 129, 130, 131, 132, 133, 134, 136, 164, 166; quoted, 130, 131n
"Langland, William" (*Encycl. Brit.*), 131n; quoted, 131
Laplace, Pierre Simon, 163, 166
Larrabee, Eric, 197n, 230
"The Last Supper" (Leonardo), 55, 66, 71
Latin (lang.), 127, 162
Latin America, 31, 218, 237, 268
Laws (Plato), 183n
Leatherstocking Corporation, 266, 267
Leavis, F. R., 166
Lebanon, 121
Lee, Rensselaer W., xiii
Lee, Robert E., 83
Legion Minervia (Rom.), 109
Leonardo da Vinci, 55, 63, 66, 71, 119
Lewis, Clarence Irving, 85; quoted, 86

279

Index

Index

Index

Index

283

Index

Index

The typographic eagle used on chapter headings
and elsewhere in this book
is a modified version of an early American
ornament. It was first cut and offered for sale by the
young American type foundry operated by
Archibald Binny and James Ronaldson
It was used by printers of the United States
during the decade 1810-1820

The illustrations were printed by the Meriden
Gravure Co., Meriden, Connecticut
The type is Linotype Primer, by Rudolph Ruzicka
Book design by P. J. Conkwright